The Profession of Authorship in America
1800–1870

The Social Foundations of Aesthetic Forms Series
Jonathan Arac, Editor

The Social Foundations of Aesthetic Forms
A series of
COLUMBIA UNIVERSITY PRESS
Jonathan Arac, Editor

The Profession of Authorship
in America
1800-1870

WILLIAM CHARVAT

Edited by Matthew J. Bruccoli

COLUMBIA UNIVERSITY PRESS
NEW YORK

PS
88
.C47
1992

Columbia University Press Morningside Edition
Columbia University Press
New York   Oxford
Morningside Edition with new postscript to preface
Copyright © 1992 Columbia University Press
Copyright © 1968 Ohio State University Press

Library of Congress Cataloging-in-Publication Data
Charvat, William, 1905–1966.
The profession of authorship in America, 1800–1870 / William
Charvat.
p.   cm.
Originally published: Columbus : Ohio State University Press,
1968.
Includes index.
ISBN 0-231-07076-4 (cloth)
ISBN 0-231-07077-2 (pbk.)
1. American literature—19th century—History and criticism.
2. Authorship—Economic aspects—United States—History—19th century.
3. Authors and publishers—United States—History—19th century.
4. Literature publishing—United States—History—19th century.
5. Authors and readers—United States—History—19th century.
6. Authors, American—19th century—Economic conditions.
7. n.-us.
I. Title.
PS88.C47   1992
810.9'003—dc20
91-46532
CIP

Casebound editions of Columbia University Press books are
Smyth-sewn and printed on permanent and durable acid-free paper.

Printed in the United States of America
c 10 9 8 7 6 5 4 3 2 1
p 10 9 8 7 6 5 4 3 2 1

Contents

Foreword

❖ ❖

IN THE death of William Charvat not only did Ohio State University lose one of its great professors but rational scholarship lost one of its most vigorous proponents. For him objective research was an end, or rather a means to an end, and not, as current doctrines of "appreciation" (dreadful word!) often assume, an obstacle to enjoyment. There are, I know, many in the academic world and too many outside it who think that literary studies are best carried on in an economic and social vacuum. They want nothing to do with the sale of books and the income of authors. Others assume that an interpretation of the march of mind takes on impurity if it stops to inquire how the ideas that influenced an age were made public to that age. Let us be fair. There is, I suppose, a kind of development from Homer to *Herzog* of technical skills in the treatment of character, the manipulation of story, the creation of atmosphere, and the transfer of sensibility from the writer to the work and from the work to the reader. In the later nineteenth century, moreover, when we were all evolutionists, studies of the evolution of genres went on without any reference to writer, printer, bookseller, or literary agent. So in our time, when a return to primitive, or primal, psychology is all the rage (can we so return?), critics and scholars interpret literary work as if the author's rational control of material were a form of hypocrisy to be stripped away in order to reveal hidden archetypal images, the mythopoetic energy of a submerged racial unconscious. Good histories of

painting, of music, and of other arts have been written without
the slightest reference to the economic support of artists and
with a minimal amount of reference to the social context of the
works of art produced. Nevertheless, if a Carl Jung may visit
with impunity Circe's island, lesser men might consider whether
they, too, can bend the bow of Ulysses.

Charvat's philosophy was that whatever the ultimate interpretation of a work of art might prove to be, the first duty of scholarship was to ascertain the relevant facts. For him relevant facts
were not only biography and technical bibliographical lore but
also the patent truth that a literary work does not exist until
it is made public—that is, somehow published. He argued, as I
think rightly, that we cannot know the full stature of a literary
artist, nor the nature of his repute, his vogue, and his influence,
until we are as fully informed as historical evidence will permit
of his struggles in the market of literary wares.

Of Charvat's great project for a definitive history of American
publishing (in the sense of a definitive history of the tripartite
author-publisher-reader relation), only fragments remain. But
what fragments some of them are! A literary work in his view
was not the original manuscript of a book, that mere object in
space; it was what had happened when the manuscript was
submitted to, and emerged from, the threefold tensions of public
production: the judgment of the author in creating the work
and submitting it for publication; the judgment of the publisher
both of the aesthetic or philosophic importance of the manuscript
and of its potential sales; and the judgment of the reading public,
expressed in opinion and purchase, on the validity of the work
as amusement, edification, or illumination. Literary history, he
thought, even before the invention of movable type, is a threefold story—the interplay of producer, distributor, and consumer.
If these terms sound harshly in the ears of sensibility, I point
out that even in classical Greece the three contending forces
existed. Somebody had to pay for staging that noblest of human

inventions, a tragedy; and a recent historical novel by Mary Renault, *The Mask of Apollo,* turns precisely upon the interplay of commercial (and political) demands and dedication to "art" as this interplay affects the life of a young Greek actor in Plato's time. Artists have to live. Dr. Johnson, a great literary critic, bluntly said: "No man but a blockhead ever wrote, except for money." If this sounds like a sad descent from high art, Charvat's remarkable discussions of Longfellow and Melville in their relations to publishing show that, descent or not, the market place and the muse cannot be severed in literary history.

Even if Charvat had lived, it is possible he could not have finished his history of the author-publisher-reader relation in America as he had planned it. His problem was virtually archeological rather than historical. By this I mean that the raw material for his study existed like pottery shards only in a scattered and fragmentary state. He had to infer and guess, to assume that such and such things were true of the lacunae in his commercial evidence, to assemble the parts of things rather than to depend on continuous documentary flow. Commercial records of publishing houses disappear. We do not possess accurate information about the business of book-selling in the United States.

This assertion may come as a surprise to many. Any large library usually has a whole section devoted to volumes that purport to be the history of this or that well-established house. The histories of publishing companies, however, tend to fall into one or the other of two unsatisfactory categories: an "official" or commissioned account, commonly issued as a centenary memorial book (or booklet); or a book of reminiscence by a prominent member of the firm. In addition to offering all the characteristic weaknesses of any commissioned history, the first type gets written on a sort of Samuel Smiles formula. The firm of Font & Folio began in a humble fashion, by industry, prudence, shrewd judgment, and the Benjamin Franklin virtues, it survived depression and disaster, beat its competitors in a perfectly nice way,

and emerged as a famous firm, the proof being the names of
prestigious authors and titles on the back list. In such a book
nothing much is said about the bargains struck with (or against)
authors, trade discounts, publicity, the ways by which a valuable
literary producer was kept with the firm, and the ways by which
the firm seduced some other famous writer from a rival company.
Publishing flops are discreetly passed over; publishing hits are
due to the insight, instinct, prophetic outlook, or fine taste of
either Font or Folio. As far as it goes, the history may be
authentic; but it does not go very far, and it certainly does not
plow very deep. And it is usually lacking in detailed and verifiable
statistical information.

The book of reminiscence written by a prominent member of
a publishing company upon his retirement is naturally filled with
a golden haze. The volume is one of happy anecdotage. Amusing
or distressing stories abound illustrating the eccentricities of
authors, the whimsicalities of taste, the oddities of print or
prudery. Publishing was once a proud profession, now it has
become commercialized; the old days were more leisurely and
the new age one of pressure; and though the author as a young
publisher may ruefully confess to this or that error in judgment,
on the whole he has had a good life, known a variety of interesting
persons in the world of books and magazines and clubs, and is
making a contribution to high culture. These volumes have value.
They do illuminate high culture. It is good to know why Henry
Holt insisted that publishing books was like practicing law, or
why Macmillan's took on so weighty a work as Bryce's *The
American Commonwealth*. Both from the commissioned history
and from the volume of reminiscence one can learn something
about the perennial puzzle of author-publisher relationship and
how this shaped publishing, and therefore literary, history. What
is lacking is what the commissioned history also lacks: exact
financial information. In this country, at least, publishing as an
industry has not yet drawn the attention of business historians,

and there are virtually no studies of publishing as a business, on a scale with the Hidy and Hidy *History of Standard Oil Company (New Jersey)*.

Of course, what is true of the records of American publishing firms has been true of most American business houses before the rise of entrepreneurial history as an important field of investigation. In the April, 1967, issue of the *Harvard Library Bulletin* Professor Arthur H. Cole relates how by a kind of accident he stumbled upon valuable records of the American wool trade, likely at any moment to be destroyed, how he secured them, and how he thus pioneered the archival use of business records. Not every area of business activity, of course, is equally valuable to the historian; not every company preserves its "dead" files; not every company finds it expedient to make these files available to scholarship. In proportion as any enterprise is relatively impersonal, like the manufacture of plows, it is easier to persuade the company that no harm will come if its business history can be studied, but in other fields of business enterprise—for example, real estate—the relations between company and customers may be highly personalized, idiosyncratic, and open to misinterpretation, or so the head office is likely to argue. Enthusiasm for archival treatment of past records is in such a case at a minimum.

Publishing is such a personalized enterprise. If, on the one hand, the connection between publishing and the development of the art of literature is obvious and close, as books of reminiscence seem to say, so that one thinks publishers would be happy to preserve the history of their contributions to culture, on the other hand, the book trade, like the real estate world, is a highly personalized world. Occasionally, of course, important records are made available; a notable instance was the publication in 1949 by the Bibliographical Society of America of *The Cost Books of Ticknor and Fields and their Predecessors, 1832–1858*, edited by Warren S. Tryon and William Charvat. But I have known of a famous American publishing company which, on

moving from its old location to its new one, dumped its back
records without regard to their historical worth for scholarship.
On the whole, indeed, publishing has not as a business come
within the sweep of interest in entrepreneurial business history
and therefore of archival preservation, and the reasons are
obvious. No business is more competitive. Publishing firms dis-
solve and reform. Heads of departments leave one house to take
a post in a competing house, sometimes bringing a string of
authors with them. Literary agents are now a hidden force in
contract-making. There are standard contracts; but as soon as
some writer becomes a notable literary property, he is likely to
demand special financial consideration known only to him, his
agent, and the publishers, and publishers are not anxious to
publicize their differentials. "Advances" are not always retrieved.
Writers are themselves careless bookkeepers. In short, no business
outside of the entertainment world is more deeply entangled with
relations of personality; and consequently, at the very heart of
the author-publisher-reader triangle there is for the scholar an
almost insoluble problem. That Charvat managed to accomplish
all he did is a tribute to his patience and to his developing and
mastering a rather special sort of economic sleuthing that seems
at first sight very far from literary study. But is it, in fact, any
more remote than the fine points of professional bibliography?

What I have been saying may be misconstrued to mean that
I think Charvat's interest in literary history became less and
less "literary" and more and more sociological. This would be
to misunderstand both the man and the enterprise. If by an aesthete one means somebody likely to die of a rose in aromatic pain,
Charvat was no aesthete. He had small patience with small
sentimentalities. But he had the graver interest of the historian-
critic. One has only to read—I find myself coming back to these,
excellent as are some of the other essays—his studies of Longfellow and Melville to see that economic determinism as a mode
of interpretation was as far from his liking as mere aesthetic

sensibility. His study of Cooper is at this point also relevant: Cooper never pretended to the high subtleties of a Henry James, but he was an imperfect craftsman of great genius, and Charvat lets us see the interplay between Cooper the imaginative writer and Cooper the marketer of his own wares. But let me get back to Longfellow and Melville for a moment.

Having established the truth that Longfellow was a shrewd bargainer, that, partly as a result of his superior market position, a certain kind of work was expected from him, and that to fulfil these expectations as a "typed" author, he had to alter basically his original literary drive, Charvat next shows that he came more and more to regret the responsibility of being a "public" poet, a responsibility he had, as it were, drifted into; and then, leaving behind the question of the price of poems and their audience, our scholar turns about, so to speak, and says in effect: There is more to this repetition of the themes of longing and regret in this poet than criticism has hitherto realized. These verses about the irrecoverable past are not mere convention. They have, on the contrary, behind them a special, a highly personalized, experience. These continual statements about labor are real cries of anguish, not Longfellow imitating Longfellow. His unease at being forced to continue as America's foremost "public" poet affects his style and it affects his soul. He tries to cut away from all his later verse the expectation of sentiment; he writes, as he wrestles to recover his artistic independence, a new, a compact, a more individualized verse. (Contrast the style of "To the River Charles" by the early Longfellow with that of "The Tide Rises, The Tide Falls," written in 1879.) Charvat does not say that Longfellow's boredom with the responsibility of being a typed poet "caused" this change in style. What he says is that the author-publisher-reader relation, supposed by careless critics to be virtually constant throughout the poet's life, was in fact a relation of shifting tension, and he argues that the change in Longfellow's attitude toward his burden should lead us to inspect his poems a little more carefully, to interpret them a little more sympathetically, and to view conventional judgments about Longfellow a little more skeptically than we now do.

We do not lack explorations of the development of American publishing. On the contrary there is a variety of books. The annual Bowker lectures tell us much. A general history like the Lehmann-Haupt, Wroth, Silver *The Book in America,* which has gone through several editions, has the value of any sound survey. We have had studies devoted to particular periods such as Donald H. Sheehan's *This Was Publishing: A Chronicle of the Book Trade in the Gilded Age,* and volumes devoted to particular types of books, like Frank L. Schick's *The Paperbound Book in America.* And we have Frank Luther Mott's magisterial, though unhappily unfinished, history of American magazines. Studies of particular publishing houses—a good example is Raymond L. Kilgour's admirable *Messrs. Roberts Brothers, Publishers*—throw occasional light on the relation of writer to book manufacturer and the effect of sales upon the publishers' faith in authors. These are valuable. But the weakness of these volumes lies in assuming that the principal fact about the book business is that it is a business—a minor business, a rather queer business, but still in the main a problem of bargain and sale, contract and delivery.

Dealing with an author, however, is not like dealing with a carpenter, or a grocer, or even an inventor. It is not even like dealing with an easel painter. Moreover, people do not buy books as they buy shoes, or meals, or swimming pools. If the swimming pool is defective, you can get it repaired. If you don't like the meal, you can complain to the restaurant. But if you don't like the book, you can't complain to anybody or get the defective article replaced by another unless it is physically damaged. In most cases most readers do not even know who manufactured the book, and in most bookstores most sales are final.

By long tradition a writer, even a hack writer, moves in mystery. He never pleads for a shorter workday like a bricklayer, or goes on strike like the electrical union, or keeps regular working hours. His habits are allowed to be nonconformist and temperamental. By long tradition also, books (that is, books that are more than compendiums of information like dictionaries and almanacs), if they are a branch of the entertainment industry, are a very special branch of that industry; and if they are more than entertainment, they are like units in symphony concerts or paintings on a museum wall—something apart from, and above, the taint of trade. To read a good book is supposed to be a meritorious act. Great authors produce good books. The fact that great authors produce manuscripts, and that crass, commercial-minded publishing firms turn these manuscripts into something called books is somehow a part of the equation of literary history people don't think much about.

From the commercial point of view the shining mediocrity of J. H. Ingraham, author of *The Prince of the House of David*, is a datum of no particular interest, since, after Roberts Brothers took over this novel in 1863, they sold more than a hundred thousand copies of it by 1898. From the point of view of art it is of no particular importance who printed Henry James's *The Turn of the Screw*, which came out in 1898, and in comparison with Ingraham's novel did not sell. But once an author gets popular, he is typed; and public and publishers are likely to discourage him from all aesthetic adventuring. If an author remains steadily unpopular, as James did during most of his life, it makes a great deal of difference whether he has found a publisher with enough insight into literature and enough stubbornness to back his insight, to keep on publishing him. In either case the personal relations of writer to book-manufacturer may profoundly affect the personality of the writer and in the long run the development of literary art. Confidence or the lack of it between editor and author may warp or warm the creative psychology of the artist: the classic case is that of Maxwell Perkins and Tom Wolfe. But the relation of the House of Scribner through Perkins to Tom Wolfe is by no means singular. The English romantic movement probably owes as much to the great John Murray and the first Thomas Norton Longman as it owes to the theorizing of Coleridge and the egoism of Byron. In the same fashion the secure place of the nineteenth-century New England men with us is as much a product of the industry of James T. Fields and Horace E. Scudder as it is of transcendental theory and abolitionist reform.

The special glory of William Charvat seems to me to be that he grasped almost intuitively the meaning of the triadic relation of author-publisher-reader in literary history. He saw that literary histories were being written in a kind of economic vacuum, whatever bows they made in the direction of social history; and that book publishing was being studied more as a branch of commerce than as a mode of culture and an expressive channel of art. He went to work to fuse the economic and the aesthetic points of view. He saw that the book is both a physical object and a spiritual fact. We have had no other scholar sufficiently tough-minded to grasp the raw materials of bookkeeping and twist cultural significance out of them, being at the same time sensitive enough to know that no quantity of statistical analysis can replace man's belief that literature is the breath and finer spirit of all knowledge. He founded no school, but perhaps he will inspire others to go on.

HOWARD MUMFORD JONES

Harvard University
February 23, 1967

❖ *Editorial Preface* ❖

THE PREVIOUSLY UNPUBLISHED STUDIES in this volume have been salvaged from William Charvat's files. They represent work in progress —or in some cases, perhaps, discarded work. All have been transcribed from his revised typescripts with no attempt to rewrite. Punctuation and spelling have been corrected; a few words have been silently supplied; and, where possible, quotations have been verified. No other editorial changes have been made. Square brackets in the text are reproduced from Professor Charvat's pages. Angle brackets have been introduced around material that he may have intended to delete or shift or rewrite. Illegible passages in the manuscript have been indicated by three asterisks.

A minimum number of stylistic changes affecting only non-substantive matters have been introduced by the Ohio State University Press in the texts of those articles that have previously been published in various journals, as a means of bringing some uniformity of style to the collection.

There is some duplication between the previously unpublished Chapter XII, "Melville," and Chapter XIII, "Melville and the Common Reader," which first appeared in 1958 in *Studies in Bibliography.* Both have been included because they show how Professor Charvat refined his own work to produce his time-saving prose.

A personal note. Near the end of his life, Bill Charvat told me that he probably would not complete his big study of the economics of authorship in America because other scholars had made his work unnecessary. He was wrong.

The selection and ordering of the material in this volume is mine, but I have been advised by Professors Roy Harvey Pearce and Claude

M. Simpson. I acknowledge with appreciation the secretarial labors of Mrs. Katharine Newland.

I am further indebted to Professor Simpson for his labors on the proofs. The Index was compiled by Miss Kathleen Addlesperger. The following members of the Ohio State University Center for Textual Studies staff contributed substantial editorial help: L. Neal Smith, John Manning, Michael Newell, and Richard Simpson.

M. J. B.

Postscript

WILLIAM CHARVAT DIED IN 1966 believing that he was a failure because he had been unable to complete *The Profession of Authorship in America, 1800–1870*, his projected "history of American literature in terms of the profession of writing and the business of publishing." The present collection of his developing work was published in 1968 to provide a sense of the scope of his project. Five years after its publication this volume seemed forgotten. Then references to the book and to Charvat began appearing with increasing frequency in literary histories as well as in studies of American publishing. But this volume was not reprinted.

Howard Mumford Jones concluded his "tough-minded" (a term he accurately applied to Charvat) Foreword to the first printing thus: "He founded no school, but perhaps he will inspire others to go on." Professor Jones, who was not a timid thinker, perpetrated an understatement that now provides a gauge of Charvat's achievement and influence. During the 16 years from 1943 to 1959 he promulgated and tested aspects of a new discipline for historians of American literature. He demonstrated how publishing evidence could be used; and he taught scholars to think in terms of an author's *career:* the combination of elements that determines a writer's reception, reputation, influence, audience, success, and failure. See Charvat's superb definition of *professional writing* in his Introduction to this volume.

Charvat's 1943 article "Melville's Income" introduced what seemed pernicious questions: What has money got to do with literature? Or: How does a writer's awareness of audience influence his work? In 1948 he contributed two stimulating chapters to the orthodox *Literary History of the United States*—"The People's Patronage" and "Literature as Business." The next year the Tryon & Charvat edition of *The Cost Books of Ticknor and Fields* provided the first such tool for the study of American literature. That year Charvat also published the rationale

for his work in "Literary Economics and Literary History." Then in 1959 he
published his Rosenbach Lectures, *Literary Publishing in America, 1790–1850*—
which Joel Myerson identifies as "one of the great unread books in American
literary scholarship."

As the result of a delayed reaction, William Charvat has in fact inspired
others—some of whom were in their cribs when he died—to follow his maps.
There are now Charvatians who may not be aware of their pedigree. The
booming field variously called Histoire du Livre, or Geschichte des Buchwesens,
or Sociology of the Book bears the impress of Charvat's thinking. He should
also be credited with encouraging the preservation of publishers's archives.
There was a long time during which such research material was routinely
discarded and destroyed. The publishers had little sense of history; the librarians
did not want to bother with all that business paper; and the scholars—who are
supposed to educate librarians—did not know what use to make of all that
business paper, either. Charvat's work has had an exemplary influence.

That William Charvat did not do all the work that was expected of him
should not diminish the proper assessment of his achievements. The work he
published is permanently usable. He was an honest scholar who cared nothing
for academic fashions. During the years of our friendship Bill conveyed a sense
of personal dignity that extended to his professional conduct. He provided
standards.

Matthew J. Bruccoli
9 March 1992

❖ Acknowledgments ❖

ACKNOWLEDGMENT is gratefully made for the permission granted to reprint the following previously published materials:

"Cooper as Professional Author," reprinted by permission of the New York State Historial Association, Cooperstown, New York, from *James Fenimore Cooper, A Re-appraisal* (1954).

"Poe: Journalism and the Theory of Poetry," reprinted by permission of the Ohio State University Press from *Aspects of American Poetry,* edited by Richard M. Ludwig (1962).

"Longfellow's Income from His Writings, 1840–1855," reprinted by permission of the Bibliographical Society of America from *Papers of the Bibliographical Society of America,* Vol. XXXVIII (1944).

"James T. Fields and the Beginnings of Book Promotion," reprinted by permission of the Henry E. Huntington Library and Art Gallery from the *Huntington Library Quarterly,* Vol. VIII (1944).

"Melville's Income," reprinted by permission of the Duke University Press from *American Literature,* Vol. XV (1943).

"Melville and the Common Reader," reprinted by permission of the Bibliographical Society of the University of Virginia from *Studies in Bibliography,* Vol. XII (1958).

"Literary Economics and Literary History," reprinted with permission of the Columbia University Press from *English Institute Essays 1949,* edited by Alan S. Downer (New York, 1950).

"The People's Patronage," reprinted with permission of The Macmillan Company from *Literary History of the United States* by Spiller *et al.*, eds. Copyright © 1946, 1947, 1948, 1953, 1963 by The Macmillan Company.

"American Romanticism and the Depression of 1837," from *Science and Society*, Vol. II (1937). Reprinted by permission of the publisher.

Acknowledgment is also gratefully made of permission to quote from manuscript materials on deposit in the Huntington Library and Art Gallery, San Marino, California; the Boston Public Library; the Houghton Library of Harvard University; the Yale University Library; and the Historical Society of Pennsyvlania.

The Profession of Authorship in America
1800–1870

CHAPTER ONE

Introduction

THIS is an attempt to write the history of American literature
in terms of the profession of writing and the business of
publishing. It is much like the effort to describe a building in
terms of internal structure—foundations, supporting beams and
columns, strains and stresses—instead of presenting photographs
of façades and finished interiors.

It cannot be a complete history because many—perhaps most
—of the documents of the profession have been lost; and because
some literature—some of the greatest—is produced unprofession-
ally and with little or no dependence on the book trade. The profession and the trade had, for example, no influence on Emily
Dickinson's production of her poems, and very little on Emerson's
Nature. The first was a private performance; the second was
addressed to a small coterie who might as well have read the work
in manuscript.

The terms of professional writing are these: that it provides a
living for the author, like any other job; that it is a main and
prolonged, rather than intermittent or sporadic, resource for the
writer; that it is produced with the hope of extended sale in the
open market, like any article of commerce; and that it is written
with reference to buyers' tastes and reading habits. The problem
of the professional writer is not identical with that of the literary
artist; but when a literary artist is also a professional writer, he
cannot solve the problems of the one function without reference
to the other.

❖ CHAPTER TWO ❖

The Beginnings of Professionalism

1. The Literary Life in New England: Barlow, R. T. Paine, Dennie

ON JANUARY 10, 1783, Joel Barlow, a "Connecticut Wit," wrote to Elias Boudinot, President of the Continental Congress, a letter which shows why professional authorship in America had thus far been impossible:

> As we have few Gentlemen of fortune sufficient to enable them to spend a whole life in study, or enduce others to do it by their patronage, it is more necessary, in this country than in any other, that the rights of authors be secured by law. . . . Indeed, we are not to expect to see any works of considerable magnitude, . . . offered to the Public till such security be given. There is now a gentleman in Massachusetts [Timothy Dwight, another Connecticut wit] who has written an Epic Poem, entitled "The Conquest of Canaan", a work of great merit. . . . It has lain by him, finished, these six years, without seeing the light; because the Author cannot risque the expences of the publication, sensible that some ungenerous Printer will immediately seize upon his labors, by making a mean & cheap impression [edition], in order to undersell the Author & defraud him of his property.
>
> This is already the case with the Author [John Trumbull, another wit] of McFingal. This work is now reprinted in an incorrect, cheap edition; by which means the Author's own impression lies upon his hands, & he not only loses the labor of writing, & the expence of publishing, but suffers in his reputation by having his work appear under the disadvantages of typographical errors, a bad paper, a mean letter & an uncooth page, all which were necessary to the printer to catch the Vulgar by a low price. The same Gentleman had by him a number of original Poems . . . which cannot be brought forward for the above reasons.

The letter closed with the request that the Congress recommend to the several states the passage of a copyright law similar to the English one, which protected a book for fourteen years after publication.

Before the month was out, Connecticut had passed such a law (the first in the United States), and the literary property of the Wits was safe within their own state. But they were not protected in other states until 1790, when the first federal law guaranteed copyright for fourteen years, renewable for another fourteen. That the country had got along without a copyright law for over 150 years does not mean that it had not had a literature worth protecting, but rather, as we shall see, that a small and scattered reading public and poor transportation depressed the commercial value of all books. Time would take care of population and transportation, but no literary profession was possible until law had given products of the mind the status of *property*.

The need for copyright was obvious and primary; but two groups of key words in Barlow's letter reveal other needs which were not to be satisfied for decades. The first group is "patronage," "Gentlemen," "study," and "the Vulgar." Barlow's phrasing here is a sign of a general condition: that when the new nation began its career, its writers were thinking of the social status of literature and authorship in terms of British aristocratic tradition, which was partly myth. In that tradition, imaginative literature was a class commodity, produced and consumed by the elite and by those on lower social levels who identified themselves with the elite and depended upon them for support. Literature, furthermore, was a by-product of learning or *study*, which presupposed leisure. The gentleman might take pride in his by-product, but he considered it as only one of many accomplishments in an active life. He never wrote for money, never put his name on what he wrote, and rarely even condescended to put what he wrote in print. His work was addressed to a small group of equals. But he met an obligation to society at large by "patronizing" the talents of men of humbler origin. Patronage took the form of outright gifts of money, hiring the writer as tutor or secretary, sub-scribing for his books, exerting influence to get him sinecures in church, court, or government, and giving him "protection"—which meant the privileges which derived from being identified with the upper classes. The writer thus patronized and protected might, from necessity, sell his work in the open market where it could be bought by "the Vulgar," but because society despised him for doing so, he published anonymously. Such status as he enjoyed was the result not of his talent but of the acceptance of his talent by someone socially secure.

Modern history and research show that this system and these attitudes, which were at their height—and depth—in the reigns of Elizabeth and James, were a burden on creative writing rather than a support; that the writers who endured the system were degraded and unhappy; and that at the moment Barlow was writing, it was in a state of final and permanent collapse. But Barlow and his contemporaries accepted the myth and did not know that it was a bubble already exploded. For four years up to the time of his letter he had been seeking a patron in the state of Connecticut, and he may even have received some handouts from a prosperous gentleman named Titus Hosmer. But the effective patron he actually found was, incredibly enough, the American army. It is a sign at once of the prestige of the clergy and of the social structure of that civilian army (many of the officers were, in the British tradition, "gentlemen" of means and education) that the chaplaincy was a well-paid sinecure—£360 a year and long vacations—for little more than a sermon a week, and now and then an ode for an officer's celebration. Barlow took advantage of this paid leisure, and the government had the plea-sure of helping to finance the writing of his epic, *The Vision of Columbus*. It is one of the earliest instance of American govern-ment patronage of the arts through job-holding.

The words "cheap" and "uncooth" are also signs of an imported tradition. In England, for two centuries, a society in which the poor consumed sensational pamphlets and broadsides, badly printed on poor paper, had emphasized the prestigiousness of expensively manufactured books for the well-to-do. It was comfortably assumed that a cheap format was the natural dress for cheap content. But note the implication of Barlow's statement that "the Vulgar" were buying a cheaply printed *epic*: the assumption of a necessary relation between content and format had broken down by the end of the eighteenth century, and the era of cheaply printed "good" literature had begun. Yet the vestiges of patrician attitude are evident in Barlow's words. Twenty-four years later he engrafted the new tradition on the old one. When, in 1807, he published his revised epic as *The Columbiad*, he reaffirmed his old assumption of a necessary relation between creative literature and the upper class by pouring ten thousand dollars into an edition which was declared the most sumptuously printed volume thus far produced in America; but simultaneously, he issued it in two cheaper grades of paper "in an effort to reach various levels of the public." But by that date Barlow had become both a rich man and a radical "republican."

Another phrase in Barlow's letter—"risque the expence of publishing"—is an index to the publishing situation in the era preceding the establishment of commercial or democratic patronage of literature. That John Trumbull paid for the manufacture of his own book describes the commercial status of almost all American literary works produced before 1820. Publishers rarely took the risk of manufacturing costs; the author paid, and the publisher served as his distributor on a commission basis. The author was thus literally in the publishing business. But in the absence of a predictable market, an efficient system of distribution, and the transportation necessary for a national market, the author tried to avoid risk by finding his buyers before he published. Almost all literary works before 1800 were published by subscription, that is, by promises to buy (on the basis of a prospectus) obtained from friends, friends of friends, public dignitaries known to be patrons of the arts, and booksellers willing to serve as agents. Subscription was another inheritance from England and an outgrowth of aristocratic patronage. At the back of the subscription book frequently appeared a list of the buyers, who thus enjoyed advertisement as patrons of the arts. But in England the system was almost moribund by 1783. It had never been very profitable, and because subscription-hunters were considered nuisances, it contributed to the degradation of the author's status.

Joel Barlow found 769 subscribers, at a dollar and a third per copy, for the first (1787) edition of *The Vision of Columbus*. (The army again appears as patron in that 117 officers are listed for an average of three copies each.) He is said to have "grossed" $1,500 on the edition, but inasmuch as he paid for manufacture and delivery, and had to give discounts for copies sold by booksellers, his profit could not have been much. And, at any rate, it had taken him five years of time and effort to find his subscribers. When the second edition failed, Barlow gave up the system. Subscription publishing, as inherited from England, probably got its death blow in 1820. In that year a young and ignorant, but later spectacular, publisher—Samuel G. (Peter Parley) Goodrich—advanced John Trumbull $1,000 on the profits he expected to make from subscribers to the Wit's *Poetical Works*. So many subscribers refused to accept their copies that Goodrich lost the thousand.

Within a year after the publication of *The Vision*, Barlow began a lucrative connection with a land company, and by 1796 he was in a position to be so careless about the copyright of his mock-heroic poem, *The Hasty Pudding*, that seven editions and innumerable magazine piracies put nothing in his pocket.

Nevertheless, Barlow has an important place in this history because he was the first American author to contribute to the growth of a genuinely democratic psychology of authorship. This growth had no direct relation with politics or with Barlow's belated transformation into an ardent republican of the French-Jefferson-Tom Paine school. A poor farmboy of undistinguished parents, he had had, to begin with, none of the sense of family

prestige enjoyed by his brother Wits. That he got an upper class
education at Yale was an accident due to the perceptiveness of a
minister who thought the boy worth encouraging, and to small
inheritances which were just sufficient to support him in college.
As a young man he naturally identified himself with the class into
which he had been able to climb, and naturally he absorbed some
of the class attitudes implied in his reference to "the Vulgar" and
in his search for patrons. But his willingness to put his name on
the title pages of his books, instead of resorting to the traditional
anonymity of the gentleman author, and his early and unique
determination to make literary work a way of life—independent
of any of the established professions—were sure signs that he did
not share all the patrician conceptions of the status and function
of the writer. For his brother Wits it was a foregone conclusion
that the writing of poetry must be incidental to a career as
minister, lawyer, or public servant. Barlow, unable or unwilling to
devote his central energies to law or the ministry, yet obsessed
with the idea of being a poet, stood between two historical
British symbols—the "gentleman-lawyer-minister-scholar-poet"
and the "beggarly poet." He was too class-conscious to be the
latter, but he would not make the compromise required by the
former. His chaplaincy (based, professionally, on a few months'
hurried study and an examination) was a solution for three years
only, and was a means to the end of poetry. When the war was
over, he had to face reality. It is of the greatest significance that
he then turned not to the professions but to "trade"—a choice
unthinkable to most gentlemen. For two years he was a publisher
in a Hartford partnership, edited the firm's magazine, and sold
groceries and cloth along with books. But the literary drive was
still central. All the while, he was finishing and revising his epic,
getting subscriptions for it, and encouraging other poets by publishing Timothy Dwight's *The Conquest of Canaan*, which found
three thousand subscribers. When the partnership broke up,
Barlow resigned himself briefly to the profession of law, but was
rescued from it by the land company.

As a professional poet he had failed because social conditions and the book trade were not ready for him. But since Barlow's verse (if we may judge by reprints for the general reader) hardly survived Barlow, one may well ask whether his failure did not also lie in the quality of his work—in his lack of some great private source of creative power. The modern reader *knows* that he lacked it: that his major work was almost totally derivative in form, language, ideas, and subject matter. But the question in this history must be whether his lack of original power made a difference in his fortunes in his own generation. Probably it did not. Poetry that is commercially successful in its time has always been *public* poetry—that is, poetry that is keyed to the culture, the sophisitication, and the language of contemporary readers. Public poetry has sometimes been written by poets of private power, but it was popular *in its time* for its public rather than for its private qualities.

Whether poetry of *any* quality is popular at all in a given society depends on the status of poetry in that society, and upon the media available for its distribution. The Elizabethan, says the historian of the literary profession in that period, loved poetry but despised the poet who was in any way dependent on his craft. Probably the same can be said of Barlow's period. In the years 1780–1810 the status of poetry was high. It was an accepted form of political, religious, moral, and satirical discourse. College students were required to write it regularly, and they vied for the honor of producing commencement poems, which they almost invariably published afterward. Verse was used universally in newspapers and magazines—not only as filler but as primary material. Editors never paid for it because the supply was unlimited: everybody wrote it. Newspaper carriers presented their customers with specially written verses on Christmas. Theater managers ordered verse prologues and epilogues for new plays. Odes were written for every important public celebration. It would seem to have been the ideal time for poetry to become a profession—for the poet to enjoy the status of poetry.

But it was not. Perhaps because poetic form and language at the end of the eighteenth century was completely standardized— a shell into which any literate person could pour his thoughts— few persons would pay for contemporary verse. Editors did not. Publishers would not. Addicts would buy the work of poets of long-established status in England—Dryden, Pope, Thomson, Milton. And a small, unified society, like Barlow's Yale-army-ministerial set in Connecticut, would patronize an equal's work. But no such society was large enough to support a poet through purchased works, and the national market was still physically out of reach.

If Barlow fared poorly in Hartford, the Boston poet fared even worse. Hartford, at least, was a river town, with a protected water route all the way to New York; but between Boston and New York was a long stretch of open sea. This fact alone would explain why Boston did not rank as a literary center until the advent of the railroad in the 1830's. With a population only half that of New York in the 1790's, it had two-thirds as many book-sellers, printed twelve novels to New York's seven, and probably more volumes of poetry. Yet it had great difficulty selling its productions anywhere else. A mass of evidence on Boston's back-wardness as a literary center is summed up in one fact: that when Barlow thought of going into publishing and bookselling in 1784, his first choice was Baltimore (because "the wealthy in that country may think libraries an ornamental species of furniture"), and that when he decided to remain in New England, he chose not Boston but Hartford. That Boston had one great publisher, Isaiah Thomas, meant little to the creative writer. Thomas was too astute to accept many literary works, and he probably published none at his own risk.

Poetry had much the same status in Boston as in Hartford, but the poet was even less gladly tolerated. Like Barlow, Robert Treat Paine, Jr., attempted the literary life at a time when it was economically impossible and socially dangerous. Unlike Barlow's, his social position was impeccable, for his father was a signer of the Declaration of Independence, a Delegate to Congress, and a judge of the Massachusetts Supreme Court, and his mother the daughter of a general. Yet after four years at Harvard, where he contracted an incurable literary itch, he became a business clerk rather than use up his vital energies in the law; left business for poetry and the theater; committed the unpardonable social sin of marrying an actress—for which he was cast out by his father; and after being imprisoned for debt, periods of drunkenness, expulsion from his house by his landlord, and sleeping in alleys, died a literary derelict, leaving his wife and children to be taken care of by his distinguished father. Society had no objection to his writing poetry; indeed, it subscribed so heavily to his pamphlet verse that, according to his biographer, who knew him personally, he cleared $1,500 on a Harvard commencement poem, *The Invention of Letters* (1795); $1,200 on a Harvard Phi Beta Kappa poem, *The Ruling Passion* (1797); and $750 on "Adams and Liberty" (1798). The figures are incredible, for the first two were pamphlets which could not have sold for more than a shilling or two, and the last was a single lyric. Yet, even allowing for exaggeration, the story is evidence of the acceptance of his verse by his own class. And it was a group of social equals who financed him to a legal education because they wanted his talents to be "employed more for his own emolument [and] his reputation" than they had been. In a word, the gentleman-turned-beggarly-poet must be brought back into line not only for his own sake but for the sake of the clan. Paine tried hard to conform by serving the numerous clients that the clan sent him. But once again the literary itch set him to scratching, and with his head full of plans for poetry, plays, editing, and even a "new system of rhetoric," he neglected his clients and sank into poverty and disgrace—"the living Muse," as he said in one of his poems, "Bound to the mouldering corpse of Penury."

The poetry left behind after this wreckage was not much. He wrote it rapidly and without difficulty, and it is now, with its standardized rhythms and tiresome figures from classical mythology, indistinguishable from run-of-the-mine eighteenth-century verse. But since Boston society clearly respected his talent, his career indicates that his class granted status not to the poet as poet, but to poetry. Paine's persistence in seeking his own way of life is admirable, but judging by the tone of commentary on him for half a century afterward, he was used as a horrible example in his community, and probably delayed the growth of a professional literary attitude in New England.

The relation between writer and society in Boston in the 1790's is even better illustrated by the career of Joseph Dennie. Lacking Paine's family prestige, he wooed Paine's class assiduously, and when it rejected him, he bitterly attacked Boston culture. As a social climber he not only adopted the social prejudices of the wealthy and well-born, but went to political extremes which even they could not stomach. Almost monarchical in temper, pro-British and traditionalistic in his cultural tastes, a leader of the witch-hunt that followed the French Revolution, he called Jefferson a political imbecile; Tom Paine a loathsome, drunken atheist; and the Declaration of Independence a "false, flatulent and foolish paper." But unlike most writers who were actually of the class he identified himself with, he set out deliberately to exploit that class by writing essays that would bring him a literary income at the same time that they fed his law practice by appealing to the politically conservative. When he went down to Boston from Walpole, New Hampshire, in 1795 with this plainly expressed purpose, he deluded himself into thinking that because of his earlier newspaper essays and satires on republicanism, he was "caressed by those who possessed the greatest Genius Wealth & power." Though experienced publishers like Isaiah Thomas and Benjamin Russell refused to encourage him to dream of literary wealth, he found one who agreed to publish his old essays on the half-profits system and to sponsor an essay-periodical called *The Tablet*. He expected his share of the profits of the latter to be £150 a year.

Believe me, my dear Mamma, it leads to property, to my legal and to my literary eminence. A design so novel has captivated all the principal characters here both in literature and politics, and all are pleased with a paper intended for amusement and rejecting the impertinence and prolixity of uninteresting news and advertisements.

Professionally he was on the right track in planning to write for diversion, but he overestimated either his ability or the size and loyalty of his audience—or both. The "tasteless and mercenary Bostonians suffered [*The Tablet*] to die and me to starve" after three issues.

Retired by Boston to the country circuit, as it were, he got a local printer in Walpole, New Hampshire, to back a magazine for him—the *Farmer's Weekly Museum*, in which his famous "Lay Preacher" sermons began to appear in 1796. For editing this magazine he was promised a salary of £110 a year (he had a £90 income from the law). But to earn his salary, he had to learn the first—and for him, bitter—lesson of the profession—to avoid political and class partisanship. "In my editorial capacity, I am obliged to the nauseous task of flattering Republicans." This led him to reflect that it was

. . . a serious evil to have been born among the Indians and Yankees of New England. Had it not been for the *selfish* patriotism of that hoary traitor, Adams, and the bellowing of Molineux [of the Boston Tea Party] I might now, perhaps, in a Literary, Diplomatic, or lucrative situation have been in the service of my rightful King, and instead of shivering in the bleakness of the United States, felt the sunshine of a Court.

He now suffered one of the chronic pains of early American authorship. His publisher, David Carlisle, who had brought out a collection of his "Lay Preacher" essays in 1796, apparently had been living off Dennie's half-profits, for in 1799 he went bankrupt, owing the editor a year's salary and all the profits on his book. Book and periodical seem to have been successful, for their time, but the village publisher could hardly have given either a wide circulation. Dennie wrote his friend Royall Tyler that his *Algerine Captive,* another famous Carlisle imprint, "has been examined by the few and approved," but that "Bostonians could not supply themselves with a book that slumbers in a stall at Walpole"—little more than one hundred miles away.

Dennie was now through with Boston, that "Jewish, peddling, and commercial quarter," whose literary folk were "mostly fools" and "all lazy"; and with New England. He had run for Congress, backed by "unbiassed citizens," of whom there appear to have been exactly six, for that was the size of his vote.

Considering his disgust with the "levity and weakness of the people" and his "profound contempt for the herd of society," he needed a change of atmosphere. He begged a job as secretary (the title of *clerk* "hurte my pride") to Secretary of State Timothy Pickering, and combined it with another as editor of a Federalist newspaper. But even as a party hack his days were numbered, for Pickering was removed by Adams because of his High Federalist sympathies, and Adams himself was succeeded in the Presidency by the loathsome Jefferson. It was high time for a man of his "feelings and principles to abandon public life, and perhaps even my country," which was full of the "Jewish and cheating and canting descendants of the Regicides." He abandoned neither. In Philadelphia he found a "ready passport into good company," was respected as a "professed man of letters," went to an Anglican church, and dreamed of recognition in England. "I love all Englishmen I meet," he wrote, and like James's "passionate pilgrim" he was sick with nostaglia for his "old home." He imagined fondly that by now his "old home" would have paid him three or four thousand pounds for a work which was a pale imitation of a British manner and matter long outdated.

Nevertheless, he continued to "drudge in literature for a mere subsistence in this execrable Country," and he now entered the last and noisiest phase of his bad-tempered career. As founder, editor, and owner (for seven years) of the Philadelphia *Port Folio,* he conducted the most thoroughly "literary" periodical in the country. As long as he owned it, he abused democracy, praised England, spread sweet rumors of Jefferson's intimacy with a female slave, and fought off libel suits. He should have remembered that his class had failed to support him and his prejudices in Boston. The *Port Folio* managed to break even, but it was not prosperous, as he bitterly complained. Long before 1809 he had alienated large segments of his reading public, and when in that year he was forced to put the magazine under commercial auspices by selling it to Bradford and Inskeep, the firm forced him to adopt a non-partisan editorial policy.

On inspecting Dennie's career as a professional, one sees that he sustained himself by combining writing with law practice, magazine editing, and political jobbery—a pattern which was to be followed by many later writers. He was at a disadvantage because his professional stock was the essay, a form which has not had, since Johnson's day, much commercial value. Short prose pieces, as Irving and Hawthorne learned later, required more work and care than longer works, and there was little demand for them in book form. Dennie's essays might have sustained him financially had magazines been on a firmer basis in his time, but the double sale which he attempted was not very profitable when neither magazine nor book publishers could exploit a national market. Moreover, unlike some later essayists, Dennie had but one string to his bow. Irving was also a biographer and historian, and Willis was a poet and dramatist.

2. *The Philadelphia–New York Center: Rowson and Brown*

Even though Dennie was unhappy in Philadelphia, the fact that he was able to maintain himself there in work closely allied to creative writing was a sign that if there was a literary center in America at that time, it was not Boston but the area of which Philadelphia and New York were the two poles. These two cities were close enough together, and transportation between them (roads and ship lines) was sufficiently well developed so that each could exploit the other's reader market. Some publishers in the one had branch offices in the other. A Philadelphia agent could distribute for a New York publisher in the upper South, and a New York agent could sell Philadelphia products in the Hudson River area. Though the population was still too small and too scattered to support an author, this middle region was beginning to be able to support an enterprising publisher.

By far the most able American publisher in the 1790's was Philadelphia's Mathew Carey. Knowing from the very beginning (1785) that the local market could not, alone, support him, he set up by 1790 a chain of over fifty agents—printers, booksellers, postmasters, general merchants, and private individuals—to distribute his books and magazines in towns from Halifax to Georgia. He flattered the subscribers to his *American Museum*, the most important American general magazine before 1800, by printing the name of each on a small strip of paper and pasting it on the cover, and publishing the entire list at the end of each volume of six numbers. He was the first extensive advertiser and promoter among American publishers. If he did not invent wholesale bookselling, he developed it so vigorously that by 1800 he was supplying the books of other publishers as well as his own to over one hundred dealers. He circumvented the currency difficulties of the time by exchanging books with other publishers rather than money. He saw to it that his travelling peddlers (Parson Weems was the most famous of them) turned up whenever crowds gathered on market days, elections, court sessions, and society meetings.

It is no wonder that with Carey setting the pace, Philadelphia attracted authors from all sections, including New England, and that during the nineties it laid the foundation for the leadership in literary publishing it was to achieve in the eighteen twenties and thirties. Yet before 1820 professional authorship flourished almost as little in Philadelphia as elsewhere. Though Carey, a writer himself, and compiler of an anthology of American verse, was known to be partial to native authors, and although he served their interests by offering to booksellers a larger discount on American works than on imported books, he had too keen a sense of commercial values to publish very many purely literary works, or any at all at his own risk.

If any literary form could have succeeded anywhere in America before 1820, it would have been the novel in the Philadelphia–New York area. The publishers there were in close touch with an important book-trade development abroad. In the 1790's England discovered that the novel was the form which was reaching the widest market—that "the Vulgar" and the idle ladies of all classes and ages were eagerly renting novels of seduction and of "Gothic" adventure. The leading publisher in this development was the Minerva Press, whose owner, William Lane, a former poultry butcher, amassed a fortune from the printing and rental of sensational fiction between 1785 and 1810. The form was not a gold mine for the authors—mostly women working in anonymous secrecy—who were paid a flat fee averaging five to twenty guineas per book. As a form which did not have, or which at least had lost, literary status, it attracted few professional-minded male writers to whom prestige was important.

The fad reached America early in the nineties. How much of Lane's trash was reprinted it is impossible to say, for the facts have not been gathered and analyzed, but contemporary American book dealers' and circulating library catalogues show that great quantities of it were imported.

That there was a market for it was proved by the persistent demand for novels by book peddlers like Parson Weems, who knew their buyers; by the fact that many village printers found it profitable to publish novels even for their small clientele; and by the universal chorus of denunciation of fiction by American critics from 1790 to 1820. American imitations appeared at once, and yet before Cooper in 1821 not one American novelist was financially successful. Of the score or more American novels before 1800 that have been identified, few went through more than one edition, and, judging by their imprints, those that did had not been copyrighted.

Not even Mrs. Susannah Rowson, the author of *Charlotte Temple,* succeeded as American novelist; but as the producer of nine works of fiction, four of which she wrote after emigrating, she is entitled to consideration as the first American professional writer of fiction. *Charlotte,* however, must be classified as a British book since she published it in 1791 before she left England. A work of purest Minerva strain, it contains a seduction, an illegitimate birth, a desertion, a murder, assorted treacheries, and a tear-soaked grave.

When Mrs. Rowson arrived in Philadelphia in 1793, she could not have guessed that *Charlotte* was destined to become the best-selling novel in America before the advent of Scott. It has gone through more than 161 editions. Of these, forty-two were printed before 1820 in seventeen cities; and the fact that ten of these were produced in New York and seven in Philadelphia, compared to one in Boston, shows that the middle region offered the greatest market for fiction. Estimates of its sales are many, but probably the most reliable was that of Mathew Carey, the American discoverer of *Charlotte* and the publisher of at least nine editions. When he was getting out a new edition at fifty cents in 1812, he wrote the author that the sales "exceed those of any of the most celebrated novels that ever appeared in England, [far exceeding] 50,000 copies," and that it was "the most popular and useful novel ever published in this country." Carey's judgment is confirmed by the fact that in 1818 the leading figures in the novel were exhibited in a waxworks show in the frontier town of Columbus, Ohio.

Charlotte, her third work, had succeeded so well in England that she had felt encouraged "to proceed in my favorite employment," and she produced two more before emigrating. In the year

after her arrival two of her old novels went through two Philadelphia editions, and another a single edition. Unprotected by
American copyright, these four works brought her nothing, yet
she had reason to hope that she could make novel-writing at least
an adjunct of her main occupation, which was acting.

That she wished to exploit the market that absorbed *Charlotte*
is obvious from the plot of her first American novel, *Trials of the
Human Heart* (1795). The heroine is the putative daughter of a
man who tries to commit incest. Her parents die, her brother is
a cad, her relatives conspire against her, she is cheated out of her
inheritance, is lusted after by every male who lays eyes on her,
is disappointed in love, marries a man she does not love, is
wrecked in the English channel, finds her real father and mother
(a lady who at one time is wooed and won by the Sultan of Tur-
key without being subjected to improper advances), and is finally
united with her real lover, now conveniently widowed. Subjected
to every misery, she nevertheless gets through all perils (including a house of prostitution) unsullied.

These delights (rendered in Richardsonian epistolary form)
were presented to the public by subscription, Mathew Carey co-
operating. But only 110 subscribers partook of them, and the
first edition was still unsold in 1812. Why *Charlotte* and not
Trials? It is worth pointing out that as in radio soap opera,
Charlotte's unmitigated miseries are presented through a simple,
straight story-line, whereas *Trials* has a wilderness of subplots.
But aesthetics is less relevant to the question than trade problems.
Subscription publishing was the wrong method for a book addressed to the general reader rather than to the discriminating
few; there must have been many who refused to have their names
publicized in the subscription list of such a book. Moreover, the
list shows that Mrs. Rowson was unable to reach many patrons
outside the Philadelphia-Baltimore area where she was well
known as actress. Finally, in order to make a profit on a work
she paid to have manufactured (there is a record of her husband's
buying paper for it from Carey), she had to charge $2.00 for the

four volumes, a price too high for people accustomed to paying a dollar, or renting.

As a professional-minded writer, Mrs. Rowson was now willing to try a new formula; as an increasingly patriotic American (attacked by William Cobbett for her apostasy, she called him a "loathsome reptile"), she was glad to apply the new formula to American materials; and as an immigrant conscious that America tolerated the seduction novel less willingly than England, she was ready to quit that genre. When she began *Reuben and Rachel* about 1796, she intended to "arouse the curiosity of the young" in the history of her adopted country, and brought to the work something of the grandiose and nationalistic spirit of Barlow's epic. But the historical novel had not crystallized as a form, and Mrs. Rowson had no good models to guide her. Hers is a fantastic tale of Columbus and his imaginary descendants down to the year 1700, replete with wars and Indians. Before she had finished it, she turned teacher, and settled down in Boston, where her novel fell dead from the press.

Most of her books were set in England, where she was born and married, and where she learned about British "high-life" in her career as governess and actress. Her firsthand knowledge of English society helps to explain why *Charlotte* was so much more successful than its American imitations. *Charlotte*'s numerous villains, male and female, were all Europeans operating on American soil. Their villainies seemed to "come natural" in the imagination of American readers who were already beginning to identify the fascinations of sin with Europe. In foreign countries, where the individual's very identification was based on his place in class and family; where the law of primogeniture produced a class of irresponsibles, frequently army men; where property laws made a woman the chattel of the male; where a woman had a social existence just to the extent that she was dependent on and "under the protection" of a male; where men of the upper classes were condoned in considering the unprotected female fair game; it was natural that fictional plots should be based on the pursuit of the female by the "gentleman officer," on lost-and-found parents, treacherous relatives, and incestuous situations which were the end product of bastardy. Raised in England, Mrs. Rowson understood all this, whereas her American counterparts learned it secondhand. Local scandals were sometimes used by Americans as the basis of seduction novels, but the home-grown female-misery plot somehow did not have the authenticity of the foreign one. Even in the late eighteenth century, the "more smiling" aspects of American life were beginning to be considered the more characteristic.

Apparently, Mrs. Rowson was not willing to continue to write as a foreigner. Having adapted herself within four years to the social and moral atmosphere of America, she was ready also to conform to American conditions of literary production. Conformity was not imposed on her by social pressure: as an emigré Englishwoman she enjoyed some immunities denied to her American counterparts. Boston frowned on Robert Treat Paine the poet for marrying an actress, but Boston sent its children to Mrs. Rowson's schools even though it had seen her on the local stage. And even as teacher she advertised herself on her title pages as the author of *Charlotte*. Her shift from the stage and from sensational fiction to the schoolroom, therefore, was not timid. When in the Preface to *Reuben and Rachel* she declared that she had become a teacher out of a compelling need to teach very young girls, she was exhibiting the same impulse that led her, quite ingenuously, to justify *Charlotte* as a book that would save somewhat older females from a fate worse than death. She was a born teacher with a strong itch to write. The English social atmosphere had permitted her to unite teaching with diversion in the form of sensational fiction. She was quite willing to continue in this line in America, but soon realized that the book trade could not yet support a novelist. As schoolmistress she had an occupation which served her as patron while she produced verse, non-sensational domestic fiction, magazine miscellanea, and textbooks for children. She was the same highly moral woman that she had been

while she was writing Richardsonian soap opera for Lane in England, and felt not at all ashamed of her past as actress or a
Minerva novelist. But the conditions of book distribution and
reader patronage were different here, and Mrs. Rowson adapted
to them without fussing.

This readiness to consult the market and adapt to it her literary
stock-in-trade, which was didacticism, gives Mrs. Rowson standing as an early American writer of true professional temperament.
Modestly but mistakenly, she thought of herself as an amateur.
Genuine amateurism, by contrast, is exemplified by a contemporary named Mrs. Wood, who was known on her title pages only
as "A Lady from Massachusetts." Mrs. Wood's gaudy mixtures
of seduction, bastardy, Gothicism, and morality, most of them
appropriately set in Europe, the home of sin, were advertised as
the work of a lady who wrote not to "remunerate herself" like
the "common English novelist, who works for a living, similar
to a mechanic," but for the "amusement of herself [and her]
friends." Mrs. Rowson by contrast did not write for pastime, but
from compulsion and for profit. All her American editions bore
her name as a selling gambit, and many of her title pages asserted
that her books could be bought from her as well as from dealers.

Charles Brockden Brown, who is called the first professional
American writer, began to publish fiction about the time Mrs.
Rowson quit. He had started out with the standard equipment of
the young dilettante: a low-grade literary infection, a distaste for
business and the professions, small talent, and grandiose, commercially hopeless, literary schemes. In 1785 he was dreaming of
epics on the discovery and conquests of America, like Barlow's.
By 1789 he was developing a melancholy, self-probing, self-con-
scious egotism which he mistook for literary temperament but
which even his friends found tiresome. Essays which he published
in a magazine that year under the title of "The Rhapsodist"
illustrate not only what was wrong with him as a young writer
but what made the prose essay before Emerson both a literary
blight and a trade hazard. When he defined a "rhapsodist" as

"one who delivers the sentiment suggested by the moment in artless and unpremeditated language" and transcribes the "devious wanderings of a quick but thoughtful mind," he was describing the slovenly, late-eighteenth century amateur impulse which lingered on in the poorer works of even such writers as Irving, Longfellow, and Hawthorne, and which publishers took seriously at their financial peril.

"The Rhapsodist" was amateurism at its worst, and Brown would have loved to continue loafing around the edges of the literary world with the other amateurs in his Philadelphia club. The writer-as-idle-man pose was to become standard among imitators of Irving, but loafing seems to be precisely what Brown did for five years after leaving in 1793 the law office he loathed. But his unprosperous merchant father seemed to have been unable to support him properly, and in 1798 he went to New York to see if he could make a living from the novel-writing he had already begun.

Considering the contrast between his early and lofty literary aims, and the low status of fiction in 1798, his choice of the form requires inspection. By the mid-nineties a group of English writers including Godwin, Bage, and Holcroft had worked out a new fictional formula which combined adventure, violence, and Gothic mystery with ideas and social propaganda. In the eyes of critics it was far more respectable than the seduction novel, and, being just as formless, could be composed at the speed necessary in Brown's ill-paid vocation. Moreover, his choice had a certain cultural logic. Unlike the Richardsonian formula, the Godwinian was importable. Based as it was, frequently, on crime and its detection, and upon discussion of social problems, it could be naturalized in a country young enough to be still somewhat lawless and ideologically still so unsettled that social theory was in complete flux.

In Godwin's *Caleb Williams* Brown found a model in which he could literally do what most Richardsonians merely pretended: combine diversion with instruction. Moreover, he saw that the native scene was a welcome setting for such stories in a time when animosity to England encouraged nativism. In advertising his first work, *The Sky Walk, An American Tale,* early in 1798, Brown had declared that his country was a rich field for the "story-telling moralist" of the Godwinian type, for whereas the "popular" (Richardsonian) tale appealed to only one type of reader—"the idle and thoughtless"—the moral adventure story could, through "eloquence, the exhibition of powerful motives, and audaciousness" of characterization, "enchain the attention and ravish the souls of those who study and reflect."

This was a truly professional attitude: Brown wished both to serve reader taste, and thereby make a living, and to exploit serious material which he had not merely manufactured to sell.

But in the publishing world logic and good intentions are never enough. In the midst of production, the printer of *Sky Walk* died bankrupt, and the sheets of the novel were permanently impounded by creditors. For half a century more, American authors were to be caught in the wreckage of shaky publishing firms.

Meanwhile, he had begun serializing another novel, *The Man at Home,* in which he again used the American scene—Philadelphia in the plague year of 1793. Against a background of death and crime, Brown discussed the virtues and follies of man and argued about social problems. Interrupted by another plague, his serial never became a book.

Both of these attempts occurred before he moved to New York in July of 1798. Tradition has it that he now became a professional because of the encouragement of friends in a typical amateur group, the Friendly Club of New York. Actually, they impeded his literary progress by persuading him to found a collaborative magazine which they failed to support. The real influence on him as a professional writer was a French revolutionary then living in New York named H. Caritat. This gentleman had come over with a mission—to promote French republican doctrine and to make a lot of money by establishing a bookstore, a publishing business, and the biggest circulating library in the United States. At the moment of Brown's arrival, the library contained 4,000 books, and within the next two years it grew to 30,000. Caritat's specialty in the circulation business was novels, and he was determined to make novel-reading a respectable, sophisticated pastime. As agent of the Minerva Press, he stocked all of Lane's trash, and as a student of Lane's library methods, he was a promoter who set up and stocked such libraries all over the country. Caritat's fiction catalogues are, for their time, marvels of salesmanship.

Closely associated with Caritat, Brown must have acquired the illusion that there was a commercial future for the author of novels as well as for the distributor, and Caritat must have shared the illusion—for he published and advertised at his own expense Brown's *Wieland* and *Ormond*. At a dollar a copy these tales of crime, insane obsession, and mystery should have been commercially attractive. But no second editions were needed, and records show that Mathew Carey, the biggest distributor in the country, ordered only twenty-eight of the one and forty-two of the other in 1799, and no more until 1803. Because the villain in *Wieland* caused some stir among critics, Brown capitalized on him in another novel, *Memoirs of Carwin*, which did not get into print in Brown's time. A Philadelphia publisher brought out two more novels for him in 1799, one of which, *Edgar Huntly*, was the only work of Brown's to go into a second edition while he lived.

In two years he had written seven novels designed to attract both the casual and the thoughtful reader, and four of them had been published in the central book market—without financial results to encourage him to go on. But he made one more compromise. Because readers complained of the "gloominess" and the "out-of-nature" incidents of his works, he tried a more cheerful formula. His last two novels, *Clara Howard* and *Jane*

Talbot (1801), omitted murders, suicides, and violence, and concentrated on the ethical and social problems of love and marriage. With happy endings. They were serious books, epistolary in form, in American settings, and full of Godwinian discourse—but so dull that they were quickly forgotten.

Brown gave up in 1801. In at least fifteen books, finished and unfinished, published and unpublished, he had tried vainly to adjust his talents to the reader. Perhaps he succeeded, but the books never got to a big enough market. He spent the rest of his life storekeeping and doing hack work for Philadelphia publishers, leaving an estate of little over $1,600 when he died in 1810.

The question of his priority as a professional is a matter of definition. If the test is intention—the wish and the attempt to live by literature alone—Joel Barlow was first, in 1783; then Paine, 1794; Mrs. Rowson, probably 1794; Joseph Dennie, 1795; and Brown, 1798. If reliance on another though allied profession disqualifies, all five must be ruled out for their work in the church, on the stage, or in magazine editing. More important is the test of professional attitude. Anonymity is only a partial clue. Paine, Dennie, and Brown adhered to the traditional prejudice of the well-to-do amateur: that the gentleman does not put his name to a work, especially in a small unified society where its authorship quickly becomes known. (Brown signed his initials to prefaces.) But this convention aside, all five showed signs of outgrowing the amateur pose, and all five showed a rare willingness to be known in their time as writers by occupation.

Financial failure, in their time, was a foregone conclusion. Poetry had cultural status, and people listened to it and read it in newspapers, but few would buy it. Fiction had low cultural status but a rapidly growing public, especially among women. Most of these women, however, were novel renters, not buyers; and what the novel gained from them, it lost in the many homes where the novel was refused a place on the family book shelves. For all these reasons no professional before Washington Irving succeeded.

CHAPTER THREE

The Condition of Authorship in 1820

THE PROFESSION of authorship in the United States began in the 1820's when Washington Irving and James Fenimore Cooper discovered that they could turn out regularly books which readers were willing to buy regularly. In England authorship had become a profession earlier, sometime between 1805 and 1820, when a few astute and daring publishers of London and Edinburgh had found that the poetry and fiction of Byron, Scott, and some of their contemporaries constituted valuable commercial property.

In 1805 Longman's of London had paid Scott £600 for the second edition of *The Lay of the Last Minstrel*; and three years later Constable of Edinburgh had startled the whole literary world by offering him £1,050 for *Marmion* before it was finished. When Byron's first two cantos of *Childe Harold* had sold 4,500 copies in six months, John Murray of London had offered him for new works prices that embarrassed him—£1,000 for the *Giaour* and *Abydos*, over £2,000 for *Childe Harold III*, and £1,575 for *Don Juan I and II*. Poetry had become a national passion with readers, and an El Dorado for poets (John Murray said that in 1817 he rejected 700 poems). By 1830 this commercial boom in poetry had collapsed, never to be equalled again, but meanwhile a bigger and more permanent one had begun in fiction. In *Waverley*, published in 1814, Scott had evolved a formula for successful fiction which had earned him an average of £10,000 for the next five years (in modern values totaling, possibly, a quarter of a million dollars).

These handsome returns depended, of course, on handsome retail prices. The first regular trade editions of Scott's novels (always issued in three volumes) sold for thirty shillings. Applying the standard formula for finding the modern monetary equivalent, i.e., multiplying thirty shillings by four, one discovers that in our terms, buyers paid thirty dollars a copy for *Rob Roy*; so if the author's share of profits was one-sixth the retail price of the book (as Scott wrote Irving it was in 1819) Scott received five dollars a copy, or $50,000 for the first edition of 10,000 copies, which sold out in three weeks!

Quite suddenly, three factors of literary production coincided to put the occupation of writing on a more profitable basis: (1) authors were writing so divertingly on subjects of broad interest that they broke down the barriers between reader groups and appealed to almost everyone who was literate; (2) readers were able to pay well for books, either by purchase or through circulating libraries; (3) publishers had the vision, the astuteness, and the business experience to bring readers and authors together in a closer relationship. But contingent were two additional factors on which the profession of writing now rests: regularity of production—the ability of a Byron and a Scott to turn out books regularly, thus establishing a taste and a demand for their products—and the respect in which authorship from Byron's time on has been held. Byron's social position helped him; but also it was inevitable that an increasingly pecuniary society should cease to be condescending to men who could grow wealthy by writing poetry and stories. No longer "poor devil" authors, far from being beholden to patrons as in previous ages, those who had the knack of writing were now wooed by publishers and readers. The fact that reader, publisher, and author all profited in England, as we shall see, helped to bring about professionalism in America.

News of the popularity of the new literature reached America quickly. Geared to British reading tastes, the American public demanded the best-sellers as fast as they became available. Our publishers—or rather, printers—paid no royalties to British authors, of course; but to get the advantage of the first sale of a new canto of *Don Juan* or a Waverley novel, they had to hire agents in Britain to secure early copies, arrange for the fastest possible transportation on the uncertain sailing vessels of that day, meet the vessel at an American port, set a dozen compositors to working day and night, hire coaches to carry editions to nearby towns, and get the work, fresher than the dull morning newspapers of that time, into the bookstores. If, as Mathew Carey of Philadelphia said, the edition had only the advantage of three or four days' priority over the next and perhaps cheaper one by a rival firm, it sold out quickly at seventy-five cents a volume for poetry, and two dollars for a two-volume novel.

On the surface, this phenomenon looked disastrous to American authorship. Who among our writers could get royalties for books when the work of Southey, Holcroft, Campbell, Crabbe, to say nothing of Byron, Scott, and the great British quarterly and monthly magazines, could be bought for the cost of manufacture and distribution? But the question is double-edged. Before Byron and Scott there *were* no professional American authors who could suffer from the competition; indeed, there were no professional authors until the success of the British writers proved that there was a kind of literature that everybody wanted to read. As soon as that became evident, we began to turn out writers whose works were so saleable that they were promptly appropriated by publishers in England and went into competition with literature there. If the availability of Scott and Dickens in cheap American editions impoverished Poe and Hawthorne, what did the sale of cheap copies of Longfellow do to Tennyson and Browning?

Lack of international copyright, then, worked both ways. Certainly American authors suffered more injury than British authors, but there were two reasons for this. One was that our authors were unable to produce as many works which appealed to an international middle-class audience; another was the immature condition of our publishing trade. Our authors suffered less from international competition than from competition among our own publishers. But of this, more later. To account for our own literary boom of the 1820's, and to explain why it was much smaller than the British boom of the first two decades, we must look at the American book trade as it functioned in 1820.

2

On December 19, 1819, Mathew Carey and Son of Philadelphia —publishers, booksellers, and jobbers for half the southern states—wrote to Ebenezer Irving, brother of Washington Irving, who was then writing *The Sketch Book* in England, that they were willing to buy 400 copies of the fifth number of that work, the earlier numbers having taken the country by storm. "Send 150 by Swiftsure State the remainder by Mercantile Line." Number 5 was a slim pamphlet which retailed for 75 cents. Orders for this first American classic had been coming into Carey from bookstores throughout the South and the Middle States, but he had been unwilling to fill them. A rival, Moses Thomas, had had a monopoly on all sales of the book in the Philadelphia area, and Carey had had to pay him 62½ cents (a discount of ⅛) for a book which he himself had to sell for 60 cents to country booksellers. But because Thomas was close to insolvency, Carey had managed to break his monopoly by appealing to C. S. Van Winkle, the New York printer of the work, who interceded with Henry Brevoort and Ebenezer, Irving's managers. Carey now got the full 25 per cent discount, four-fifths of which he gave up on those copies which he sold to his retailers in the hinterland. It was a small profit for a wholesaler; but he had to supply the demand, for many of his booksellers bought their whole stock of all books from him.

Reconstructing the account from such correspondence as survives, one finds that the score on *Sketch Book No. V* was somewhat as follows:

Printing	26 1/4 cents	35%
Discount (Retailer 20%, Wholesaler 5%)	18 3/4 cents	25%
Author's Profit	30 cents	40%

These figures tell a story about American literature: why our popular authors flourished in the 1820's, and why the profession as a whole slid steadily downhill for over fifteen years in the 1830's and 1840's.

The bright side first. The set of seven pamphlets which constituted *The Sketch Book* cost the buyer $5.37½—an enormous price in those days. But an estimated 5,000 American readers were willing to pay that price (not without some protest) during the first two years of sale—at a time when Scott's novels could be bought for $2.00. Obviously, the American people were willing to pay well for American books that they liked. Irving's profit for this period of two years must have been near $10,000; Cooper's rate and amount of profit a year or two later was similar. For these two, at least, and for some others in lesser degree, the golden age continued through the twenties and early thirties.

But the facts displayed show also that this prosperity contained the seeds of its own destruction. Irving was his own publisher, invested and risked his own money, had all the work of management (by proxy), which a skilled publisher could have handled better. Carey was probably the only one in the country at that date who could be trusted; but printers and proofs had to be watched carefully; Irving's agents were in New York, and they could not trust the proof to the mails of those days.

Thomas' near-insolvency was characteristic of the trade. He was one of our first genuine publishers, that is, he was not a printer, but a man who sold and "promoted" books. But like most of his colleagues he worked on a shoestring, financially. It was one of the discouraging facts about American authorship that few of our writers before 1850 escaped loss through the bankruptcy of a publisher.

Worst of all were the conditions of marketing, distribution, and discount. Carey's country booksellers could not order *The Sketch Book* direct from the publisher because of a regional monopoly system which gave one firm in each major city exclusive rights for an important book for a whole area. This meant a split discount. Now it was becoming a custom at this date to reduce the regular discount of one-third (which had become standard about 1800) on "non-copyright" books, to 25 per cent on native works on which the author received "copyright" or royalty. Thus, the author's returns were taken out of the publisher's and retailer's profits. This in turn meant that many booksellers were unwilling to "push" native works on which they made a smaller than normal profit. This fact bears upon the sale and circulation of almost all American works of the 1820's. Irving and Cooper found that they had to increase their discounts, and when the able Carey took over their business, he found that he had to reduce his own profits drastically to keep his writers in competition with British authors. The problem of the publisher of American literature was, then, as difficult as that of the American author. When Richardson and Lord of Boston went into partnership in 1820, their articles of agreement stated their intention of engaging in "the art, trade, and mystery of bookselling." It was all of that, as the following facts will show.

3. *Transportation: Localized Publishing*

Publishing in 1820, to a much greater extent than now, was devoted chiefly to "useful" and educational works, but there was plenty of luxury money for the purchase of "merely literary" books, as Irving called his own. The proof is that by 1820 a half-million volumes of Scott had been reprinted and sold in America. The great problem was to get the works of our authors to the people who had the money. The fact that transportation was by poor roads and unreliable rivers made the delivery of books in quantity difficult, but fewer books had to be transported long distances then than now. Partly because of poor transportation and partly because of the primitive state of business, printing and publishing were localized, though the process of concentration was going on rapidly, as this table will show:

AMERICAN FICTION, PLAYS, AND POEMS
PUBLISHED IN BOOK FORM IN THE UNITED STATES

	1801–10	1811–20	1821–80 *
New York	81	101	117
Boston	52	58	64
Philadelphia	49	64	85
Other places	139	180	87
Approximate per cent of total	44	45	33

* Fiction and plays only.

The proportion of non-American and non-literary works published locally was probably even larger. The small printer of Harrisburg or Poughkeepsie, for example, who could not afford to pay a writer anything, found enough local demand for a British best-seller like *Charlotte Temple* that he turned out over half the American editions of that work; and a teacher like Longfellow at Bowdoin was likely to make up his own textbooks and have them printed at a nearby town like Portland, Maine.

Transportation, therefore, was not so great a problem as it seems on casual inspection. Nevertheless, some publishers in the few large cities tried to reach the country market. The Atlantic coast region was, of course, accessible by sea. Carey's records show that his books and stereotype plates reached New York, Boston, Baltimore, Hartford, and Albany by sloop and schooner. But it was so difficult for him and other coastal publishers to exploit inland regions that, until the West was opened up by canal and railroad, the printers and publishers of upper New York state and the Ohio Valley had a decade or two of prosperity. The Phinneys of Cooperstown—publishers, booksellers, and printers— had reached out to the farms with book wagons; and when the Canal opened, they fitted up a book boat with a large stock and kept open even in winter by tying up at a large Erie town. In the West, the store-boats of Cincinnati merchants brought books to remote villages on the tributaries of the Ohio, so that even now rare-book hunters find treasures by following the course these vessels took.

This was all very well for six or eight months of the year, but during the winter most of the waterways froze up, and for part of the summer the rivers were too shallow for navigation. Thus, to the literary man the temperature of the inland waterways was a matter of some importance. Cooper hurried his London publishers so that the sheets of his novel *The Bravo* would get to Carey during the summer of 1831. But the American edition was delayed until November 29, and Carey wrote him the following January, "*The Bravo* has been much liked, but the unfortunate close of our navigation immediately after it was published has prevented it from reaching over half the interior towns and has affected its sale." In 1827 the *Methodist Magazine* increased the size of its first ten numbers and omitted the last two so that the volume could be bound up in October and dispatched to subscribers before the rivers closed. As late as 1843, the Harpers' literary adviser instructed them to bring out Theodore Fay's *Hoboken* "so soon as navigation opens." This explains partly why most first editions, before the era of railroad networks, were brought out between March and October. It also shows that the western reader began to be a cultural influence as soon as he became accessible to eastern publishers.

4. The Retail Book Trade

The organization of the retail book trade in 1820 was not very different from what it had been in the eighteenth century. Of course their number had improved. Things had improved considerably since Dr. William Bentley of Salem recorded in his diary in 1792 that there was not "a proper bookstore this side of New York." What he meant was that there were few shops which specialized in books and whose proprietors knew their stock. In the smaller towns general stores stocked some books along with candles and dried fish; and almost all newspaper offices sold books, as did some postmasters, apothecaries, and milliners. But "proper" bookstores were not long in coming. By 1806 Salem had half a dozen, and by 1820 its firm of Cushing and Appleton was on the list of every large firm on the East coast. By 1820 there were twice as many bookstores in Boston as there had been in 1800; and its lending libraries, which had been static in number for over twenty years, doubled and tripled between 1819 and 1825. These years, it will be noted, were the heyday of Irving and Cooper.

If Salem's bookstores were representative of those in the East, Cincinnati's shops were in the vanguard in the West. By 1810 books were available in the newspaper offices and drug stores of the river town, and by 1812 it had its own "proper" bookshop. Culturally, the town must have grown up quickly, for some seventeen years later a friend wrote J. P. Kennedy that on the day of publication fifty copies of his *Rob of the Bowl* had been sold by one bookseller. Farther north the retail trade was flourishing by the 1820's. One book and stationery jobber, James D. Bemis, set up a string of fifteen stores along the waterways from Canandaigua to Detroit.

The rich South was the despair of the book trade. There was money there for the luxury trade, and it was a happy hunting ground for peddlers of Carey's expensive Bibles and atlases, and for richly bound special editions. But as a staple-crop region, it was hit hard by all depressions, which meant bankrupt book-sellers and bad debts. Moreover, its retailers were sluggish; customers might besiege them for a new book, but it required more energy than they had to reorder promptly. "Your book-sellers," wrote Carey to Kennedy in 1833, "are the most inert people on earth. They complain that business is bad and take good care that it shall not be otherwise, for they make no sort of exertion."

Nevertheless, for the first third of the century these "infernally lazy" bookmen were the most important resource of the Phila-delphia publishers. By 1814 the firms of Carey, Conrad, and Bradford and Inskeep had set up branch offices in Baltimore, Alexandria, Fredericksburg, Richmond, Petersburg, Norfolk, and Charleston. In 1827 Carey's balance against its Charleston store was $17,756; and in the same year a canvasser for a Boston firm was being paid $137.50 a month to get subscribers to Jared Sparks's edition of the works of Washington in the lower and middle South.

The man who first recognized the coastal South as rich book territory was Parson Weems of Dumfries, Virginia. Starting as a peddler of Carey's stock in 1794, Weems soon yearned for a middleman's cut on sales to new outlets which he saw everywhere in his territory. By 1796 he was urging Carey to send books to stores that had never sold them before. His plan was for Carey to make up trunks of assorted "school books, little histories, voyages, travels, fine novels," to the value of $150–200 each, and to distribute these in every large neighborhood throughout Maryland and Virginia—a 25 per cent discount to be split between Weems and the stores. The catch, of course, was credit—the perennial problem of the South and of booksellers—and Carey cautiously insisted on exact and specific credit arrangements with these retailers. Such caution was necessary and natural, but Weems's vision paid off for the firm. Though Weems still felt in

1819 that Carey had failed to exploit fully "a Country of such boundless extent and rapidly growing population . . . where the passion for Reading is rising with a flood beyond all former notice of Man," Carey could truthfully argue, in 1822 when he was bargaining for the southern agency of Cooper's *Pioneers*, that he supplied "many places [in the South] to which not a single copy will go unless through us." The popularity of Cooper and Irving in the South must be credited in part to the Parson and his employer.

On the whole, however, peddlers and subscription-book canvassers like Weems had little to do with new literary works, their specialty being "complete works" of Franklin, Washington, and other notables, and useful works in general. By the 1840's the system had fallen into disrepute. The depression of 1837-41 was particularly hard on the South and West, which was the best canvassing territory, and much money was lost to publishers through bad currency, revoked subscriptions, and absconding agents. Lea and Blanchard wrote J. P. Kennedy in 1848 that they had long since given up the system which they had done so much to establish over fifty years earlier, and remarked scornfully that it now required an "organized band of Yankees."

5. The Publishing Economy

In 1820 the relation between the retailer and the printers, publishers, and jobbers was extremely complex. Almost all publishers were retailers; many printers were also publishers and sometimes also retailers; all jobbers were retailers; no jobber could deal profitably in the books of all publishers; and sometimes the bookseller who served as jobber in his territory for a firm in another state advertised the books of that firm for him. Of advertising and "promotion"—one of the chief functions of the modern publisher—there was very little. In 1820 publicity was a primitive gesture rather than an art. In fact, the whole structure of the book trade was primitive. Perhaps the major cause of the disparity between the fortunes of British and American authors at the time was the contrasting maturity of the British system. The British kept competition under control through "courtesy of the trade" and other more coercive devices; kept retail prices high through collusion, even to the extent of destroying "remainders" rather than dumping them at low prices; had a closely predictable market for every type of book; had good publicity methods (some book publishers owned critical journals); and in general enjoyed all the advantages of a geographically small and homogeneous market.

In America, by contrast, no publisher could reach directly all markets in the country; few firms had sufficient capital to take the whole risk on their titles; and money and credit were so undeveloped that the mere process of paying and getting paid was difficult. The result was a system of distribution so complicated that the publishers were almost as confused as the historian who tries to read their surviving records and correspondence.

The basis of the system was a loose intercity structure of tie-ups between particular booksellers. A large publisher had agreements with one or more firms in every other large city. These firms were called "correspondents" and acted as bankers, post offices, retailers, co-publishers, and sometimes jobbers for their principals. The correspondent was a co-publisher when he co-operated in the issue of a book under the multiple imprint system, whereby a firm split the risk on a book which it had contracted to publish. Suppose, as in the case of *Sketch Book No. I*, a first edition of 2,000 copies was published simultaneously in four cities—New York, Philadelphia, Boston, and Baltimore. The printer and quasi-publisher, C. S. Van Winkle of New York, arranged with his correspondents in the other three cities to take, say, 500 copies each, at a 25 per cent discount, the names of all four firms appearing on the cover as a multiple imprint.

Each of the correspondents took charge of publicity for the work in his region. Probably no returns of unsold copies were allowed: the correspondents shared the risk. But their risk was mitigated by their monopoly: no copy could be bought in New England, for example, except from the Boston correspondent, who split his discount with retailers who bought from him.

If the work was a book rather than a pamphlet, the publisher usually sent sheets (or folded gatherings) to his correspondents, who had them bound up locally. This explains why so many first editions of the time survive in a number of different bindings. Somewhat later, it happened occasionally that a publisher had one or more extra sets of stereotype plates cast for him. He would sell a set of these to a bookseller, say, in Cincinnati, who would set up a new title page bearing his own imprint and that of the original publisher. This, again, was a way of dividing risk, for extra sets of plates, inexpensively cast from the same forms as the first set, were sold at a considerable profit, or were paid for in the shape of a charge for each copy printed therefrom.

The multiple imprint system was probably at its peak in 1820; certainly, so far as literary works were concerned, it was on the downward path from then on. By 1850 most publishers had enough capital to manufacture their books at their own risk; and distribution had so improved with the spread of railroads that many booksellers in the interior did their buying direct from publishers.

Necessary in its time, the multiple imprint system was doomed. Its vices were regional monopoly and an unprofitable division of discounts. A potential purchaser in Boston might know, through advertisements, that *The Sketch Book* was available in the correspondent's shop; but if he lived on the other side of the town, he might not bother to make the trip. The correspondent was willing to supply, and to split his discount with, a bookseller in Salem; but in Boston he was likely to prefer to monopolize the retail sale and keep the whole discount himself—if he was sure his whole stock would sell. This was nice for the correspondent, but poor for the purchaser—and for the author.

The same objections applied to the "exchange" system. Periodically, the publisher printed a list of his publications, sent it to his correspondents in other cities, and received their lists in return. Each ordered from the other as many books as he could use. No cash exchanged hands until the end of the year, when the books were balanced and the debtor paid the creditor. In 1822 Carey's correspondent in New York was Wiley and Halstead; in Boston, Wells and Lilly. Apparently (the facts are not entirely clear), in Philadelphia some of Wiley's titles could be bought only at Carey's; and in New York, some of Carey's only at Wiley's. However, the larger publishers sold some books— especially the less popular or the more doubtful ones—to non-correspondents as well. These were either purchased outright on credit or taken "on sale" or "commission," the retailer returning unsold copies at the end of a stated period. About the latter there was constant bickering because sometimes, for example, a Boston book, sent to Louisville on commission, was returned at the end of the year, in shopworn condition, and when the popularity of the work had passed.

For a period in the twenties New York and Philadelphia publishers competed through their correspondents for the first sales of new books in the smaller towns of New York, Pennsylvania, and New Jersey. Carey complained bitterly about a clever co-operative move among New York booksellers to corner the small-town market for themselves. Apparently, when one of the New York firms published a new and popular British novel, it divided up the whole edition among half a dozen of the booksellers of the city. All these firms then supplied their correspondents in Philadelphia and smaller Pennsylvania towns before they sold in quantity to a large Philadelphia jobber like Carey. When Carey tried to buy a large quantity at a big discount, he was forced to take small lots from six New York firms at small discounts. "It is the case with almost every book published in New York for a considerable time," he wrote Wiley and Halstead in 1820. The result was that he was squeezed from two directions: he could not get a discount large enough to make jobbing profitable, and he found towns supplied before he could get to them.

Such schemes were profitable for the New Yorkers, but they were not good for the trade—or for authors. Even the allotment of territories to specific booksellers operated unfairly. Ebenezer Irving gave the Charleston rights to *The Sketch Book* to Mills; when Carey sent Irving an order to ship a number of copies direct to his own correspondent in Charleston, he was refused. Thus Carey, a legitimate jobber with correspondents who depended on him, was unable to supply them with a popular work.

Obviously the techniques of book distribution were inadequate; and certainly publishing did not mix well with jobbing and retailing. The most prosperous, stable, and long-lived publishing houses avoided the confusion. Carey gave up his retail business in 1830, and probably his jobbing for other publishers at the same time. One reason why his rich and powerful neighbor to the north, the house of Harper, became the oldest general publisher in America was that it restricted itself to printing and publishing from its founding in 1817.

But conditions, such as they were, had to be faced, and no one did more to improve them than Mathew Carey. Earlier than anyone else he saw the need for book-trade organization and co-operation. In 1801 he set up the American Company of Booksellers, whose purpose was to regulate the book trade. Following the example of the literary fairs of Leipzig, his company of New York, Philadelphia, and Boston booksellers held a literary fair in New York in 1804 and offered prizes for fine inks, paper, and binding. For some reason, the organization disintegrated in 1806; but meanwhile in 1802, the New York firms had formed an Association of Booksellers to encourage the publication of American editions of texts and correct editions of the classics. More practically, the Philadelphia booksellers met in 1803 to establish a standard of twelve months' credit and a discount of one-third. On the other hand, there were no good book-trade journals or catalogues until the 1850's.

The early attempts at co-operation probably led, in the 1820's, to the establishment of an important but ill-starred institution for the wholesale distribution of books. This was the trade sale—a meeting of publishers and retailers at which publications were auctioned off in wholesale lots. From their beginning— presumably in 1824—these sales were a cause of bickering and quarreling. Theoretically they were an opportunity to bring publisher and retailer together without benefit of a middleman; and they were in fact useful in promoting contacts between publisher and retailer in the days before the traveling publisher's representative. Actually, however, they very soon turned into occasions for working off sluggish books at cut prices. To authors working with their publishers on the basis of half-profits, the sales were a nuisance. Rarely did books bring as much at auction as they did on regular sale, and writers whose books were thus sold could well suspect that their publishers were trying to unload because of lack of confidence.

Discounts were at the core of the American writer's problem. In 1820, in both England and America, the average discount to the trade was one-third, though the range was from 25 per cent to 40 per cent—even 50 per cent depending on quantity. These rates, however, applied only to books on which little or no royalty was paid. In the twenties works for which American writers were paid rarely discounted for more than 25 per cent, many for less. In 1821–22, 25 per cent was the regular discount for Irving's *The Sketch Book,* Cooper's *The Spy,* Dana's *Idle Man,* and Halleck's *Fanny.* Two documents from the beginning and end of the twenties show what this situation meant in the competition. On May 5, 1820, Moses Thomas wrote Carey, "I will take 50 [Scott's] *Monastery* at 40pc. and pay for them in *Salmagundi* [Paulding's second series] at 25pc. The terms on which I get the *Sketch Bk.* are such that I cannot include that." (On the latter he offered only ⅙.) In 1829 Carey printed a list of his prices to the trade: Scott's, Disraeli's, and Moore's works were discounted at from 50 per cent to 66 2/3 per cent—Cooper's oldest works at 50 per cent, a later one at 40 per cent, and two new ones at 25 per cent. In Boston the situation was even worse. A 20 per cent discount on American works was common, and in the early forties Emerson decreed discounts as small as 10 per cent on some of his books. It is small wonder that the reputation of many New England writers before 1850 was local: booksellers outside the area could not make a reasonable profit on their books.

Publishers' records of the 1820's are so scarce that it is impossible to make an accurate estimate of manufacturing costs, but probably they were somewhat higher than in England, where, according to Scott, manufacture was one-third of retail price. The cost of Irving's *Columbus* (1828) was 36 per cent, and Ticknor's costs in the 1830's averaged about the same. There were reasons for higher costs in America. Printers' wages were probably higher; the better grades of paper had to be imported from England and a tariff paid on them; much printing machinery had to be imported, as well as cloth for binding. A persistent shortage of type ran up costs because, since frequently a whole book could not stand in type at once, books had to be entirely reset for successive editions. As late as 1832 H. C. Carey wrote J. P. Kennedy that

> to send you one form [of proofs of *Swallow Barn*] per day, it is necessary that we should always have six forms in type, and that quantity is about twice as much as an ordinary fount of type will set up. The printers have, most stupidly, so great a variety of [styles] in the type now used that although one of them may have two thousand weight of one size in the office, it will be of three or four different founts, differing from each other so much that they

cannot be used together. Such is exactly the case with the printer of this work.

Obviously printers had not yet started to think in terms of large production and low cost.

This problem was mitigated somewhat by the use of stereotypes. By the early 1820's stereotyping was a branch of the printing industry in Philadelphia, where some Bibles, schoolbooks, and standard works were being printed from plates. Paulding's *Diverting History of John Bull and Brother Jonathan* (1815) was probably the first American "literary" work to be stereotyped, as Cooper, in 1826, was the first "literary" author whose collected works achieved that honor.

In the late twenties case binding (mass production of cloth and board cases as a separate process) was found to be much cheaper than bindings prepared individually for each volume. The general use of power presses in the thirties still further reduced costs: in 1816 it took three men one day to print 4,000 sheets; forty years later three men, plus machines, turned out 56,000 sheets. Kennedy's first novel, in 1831, cost 63¼ cents to print; his third, in 1838, cost 44½ cents. But by this date such savings were being passed on to the reader rather than to the author and publisher.

Too small a portion of the cost of publication was advertising, and almost certainly our American authorship suffered for lack of proper publicity. A retailer might announce in the papers that such-and-such books were available at his store, but there was no advertising per se by publishers. The core of the promotion system was the "review" copy, which constituted a large proportion of advertising expense. An editor received a free copy of a new book, and turned out a "notice" of it. If the author or publisher had a friend on the staff of the paper, a more extended notice, called "a puff," was likely to appear as filler. How this system developed into a racket in the thirties and forties we shall see later on, but in the twenties the "gentleman" author was squeamish even about review copies. Irving refused to allow his English publisher to send copies of *The Sketch Book* to editors because he did not want to seem to be currying favor. Like other authors, he preferred to have his influential friends work quietly behind the lines in newspaper offices.

There were minor types of advertising. Publishers printed up show cards or posters to be displayed in store windows, just as circuses and movies advertise themselves in laundry windows today. But the publisher's chief concern was publicizing his list to retailers. By the 1830's the larger firms like Harper and Carey were printing circulars concerning their new works which they dispatched to every retailer they could reach. By the 1840's these must have evolved into handbills advertising individual books, which were distributed by retailers, for Harpers wrote Prescott in 1847 that the number of circulars on his *Conquest of Peru* was 100,000.

But in the early twenties the modern concept of "promotion" was not yet born. Parson Weems had a glimmering of it, but his publishers' attitude toward it was probably characteristic of the time. They, Carey and Lea, who were probably more progressive than most firms, wrote John Neal in 1821 that "We have so many books to manage that unless a work will sell itself we can do little about it."

In the years when Irving and Cooper established the American literary profession, then, the waters of American publishing were not only calm but sluggish. The popularity of *The Sketch Book* and *The Spy* made the more alert firms lift their heads and sniff the wind for commercially desirable literary works. Venturesome small fry like Van Winkle and Wiley and Halstead in New York were literary-minded and popular with authors, but they lacked capital and techniques—and they were slovenly. Year after year they went out of business, or formed new combinations and died again—unable to keep up with the bewildering changes in the

American economy. In 1815, when Bradford and Inskeep, the Philadelphia publishers of Irving's *History of New York,* went bankrupt, dragging Moses Thomas down with them, the author wrote that Thomas was

> not to be censured in the affair otherwise than for having conducted his business in the same diffuse, sprawling manner in which all our principal booksellers dash forward into difficulty. . . . These failures I am afraid will sensibly affect the interests of literature and deter all those from the exercise of the pen who would take it up as a means of profit.

Professional authorship, obviously, was ready to begin, but the publishing world was not: the classics that Cooper and Irving produced proved more enduring than the business structure which brought them into the world as printed books.

It is no wonder that in the early twenties our successful authors used publishers only as agents and directed the business of manufacture and distribution themselves. Until the 1850's those of our writers who had the capital took over many of the functions of the publisher in order to protect their profits. This was a load that the contemporary British author did not have to bear.

CHAPTER FOUR

American Romanticism
and the Depression of 1837

THE GREAT LAND BOOM which followed the completion
of the Erie Canal in 1825 and lasted for twelve golden
years coincided with America's first great literary boom. While
money poured into the coffers of speculators and infant industries
prospered, romantic literature and philosophy were being born
or incubated. Poe turned out three volumes of aesthetically revolutionary poetry and learned to write short stories. Hawthorne
hibernated in Salem throughout the whole period and wrote
many of his best tales. Irving traveled through the West gathering material for eulogies of Astor's single-handed imperialism.
Longfellow, in his library or in Europe, absorbed great quantities
of romantic legend which he was to transmute shortly into incredibly popular rhymes. Still more important, American Transcendentalism was given an impetus as American editions of Wordsworth and Coleridge appeared and echoes of German philosophy
reached New England. Alcott evolved exhilarating theories of
education and practiced them on well-to-do Boston youngsters,
and Thoreau began to be Thoreau while still at Harvard. In 1832
Emerson made his fruitful decision to leave the arid Unitarian
Church, and four years later came the first meeting of the Transcendental Club and the first coherent statement of the new
philosophy in Emerson's *Nature*.

Suddenly the land boom collapsed. The panic began in May,
1837, when the banks suspended specie payment. By September,
nine-tenths of the nation's factories had closed. Banks failed
every day, and New York City alone had two hundred and fifty

bankruptcies in two months. As in all economic depressions, the rank and file of the population suffered most. During the bitter winter of 1838 families suffered from starvation and exposure, and the almshouses and poorhouses were full to overflowing.[1] In the cities riots raged in the streets, food stores were raided, soup kitchens were set up, and labor groups clamored so loudly at their Locofoco meetings for relief and remediary laws that the editors of the New York *Knickerbocker* nervously suggested a campaign against agitators, and several states revised their debtor laws.[2]

The depression lasted five years. The literary boom, on the other hand, not only continued but flourished. In the year of the panic Hawthorne published his *Twice-Told Tales*, and Prescott his first history, which was quickly sold out at $7.50 a set. During the depression Poe, Whittier, Longfellow, and Lowell, all published volumes of verse or prose. Longfellow was particularly fortunate. During the depression his first volume of verse went through five editions, and it was during this period that he wrote "A Psalm of Life," "The Village Blacksmith," and "Excelsior." As for Transcendentalism, economic distress seemed to nourish it. In 1837 Thoreau began his *Journal*, and at the height of the panic, in August, Emerson published his "American Scholar," our "declaration of intellectual independence." In the dreary years that followed, his group published the *Dial* and established their experimental Brook Farm. Optimistic philosophy flourished at Concord, fifteen miles south of the cotton-manufacturing towns of Lowell and Lawrence, where operatives practiced the transcendental doctrine of plain living, if not of high thinking.

It was not that the New England romanticists and intellectuals were ignorant of the forces that were building factories and creating a new and unpicturesque destitution, unrelated to the scenes of genial rustic poverty they had learned to love in the poetry of Gray and Wordsworth and of contemporary German sentimentalists. They still thought of the American workman as a farmer and artisan, and starvation was to them a European rather than an American reality; but some of them had been through the panic of 1819, and all of them must have been aware of Unitarian concern with the problem of pauperism, for at least three-quarters of the literary men in New England belonged to that prosperous sect.

It was in 1819 that urban pauperism became conspicuous for the first time in American history. As John Q. Adams wrote in 1820, "multitudes [are in] deep distress . . . and [are] looking out anywhere for a leader." In Philadelphia an investigating committee found that in thirty industries employment had dropped from 9,672 to 2,137. In New York twelve to thirteen thousand persons received relief, and a newly organized Society for the Prevention of Pauperism estimated the number of paupers in the city at 8,000.[3] In Boston the Unitarians began the humanitarian activity for which they became famous. In 1822 they established the Ministry at Large, the purpose of which was the administration of charity and religion—not Unitarianism, they explained significantly, but religion. Under Joseph Tuckerman they established missions among the poor who were without religious affiliations, studied the slums and the causes of poverty, and worked out a technique for charity. In *Principles and Results of the Ministry at Large in Boston* (1838) Tuckerman drew such a useful distinction between pauperism and poverty that the French "sociologist" De Gerando published a translation of it. More practically, his work led to the establishment of a legislative Commission on Poverty in 1832. Tuckerman's paternalism was indicative of a new attitude in the twenties which received the moral and financial support of the Unitarian businessmen. Unitarian leaders stressed the duties of the upper class toward the lower, and charity provided a means of performing them. The Unitarians established most of the prominent institutions for the poor at the time, including the Massachusetts General Hospital, the McLean and Perkins Asylums for the Blind, and a number

of institutions for the orphaned and the insane. Of course, the
Unitarians were not alone in their concern about a depressed
class uninstructed in the principles of Christianity, for in New
Haven the Trinitarians noted with joy that the concentration of
workers in factory towns made somewhat easier the labors of
their evangelists.[4]

Even if our writers had not kept in touch with institutional
activity, some of them had ample reason to be aware of such
realities as dividends from the manufacturing corporations and
railroads which were laying off workers. Indeed, Longfellow,
Prescott, and Lowell were related or married to manufacturing
and banking families, and had learned to keep an eye on business
conditions. Transcendentalists transcended this narrow interest,
for with the exception of Emerson they were practically free of
investment worries; but if the latter's *Journals* may be considered
a guide, they must have discussed frequently the new phenomena
of railroads and factories. As early as 1835 he had taken note of
the number of spindles at Waltham and Lowell, and when the
panic came, he watched the figures on bankruptcy, wholesale
prices, and discount rates. Even the impractical founders of
Brook Farm had to face the unpleasant reality of a mortgage
administered by the bourgeois officer of a railroad, when in the
midst of the depression they made their heroic effort to escape
the evils of life under a capitalistic economy; and they must have
felt badly let down when Hawthorne untranscendentally sued to
recover the thousand dollars he had invested in their enterprise.

Certainly all New England writers at the time must have
been familiar with the thinking of William Ellery Channing on
the subject of industrial poverty, for as the leading Unitarian
minister of the day and as the forerunner of the Transcendentalists, he enjoyed the audience of both the radicals and conserva-
tives. He had been active in the organization of the Ministry at
Large after the panic of 1819, and even at the height of prosperity
in the middle thirties, he had been fully aware of the degrading

living conditions of the mill operatives and had even rejected intemperance as the basic cause. Nevertheless, he believed with his generation that "the chief evils of poverty are moral in their origin and character," and that "moral and religious culture is the great blessing to be bestowed upon the poor."[5] This was anything but the pious complacency of a comfortable clergyman. Rather, it was the product of a background of hard work, frugality, and asceticism; of a belief that there was little real difference between the lot of the laborer and his own; and of a pardonable misunderstanding of the nature of economic forces in a transition period. When the panic came, he was sincerely distressed at the suffering of the poor and at the spectacle of class animosity. His answer was the familiar specific offered in that day for social and economic ills: education. He would teach the working class to rise above the physical and the sensual, and to use the resources of mind and soul, which he himself had in abundance. He would show them how to educate themselves morally and spiritually, a plan which would have the double advantage of saving other people's money and preserving the workers' independence. Throughout the thirties and forties he lectured to workingmen's societies on self-culture, showing them how to use their "spare" time to the greatest moral and spiritual advantage.

Such was the temper of the time that the workers not only listened but rejoiced, and Channing told with pride how his lectures were reprinted in England and "widely circulated among the overtasked operatives," and that he received letters of thanks from English Mechanics' Institutes.[6] In that period the fallacies of his system went unchallenged. The question of how the operative who worked twelve hours a day was to find the time, energy, or money for "self-culture" seemed to present no great problem. Only a little time each day was needed; the will would supply the energy and books were unnecessary, for intellectual improvement was not to be confused with book-learning. As an honest thinker, Channing acknowledged the imperious force of the facts and admitted that often the worker "can live for but one end, which is to keep himself alive"; but he left the answer to the future. "I wait for the judgment of profound thinkers on this point, a judgment formed after patient study of political economy, and human nature and human history; nor even on such authority shall I readily despair of the multitude of my race." [7] In the midst of the depression, shocked by statistics he had found in Marshall's *Statistics* of the British Empire, he wrote Harriet Martineau asking her to "recommend any books which treat of the distribution of wealth, and which particularly consider the question, how the most equable distribution may be effected in consistency with private rights and industry. The subject has always been to me beset with difficulties. The tending of all societies is to the depression of the multitude of men, and freedom promises no remedy." [8]

Had he pursued further the question of freedom—of "laissez-faire"—he might have found a way out, for his confusion was clearly rooted in his agrarian sympathies. The forces of commerce and industrialism he understood superficially, but like most liberals of that day, he fancied that they were subject to moral control. Instinctively he hated the new industrial world. Everybody was overworked. "My own constitution," he says, "was broken by early toils." The division of labor in the factories— the "monotonous, stupefying round of unthinking toil" which "dwarfs the intellectual powers"—appalled him. [9] Realizing that "at the present time a momentous change is taking place," he asked whether "the mass of the people will be permanently advanced in the comforts of life . . . and in the culture of their highest powers and affections." [10] Could the American workman "stand his ground against the half-famished, ignorant workmen of Europe, who will toil for any wages, and who never think of redeeming an hour for personal improvement"? His reply was typical of liberal agrarian thought in America. "If this end should require us . . . to desert from the race of commercial and manufacturing competition with Europe; if it should require that our great cities should cease to grow, and that a large portion of our trading population should return to labor, these requisitions ought to be obeyed."

Whatever his confusion about the problem of poverty, Channing was one of the few literary men of the day who were deeply disturbed by it, and except for Orestes Brownson, he was the only one of them who gave much thought to the distress of the workers during the depression. As an active social worker, Channing made it his business to see the slums which most of the other writers avoided. Perhaps also it was physical contact with poverty that made Brownson speak plainly and to the point during the depression. As early as 1829, he had been active in the Workingmen's Party, and had adopted Channing's theories on the education of the worker.[11] When the panic came, he dropped these theories. After a series of blasts against the banks as the chief offenders, and a controversy over the health and morals of the women operatives at Lowell (whose average working life, he said, was three years), he published in 1840 his famous article on "The Laboring Classes."[12] He told an incredulous world that in the United States death by starvation was not uncommon, and the only remedy was to "emancipate the proletaries." How? Not by inner reform: that theory had been condemned by six thousand years' experience. Channing's "self-culture" could not abolish inequality nor restore men to their rights. The system must be changed, not its managers. The priesthood must be destroyed, the Christianity of Christ must be revived, control of the government must be taken away from the banks and given to the workers, and privilege must be wiped out by prohibiting the inheritance of property. He even hinted that the change must come through force, though the time was not yet ripe.

To his liberal contemporaries such talk occasioned raised eyebrows, and their skepticism concerning his sincerity turned out to be justified. By 1844 Brownson had been converted to Catholicism and had run through four religions and perhaps as many economic creeds. Whether or not his championship of the labor movement did more damage than good, his factual articles on labor conditions in his own magazines stimulated Theodore Parker to do much sounder thinking on the problem. Decidedly, Brownson and Channing were forerunners of the group who were to investigate industrial poverty in the middle and late forties.

Meanwhile, what of the major writers? To all of them the depression must have been a fact, whether personal or social, and their reactions to it are an interesting commentary on the relationship between the writer and his mileu. One thing is immediately apparent: few of them published anything which reveals any particular consciousness of the distress of the worker. Melville, eighteen years old in 1837, saw poverty in New York and Liverpool which must have contributed to the cosmic bitterness of his mature works,[13] and young Russell Lowell printed some juvenilia concerning "hunger and cold"—a subject to which he did not return. The rest of them, though they all showed signs of being aware of the panic, made no mention of human suffering. If they worried at all, it was about the damages that hungry mobs might do to private property. Thus Emerson's first reaction to the panic was that the sixty thousand laborers "to be presently thrown out of work . . . make a formidable mob to break open banks, rob the rich, and brave the domestic government." [14] If they felt any pity, it was for the solid merchant who had been damaged through no fault of his own. As Emerson said, "The merchant fails. He has put more than labor, he has put character and ambition into his fortune, and cannot lose it without bitter mortification. . . . It seems that he could and should have been content with safe wealth, and not ventured and so fallen." The honest merchant sees that "a great fortune has not an evil, a dishonorable influence. . . . Its influence is very far from being built on the weakness and sycophancy of men, but it is a certificate of great faculty, of virtues of a certain sort. Moral considerations give currency every day to notes of hand. . . . Success and credit depend on enterprise, on accurate perceptions, on honesty, on steadiness of mind. *This man* in the land-fever bought no acre in Maine or Michigan." [15]

This attitude was typical of the times. When Dion Boucicault later wrote his play *The Poor of New York*, based on the panics of 1837 and 1857, he wasted no words on the workers. "The poor! Whom do you call poor! . . . They are more frequently found under a black coat than a red shirt." All of them are, like his hero, once prosperous people, cheated by Wall Street. "These needy wretches are poorer than the poor, for they are obliged to conceal their poverty, with the false mask of content—smoking a cigar to disguise their hunger—they drag from their pockets their last quarter to throw it with studied carelessness to the beggar, whose mattress at home is lined with gold."

Aside from the traditional acceptance of a poor class as a law of nature, there were several specific reasons for the indifference of the romantic writers. It is not unfair, perhaps, to inquire into the personal financial condition of these authors, since a real relationship frequently exists between a writer's comfort and his sensitivity to social catastrophe. Well-to-do authors like Prescott were interested in the mechanics of the decline. Prescott's securities were damaged a little, but his history of Ferdinand and Isabella had a big sale. Longfellow was safely established on the Harvard faculty and probably received help from Judge Longfellow which enabled him to travel. Irving was comfortable, having hired out to Astor for sums unknown but reputed large.[16] The sale of Hawthorne's *Twice-Told Tales* was probably hurt by the panic, but in 1839 his friends in politics obtained a lucrative job for him in the Boston Customs House which protected him from the financial bad weather of the next two years. Brownson likewise enjoyed a political job as steward of the U.S. Marine Hospital throughout the depression. Poe, of course, was rarely out of financial difficulties, be the times good or bad. Ministers like Theodore Parker received small but steady salaries in stable farming communities whose respectable citizens had not caught the gambling fever. Thoreau lived from hand to mouth and liked it. Emerson wrote in 1838 that he owned a house, $22,000 worth of stocks earning 6 per cent, and an income from lectures varying from $400 to $800 a year.[17]

These facts may mean little or nothing, but they are significant in this respect: the New Englanders' incomes, whether from work or investments, suffered very little in the panic of 1837. The circumstance that their books had fair sales, that their lectures were well attended, and that their holdings were not wiped out, throws light on the situation, and suggests that romanticism and optimistic philosophy grew and prospered during very trying years in our economic history. The fact is that New England, especially Massachusetts, was in remarkably good condition from 1837 to 1843, while other sections of the country were prostrated. For although many of the textile factories were closed by the fall of 1837, and the operatives lost their jobs, New England railroads and banks suffered hardly at all. "Boston securities," say the economic historians of the period, "passed through the relatively troubled times of 1816-1819 with hardly a tremor, and they coursed through the even more active forties with much less movement than the index of New York bank stocks reveals. . . . One is forced to conclude that Boston securities were strikingly insulated from forces which were active in other parts of the country." [18]

New England railroad stocks were so divergent from main movements that Messrs. Smith and Cole charted them separately in their statistical records for the period. In 1843, with Central Atlantic roads at an index of 35, New England roads were at 90, not 20 points below the great peak of 1835. Nor was the construction of new roads checked by the depression. The Boston & Worcester, even in the difficult early years, earned an average 7 per cent, and the Western Railroad, chartered in 1833, and begun in

1837 with the aid of a grant from the state, obtained the rest of its funds by a canvass of Boston and main-line towns. By 1847 it was paying 8 per cent.[19] Professor Cole explains this in part by the attitude of Massachusetts toward railroads. "While the roads were permitted to fix their own rates (and these rates were the lowest in the United States), the legislature reserved the right to lower such charges if the net income of the company exceeded ten per cent of the cost of the property. The legislature also reserved the right to purchase the railroads for the state at the end of twenty years from the date of their completion. Such a threatening attitude might well curb speculative enthusiasm for the shares of railroads incorporated in Massachusetts." Of course, Massachusetts was a region already well settled, whose potentialities were easily gauged, but the conservatism of New England stock purchasers was well known. "Moreover, the securities of the New England railroads may have been closely held. . . . Possibly their acquisition had been dictated as much by the desire for an income-yielding investment as by an itching for marked appreciation in values."

The New England banks acquired a like reputation for sound policy. Controlled by a banking aristrocracy made up of the Amorys, the Perkinses, the Appletons, and the Lawrences (the group that supported Daniel Webster in politics with a fund of $100,000), Boston institutions not only sustained the values of their stock (Massachusetts scrip, issued in 1838, commanded the highest price of loans placed by any American state in London) but did their best to restore credit by importing British gold.[20] It is worth noting that Massachusetts banks offered the only bank statistics available for the period from 1790 to 1820. New England investors had every reason to feel confident in local enterprises, and indeed, there was no great gap socially and intellectually between the old mercantile group, who were now going into railroads and manufactures, and the literary men. Prescott and Longfellow married into capitalist families through the Lawrences and the Appletons; John Murray Forbes was an intimate of Emerson's and a member of the Saturday Club; Francis G. Shaw and Lucy Cabot took a second mortgage on Brook Farm; and the Peabodys have been called the patrons of the Transcendental movement. It was only natural, then, that bank, railroad, and industrial stocks provided a substantial part of the income of those New England authors who had money to invest. Specifically, Emerson and Prescott had such holdings, and though they complained of a slight depreciation and an occasional passed dividend, there is no indication in their letters and journals that they were seriously affected at any time during the depression. What is more important, it was probably this same group of investors in Boston and "the main-line towns" who were able to attend Emerson's lectures (his audiences averaged four hundred between 1837 and 1841) and to buy Prescott's $7.50 history when times were hardest. And it was Massachusetts economic soundness generally which made possible the progress of New England idealism through such specific circumstances as Emerson's gift of $500 to Alcott for a trip to England in 1842, and his financing of Carlyle's books in America; the "kind friend's" gift of $600 to Parker for his trip abroad in 1843; the ease with which the Brook Farmers mortgaged their property for $500 more than it cost them, through the generosity of such local aristocrats as Francis G. Shaw and the co-operation of the Commissioners of the Sinking Fund of the Western Railroad Corporation.[21] It also helps to explain how prominent Unitarian laymen—the Lowells, the Appletons, the Lawrences, and other members of the banking, railroad, and manufacturing aristocracy—were able to establish such paternalistic humanitarian institutions as the Perkins Institute for the Blind in 1837 and the Lowell Institute in 1839, and contribute heavily to various reform movements.

New England was "sound," and it is not surprising that the writers refused to be disturbed by talk of bread-lines in other regions. Even the distress of the working class in the manufacturing towns was not particularly conspicuous. Boston had its slums, it is true, but they were full of unassimilated Irish. The native factory workers in Lowell, Bedford, and Lynn fared better, since for the most part they came from neighboring farms to which they could return when the mills closed down. What was more, most of the writers themselves lived simply and frugally according to our standards, and were not conscious of a great gap between their standards of living and that of the worker. The real difference, they thought, was in the mind, not in material comforts.

What really disturbed the writers of the day was not the poor, whom we have always with us, but the new commercial middle class, whose feverish expansion had brought about the crash. Channing, for instance, not only held the speculators responsible for the panic but accused them of endangering the whole social structure through their efforts to become prosperous without labor. "Thus prosperity is in more danger from those who live by the sweat of their brow." [22] It was the pushing middle class, he felt, which made the masses dissatisfied, put a deplorable stigma upon physical work, and contaminated American culture with its cheap penny papers, its vulgarity, and its false standards. Poe's only literary reaction to the depression was a satire on "The Business Man," attacking his lack of taste, his spineless subjection to the banks, and his pretensions to genius. Hawthorne, in "Peter Goldthwaite's Treasure," mocked the speculators and Colonel Sellerses of his time.

Emerson's entries in his *Journal* through the depression years contain the essence of the rebellion of his class against Jacksonian democracy. Even before the panic he had expressed his dislike of the new regime. "In a former age," he wrote in 1834, "men of might were men of will; now they are men of wealth." [23] He might have added that that age was not far past and that he had lived in it, for up to Jackson's time the men of might had been men of his own class. Now all that was changed. It was "rather melancholy . . . to find no more receivers of your doctrine than your own three or four, and sit down to wait until it shall please God to create some more men before your schools can expect to increase." [24] Moreover, the new class in power seemed not to be hardworking members of a profession. "The virtue of the intellect consists in preferring work to trade."

The weakness of the business class would seem to be their lack of any working philosophy. Emerson talked with many of his business neighbors in Concord and came to the conclusion that "the most wonderful men in our community have no theory that can stand scrutiny. . . . They are devoid of remote aims." [25] Yet he did not undervalue legitimate business as a calling, nor the business man per se. John Murray Forbes, the railroad man, he honestly admired, and he spoke no word against the financial barons who seemed to conduct legitimate enterprises. It was the lesser fry, the new middle class, who speculated in land, whom he criticized. They were turning us into a money-mad nation without value, without principles. As the depression wore on, Emerson became more bitter about the materialism of which it was a symbol and gradually came to identify it with democracy. "Bancroft talked of the foolish *Globe* newspaper," he wrote in 1838. (It had a circulation of thirty thousand and reached three hundred thousand readers.) "I ought to have said what utter nonsense to name in my ear this number, as if it were anything. Three million such people as can read the *Globe* with interest are as yet in too crude a state of nonage as to deserve any regard." [26] The Van Buren-ism which gulled these millions disgusted him, as did the "progress" which they admired. "The rapid wealth which hundreds in the community acquire in trade . . . enchants the eyes of all the rest, the luck of one is the hope of thousands, and the whole generation is discontented with the tardy rate of growth which contents every European community." [27] "This invasion of Nature by Trade with its Money, its Credit, its Steam, its Railroads, threatens to upset the balance of man, and establish a new universal monarchy more tyrannical than Babylon or Rome." [28]

The total effect of these phenomena was to send Emerson deeper into his idealism and to make him preach more vigorously than ever. Seen against the background of the depression and of his thoughts concerning it, his "American Scholar," conceived and written while banks were collapsing, and the famous *Essays* published in 1841, gain a fresh significance. The crash supplied him with an object lesson, a factual point of reference, which gave his still-developing idealism a special cogency and a vindication. "I see good in such emphatic and universal calamity as the times bring that they dissatisfy me with society. Under common burdens we say there is much virtue in the world and what evil coexists is inevitable. . . . When these full measures come, it then stands confessed—society has played out its last stake. . . . Young men have no hope. Adults stand like day laborers idle in the streets. . . . The present generation is bankrupt of principles and hope, as of property . . . behold the boasted world has come to nothing. . . . Pride, Thrift, Expediency, who jeered and chirped and were so well pleased with themselves and made merry with the dream, as they termed it, of Philosophy and Love—behold they are all flat, and here is the soul erect and unconquered still." [29]

These words were written in private in May, 1837, but the essays published in the next few years were written in the same triumphant mood. To us it may seem that he was somewhat callous in raising this slightly vindictive paean of joy at a time when thousands of workers who had taken no part in the gambling were suffering acute privation. It is in the essay on "Self-Reliance" (1841) that we find the statement, "Do not tell me, as a good man did today, of my obligation to put all poor men in good situations. Are they *my* poor? I tell thee, thou foolish philanthropist, that I grudge the dollar, the dime, the cent I give to such men as do not belong to me." It is in his attitude toward the lowest social strata that Emerson reveals the class basis of his thinking and the essential similarity between his social point of view and that of such complacent patricians as Longfellow and Prescott. Even his antipathy to slavery was lukewarm until his personal moral code was outraged. In 1846 he wrote in his *Journal*, "Does he not do more to abolish slavery who works all day steadily in his garden than he who goes to abolition meetings and makes a speech," and in his "Ode to W. H. Channing" in 1847 he rebuked that zealot for trying to draw him into a cause which would "rend the Northland from the South." But when the new Fugitive Slave Law was passed in 1850, and his moral independence was violated through the complicity of his own state in the slave system, he forgot his philosophic calm and stumped in Concord, Boston, and New York for John Brown and the Kansas settlers, as zealously as Mr. Channing.[30] Emerson refused to get excited over human chattels, but he fought like a tiger when the state violated his own integrity.

In the thirties the real class animus was not between the "haves" and the "have-nots." So far as the writers and intellectuals were concerned, the struggle was between their own homogeneous patrician society and a rising materialistic middle class without education and tradition, who were winning cultural and economic power and changing the tone of American life. The patrician group, molded by college education and Unitarian and Congregational churches into a traditional cultural pattern, had for a generation controlled the national culture through the professions of law, ministry, and politics; had written their own books and edited all the critical journals; had represented the people in their legislatures and garnered all the diplomatic appointments.

But with the widening of the franchise and the advent of the new politicians of the Jackson and Van Buren regimes, their power had begun to weaken: the lower middle class had begun to feel their political strength and to demand their share of patronage, and as their power grew, their own culture took shape and engulfed the old. As a class, they were aggressive, materialistic, and vulgar. Impatient of the slow returns from professional work, they were speculators and gamblers. Careless of traditional "taste," they were ostentatious in their preferences in dress, architecture, and interior decoration. Lacking college education, in literature they preferred novelty, brevity, sensationalism, and sentimentalism to the solid learning and stately prose of the *North American Review* and the serenity and authority of the classics. By 1840 they had established academies whose curricula had profound effects upon those of the colleges, and lurid newspapers which at a penny a copy drove out the solid but dull sheets which only gentlemen had read. They were building horrible Gothic residences whose elaborateness excited the public far more than the quiet classical Georgian houses of the aristocrats. They had established magazines like *Graham's* which had such big circulations and paid so well that patrician writers who depended upon their art had to succumb to them.

Emerson's speech "The American Scholar" (which, it must be remembered, was addressed to the Phi Beta Kappa Society of Harvard) was essentially a plea to his own class to recapture cultural power and leadership by reforming its education and vitalizing its ideals. For Emerson had perceived the spiritual aridity of the colleges and of Unitarianism, and knew that they no longer had sufficient energy to cope with the needs of his class in a new age. For the new generation it was important to learn more from nature and less from books and tradition. It was necessary also, he pointed out, to act and assume leadership. Above all, the scholar must be independent and "defer never to the popular cry." "Self-Reliance," likewise, may be interpreted as a protest against the tyranny of public opinion in a society in which numbers were beginning to be more powerful than the prestige which Emerson's class had always enjoyed. In the privacy of his *Journals*, protest became pugnacity:

> Look danger in the eye—it vanishes:
> Anatomize the roaring populace,
> Big, dire, and overwhelming as they seem,
> Piecemeal 'tis nothing. Some of them but scream
> Fearing the others; some are lookers-on;
> One of them hectic day by day consumes,
> And one will die tomorrow of the flux.
> One of them has already changed his mind
> And falls out with the ringleaders, and one
> Has seen his creditor amidst the crowd
> And flies. And there are heavy eyes
> That miss their sleep and meditate retreat.
> A few malignant heads keep up the din,
> The rest are idle boys.[31]

The whole romantic movement in America may be considered in part as a protest against the new bourgeoisie. Poe's natural bitterness was aggravated by the necessity to pander to it. Cooper, from 1834 to the end of his life, waged a bitter war against its newspapers. Holmes's essays and such of his poems as "Rhymed Lesson" are attacks upon their manners and speech. J. G. Holland's best-selling *Titcomb's Letters to Young People* were intended to improve their manners. When Edward Everett, lured by the offer of $10,000 for a series of articles, sold out to the most blatant of their journalists, Robert Bonner of the famous *New York Ledger*, he was attacked as a renegade, and Irving lost the respect of his class when John Jacob Astor bought up his talents for propaganda purposes. Here was intramural, class warfare which overshadowed completely the conflict between laborer and non-laborer, and it was the factor which chiefly determined the attitude of the romantic writers toward the Panic of 1837.

1. H. J. Carman, *Social and Economic History of the United States* (Boston, 1934), II, 165.

2. Samuel Reznik, "Social History of an American Depression," *American Historical Review*, XL (July, 1935), 662.

3. Samuel Reznik, "The Depression of 1819–1822, A Social History," *American Historical Review*, XXXIX (October, 1933), 28.

4. "The Moral Influences of Manufactures," *Christian Spectator*, IV (1932), 375.

5. "Ministry for the Poor," *Works* (Boston, 1879), p. 78.

6. W. H. Channing, *Memoir of W. E. Channing* (Boston, 1848), p. 56.

7. *Ibid.*

8. *Ibid.*, p. 115.

9. *Ibid.*, p. 39.

10. *Ibid.*, p. 64.

11. Henry F. Brownson, *Orestes A. Brownson's Early Life*.

12. *Boston Quarterly Review*, III (1840), 358.

13. See his *Redburn*, chaps. iv and xxxvii.

14. *Journals*, April 22, 1837, IV, 209.

15. *Journals*, May 5, 1837, IV, 216.

16. See Stanley Williams' *Life of Irving*, II, 7 ff.

17. *Correspondence of Thomas Carlyle and Ralph Waldo Emerson, 1834–1872* (Boston, 1883), I, 160.

18. W. B. Smith and A. H. Cole, *Fluctuations in American Business, 1790–1860* (Cambridge, 1935).

19. B. H. Meyer, *Transportation in the United States before 1860* (New York, 1917), pp. 321–28.

20. Arthur B. Darling, *Political Changes in Massachusetts, 1824–1848* (New Haven, 1925), p. 236.

21. Lindsay Swift, *Brook Farm* (New York, 1900), pp. 19 f.

22. *Works*, p. 28.

23. *Journals*, II, 250.

24. *Ibid.*, p. 371.

25. *Ibid.*, p. 458.

26. *Ibid.*, IV, 440.

27. *Ibid.*, V, 529.

28. *Ibid.*, p. 285.

29. *Ibid.*, IV, 241.

30. Emerson's philosophic calm was also shaken by the panic of 1857, which New England did not escape. See the statistics for the period in Smith and Cole, *op. cit.*; note also Emerson's indignation when his railroad stocks depreciated seriously, in *Journals*, September 22, 1856, IX, 122.

31. *Journals*, 1838, V, 30.

CHAPTER FIVE

Cooper as Professional Author[1]

I BEGIN with the proposition that Cooper's significance today lies not in his mastery of fictional art (which is at least questionable), or in the viability of even his best books (which do not crowd the lists of the reprint libraries), but rather in his personality and in his character as an American citizen. For this reason he belongs with those other Americans—Franklin, Mark Twain, Thoreau, perhaps even Scott Fitzgerald—whose art and whose intellects are of less significance than their representativeness as American personalities.

Such personalities become interesting—become illuminating—for American cultural history only as they develop through contact and conflict with the forces of our national life. I hope to contribute a little to our understanding of Cooper's public character by telling something about his professional character, and by showing how that character developed through his experiences with his publishers and the book trade.

Let me start with some generalizations about Cooper's place in the history of professional authorship. In his thirty-one-year writing career he averaged a novel a year, and turned out twenty other separate book publications and a still unknown quantity of periodical contribution. He was, therefore, the first American writer of imaginative literature to make a living from writing, continuously and successfully. By these terms, he, rather than Irving, was our first professional author. By the same terms, he was the *only* commercially successful writer of belles-lettres up to 1850. Irving and Hawthorne are excluded because of their years in government office and the long hiatuses in their productivity; Bryant and Poe because of their work as editors; Emerson because he was primarily a lecturer; and others for reasons similar to these. Contrary to general opinion, his popularity did not decline at the end of his career; it increased. Such works as *The Wing-and-Wing* and *Wyandotté* in the 1840's sold twice as well as *The Spy* and *The Pioneers* in the early 1820's. In the last three years of his life three more or less complete editions of his novels were brought out by different publishers, and in the four years after his death one house is said to have sold 300,000 copies of his works. Yet by the late 1840's he had become a tired hack, forced to grind out two novels a year for much smaller returns than he had received in the twenties for one novel a year—and this in spite of the fact that some of the novels of the last decade were as good as those of the first. The explanation of this paradox of continued popularity, continued skill, but increasing drudgery and penury, lies partly in publishing history.

Let us go back to the author. A more complete extrovert has never been known in American letters. No temperamental artist could have produced as regularly and steadily as Cooper did. After *The Spy* he suffered none of the tortures Irving endured in waiting for the "right mood." Nor did he, like Hawthorne, have to lie fallow in summer. G. C. Verplanck may possibly have been right in 1824 when he said that Cooper was "not a regular literary artizan who can do his job within a year or work by the day at so many pages a morning," but that was before Cooper could have been sure that writing was his proper business and his lifework. Before many years he was writing on schedule—by the clock. "I said to Scott," he wrote a friend, "that I always invented twice as much as was committed to paper, in my walks, or in bed, and in my own judgment, much of the best parts of the composition never saw the light; for what was written was usually written at set hours, and was a good deal a matter of

chance." Note the implication: that he threw away many inspirations and inventions simply because they did not turn up at the
right point in the course of composition.

The power of invention, apparently, never failed him, as it
often failed Hawthorne. His tank was always full; he always
had more novels in his head than he had time to write. He could
promise two or three novels, in advance, on specific subjects.
This fertility was sometimes a nuisance to his publishers. On
one occasion he promised them one novel set in Italy and
another on Lake Ontario. By the time he had finished the first,
he was hot with inspiration for two other novels set in Europe,
and the publishers had to wait eight years for the Ontario story,
which was the only one of the lot they really wanted.

He was like his assassin, Mark Twain, in letting his books
write themselves. He was never bothered or slowed up by problems of form or method. Sometimes, when he was well along in a
book, he had no idea what his last chapter would contain. He
was not alone among novelists in starting one end of the book
through the press while the other was still unwritten, but few
writers have had his naïvely objective curiosity about how
his own plot was going to turn out. He had an unshakable
confidence, which he reiterated again and again to his publishers
when they worried about the drag in the first two parts of his
manuscript, that the last part would be full of torpedoes which
would save the story. And here is an odd fact for the critic.
Though Cooper wrote primarily for his American public, and
though all his full-length novels were published in two volumes
in America, he *thought* in terms of the traditional British three-
volume structure, in which form his novels appeared in England.
Thus he wrote his American publishers, Carey and Lea, who
had printed his *Red Rover* in two volumes as usual, that the
first and last volumes "are the best I have ever written." Any
analysis of the form of Cooper's novels ought to take this fact
into consideration. One suspects that the structural weakness of

some of his books is similar to that of many three-act plays: the dramatist writes inspired first and third acts but does not know quite what to do in the second. Sometimes Cooper's second volume seems to exist simply to separate the first from the third.

Rewriting and revision of manuscript seem never to have caused him any pain—simply because he did not rewrite. It is perhaps unkind to say that he sent his first drafts to the printer and did his revising in later editions, but it sometimes happened. He depended heavily on publishers' proofreaders, and on that account he wrote Bentley airily, "I pay no attention to any of the spelling." Of course he grew wary after some early disasters. *Precaution* was so full of blunders that Bryant was puzzled and repelled by it. A typical sentence read, "To this Sir Edward cordially assented, and the old gentle*man* separated." This typographical homicide so infuriated Cooper that he threatened to sue the printer.

When he did do a thorough job of revision of an old novel, he demanded handsome extra pay for it. He was quite willing to adjust the quality of the "purification" (as he called the work of revision) to the rate of pay. He told Bentley that he would revise his old novels five pounds' worth or fifty pounds' worth, as Bentley pleased. "This is an age," he said in self-defense, "when good company [meaning Scott] makes an author shameless, and I believe it is very generally understood that the genius finishes to order." "Recollect," he wrote Bentley in the course of this bargaining, "it is harder work to read [these novels of mine] than it is to write them." Three hundred pounds, he added, would hardly reward him for the "vexation of spirit caused by reading nine novels written by myself."

Cooper's stylistic slovenliness was recognized by some critics, and was attributed by his enemies to the over-rapid writing of a mercenary author. This, of course, was nonsense. But it is true that Cooper had no very high regard for the niceties of style; he was capable of saying, "I find the mere composition of a tale a source of pleasure." The adjective *mere* is revealing, but it reflects no particular eccentricity in Cooper. Contemporary attitudes toward rhetoric, inherited probably from the eighteenth century, sanctioned what seems to us an unnecessary distinction between fine finish in prose and strength in prose, and assumed that much finishing reduced strength. These attitudes are suggested in a comforting letter written to Cooper by his friend Charles Wilkes: "Certainly every man has a perfect right . . . to exert his talents in the way he likes best. If he chooses to employ more of the *labor time,* to polish his works to the utmost, he may have the pleasure of thinking his fame will be more lasting, but even this advantage over more hasty productions is by no means certain, and strength is often sacrificed to polish. The one I fancy is generally an irksome task—the other often a delightful one—to embody fleeting visions which pass thro' the mind." This was poor advice to give to Cooper: early nineteenth-century prose is full of unpolished visions which were fleeting in a sense the authors never intended. But in an age which preferred oratorical flux to concise and economical statement, Cooper's style was the norm, and he properly concerned himself with broad rather than fine effects.

About the story quality of his novels, he had no doubts, no diffidence. The man whose second book was a best-seller went through no harrowing years of trial and error, as Hawthorne did. He burned no manuscripts in despair, and put by few if any for later rewriting. The novel he was writing was always his best, and he was all the more certain of this if his critics and publishers thought otherwise. *The Bravo,* he was sure, would be a hit. *The Headsman* would be better than *The Bravo.* When Carey told him that *The Monikins* was the worst failure of his career, he replied flatly, "It is my favorite book." When he was writing *Mercedes of Castile,* he thought it would become one of the "standard works of the language," but it failed so badly that his publisher asked him for a refund. There was a touch of Colonel

Sellersism in all this. He was capable of counting on receipts of $15,000 from a book which brought him one-third that amount, and five hundred dollars a year for life from another which breathed its last after three years on the market.

It was perhaps part of the secret of Cooper's success that he was never haunted by any sense of inferiority to British novelists. He had good reason not to be. He had intended his tour de force, *Precaution*, to be mistaken for an English tale. "No book was ever written with less thought or more rapidity," he slyly confessed; but though he had to remainder the American edition of a thousand copies to Harpers to get rid of it, in England it had twice the sale of *The Spy*, and by 1851 the British had bought five editions of it. "I take more pains with *The Spy*," he said impudently, "as it is to be an *American* novel professedly."

Though his self-respect as a writer was unmitigated, he exploited literature in a brisk and business-like fashion. In his correspondence with James Ogden, his agent in the cotton market, discussions of the salability of his novels mingled naturally with shoptalk about other commodities. For an unwritten novel on the Great Lakes he demanded of his English publisher one hundred pounds extra because it was not only nautical but had "Indians intermingled." A letter of 1826 to Colburn of London sets the keynote: "It is necessary to speak of these works as mere articles of trade." The most famous of his contemporaries— Emerson and Melville—felt much the same way about their books.

These are a few of the high lights of Cooper's professional personality, but to understand it fully we must stand as far away from it as possible and see it as a small shadow on the screen of economic and book-trade history. His thirty years of professional authorship (1821–51) began when the business cycle was on the upswing, and ended when another era of prosperity was dawning. During those three decades there were only five years of really serious depression—the Panic of 1837 and the

Debt Repudiation Depression of 1840–43. When *The Spy* was published in 1821, the country had just emerged from a primary postwar depression, and the great age of river and canal traffic was under way. When *The Ways of the Hour* was published in 1850, the railroads had just crossed the Alleghenies, and the era of national marketing had begun. Though Cooper died just as huge editions of his novels were about to be distributed in the now easily accessible trans-Allegheny region, he was historically lucky. He had reaped his biggest harvests in the two decades preceding the economic and book-trade crisis of the early forties.

It was perhaps a coincidence that the depression of 1840–43 was contemporaneous with the worst period in the competition of British and American literature. Literary history sees the early forties as bright with promise and fulfilment, but let us look at these years from the American author's point of view. Emerson's *Essays* were on the market, but the author had to pay for their manufacture and they had a very small circulation. Poe's *Tales of the Grotesque and Arabesque* were available because Carey and Lea could not get rid of the 750 copies they had printed. Hawthorne was wearily contriving one magazine story a month, stamped out by formula, because his collections would not sell. Irving had stopped producing temporarily, and his works were almost out of print. Thoreau inquired into literary opportunities in New York, and gave up. In a word, the commercial value of the works of these masters was close to zero. The cause was mainly—but not entirely—the competitive reprinting of British books.

Cooper was better off than most because he wrote the kind of thing that had some commercial value in any market, but consider what the competition did to him. In the 1820's novels by Scott and Cooper sold for two dollars. In 1840 Disraeli's novels sold for seventy-five cents and Cooper's for a dollar fifty. In 1843 one could buy a new novel by Dickens for ten cents and a new one by Cooper for fifty cents. A revised postal act of 1843 took the profit out of ten-cent novels, competition finished off the "mammoth weeklies" which had been publishing them, and "courtesy of the trade" brought some order into the reprint business. By 1850 the retail price of American novels was back to about a dollar fifty in terms of the length of the old two-volume novel, but the conventional two-volume format itself, fortunately for the art of the novel, was on the way out. The one-volume *Ways of the Hour* sold for a dollar and a quarter in 1850, but Cooper's time was almost up.

Nevertheless, he was lucky to have suffered only ten years of the competition. He was lucky in another way. During the first two decades his profits on early sales of his novels was sometimes as high as 45 per cent of the retail price—a profit never equaled by any other American author from that day to the present. The explanation of this high return is complicated, but the answer lies partly (and paradoxically enough) in the immature state of the publishing business in the 1820's and partly in the fact that Carey and Lea carried Cooper as a kind of loss-leader. But his rate of profit slipped in the 1830's, and in the 1840's he had to be content with a mere 20 per cent. Put the decline of retail prices and of royalty rates together and the result is this: In 1826 *The Last of the Mohicans* sold for two dollars, sales were 5,750, Cooper's profit was 43 per cent, and his total take was $5,000. Sixteen years later, in 1842, the newly published *The Wing-and-Wing* sold for fifty cents, sales were 12,500, the royalty was 20 per cent, and his profit was $1,187.50. Thus, though the sales of the later book were more than twice that of the earlier, his returns were less than one-fourth. If these facts explain why Cooper had to overproduce in the forties, they also suggest a reason for his return to the adventure story after a decade of slow-selling propagandistic prose.

Book-trade forces affect an author's pocketbook, and they often affect the quantity and quality of his production. But between these forces and the author stands the individual publisher, who can, if he is as competent in his line as the writer is in his, serve as a buffer between the brute economic pressures of trade and the writer's desire to create according to his inner drives. If there had been no Charles Wiley in New York in 1821, no Carey and Lea in Philadelphia in 1826, and no John Miller or Richard Bentley in London, Cooper's career and fortunes would have been different—economics or no economics. It could not have been mere luck that he gravitated toward the best literary publishers of his day. The best are always those who have a genuine interest in writers and writing, take pride in getting good names on their lists, and joy in making attractive books. Cooper might have worked with the Harpers in New York, but he sensed that in those days the powerful brothers were mere merchandisers. He might have worked with the great John Murray of London, and did for a while, but he found Murray cold, supercilious, and unapproachable.

The fact is that the hard-boiled Cooper needed appreciation, comfort, and encouragement from his publishers. He required of them also an integrity, candor, and loyalty equal to his own. Two of them, Wiley and Miller, he stayed with even after he knew they were bankrupt, and he helped to finance them. The two stronger ones, Carey and Lea, and Bentley, he stayed with for seventeen years—a record equaled by no other American writer of his day. The connection was not an easy one for either of these publishers. Cooper was bad-tempered, imperious, often unreasonable, dilatory about meeting crucial deadlines, and almost completely unwilling to accept advice. As trade and copyright conditions backed the publishers against the wall, he fought their reductions of payments to him dollar by dollar.

There is no place here for an account of either Miller or Bentley, or of the immense differences between the British and American book trades. It is worth pointing out, however, that his English receipts, though large, were much smaller than his American ones; and that in spite of the fact that America exasperated him, he wrote for his American public rather than his English one. "With me," he said, "it is a point of honor to continue rigidly an American author." And when Bentley on one occasion annoyed him, he wrote him bluntly, "You know I consider all editions but the American as reprints, and if you cut capers with the book I [shall] wash my hands of it."

On the American side, Charles Wiley was one of the major personalities of the publishing world. His contribution to the first American literary renaissance—or rather nascence—was great, for he was one of the very few publishers of the time who had any faith in native literature. He and the printer, C. S. Van Winkle, with whom he was closely connected, saw through the press during the years 1819–21 most of the works that constituted that early flowering. Irving's *Sketch Book,* Halleck's poem *Fanny,* Cooper's *The Spy,* and Dana's *Idle Man* were on their lists. Indeed, of the major titles, only Bryant's 1821 *Poems* was out of their hands, and Wiley assisted in the distribution of that too. This flowering, though less lush than that of 1850–55, is of great historical importance, for it brought about the transition from the gentleman-amateur-author phase of American letters to the professional and commercial phase. It was the unexpected but well-publicized commercial success of *The Sketch Book* and *The Spy* that drew scores of hopeful writers into the market and led to the establishment of the literary profession in the United States.

But if Irving and Cooper began as amateur writers, Van Winkle and Wiley were also amateur publishers. They had poor facilities for distribution, and for lack of capital they had to serve as agents rather than as genuine publishers for Irving and Cooper, who financed their own works. In fact, the position of the two pairs of men represents an odd reversal of what we think of as the norm, for the authors in this case supplied the capital, and took the risks and profits, and the so-called publishers received a commission equivalent to an author's royalty.

Wiley's great distinction lay in his being (except perhaps for Mathew Carey) the first of America's "author's publishers"— that is, the kind of publisher who takes a deep personal interest in writers and in the contents of their books. Long before the reign of G. P. Putnam in New York and James T. Fields in Boston, this prototype of Maxwell Perkins rejoiced in the society of writers, encouraged them, and entertained them in the back room of his store in Reade Street which Cooper christened "the Den." But, though he put his imprint on five of Cooper's novels, he was financially so unstable that when he died in 1826 the novelist got back a number of his unpaid promissory notes to remember him by. But Cooper's loyalty to him never wavered, and in after years he thought of him as "Poor Wiley, whom I loved, credulous and weak as he was in some respects, though at bottom an excellent fellow, and of great good sense—nay, even of talent."

After Wiley's death Cooper felt free to go to the firm of Carey and Lea of Philadelphia, which had been beckoning to him for several years. Mathew Carey, who founded the firm in 1785, was, with Isaiah Thomas, one of the two great bookmen of the late eighteenth century—not merely a bookseller but a distinguished editor and author in his own right. In 1817 he took into the firm his son Henry C. Carey, who was to become a noted economist; it was with this Carey that Cooper carried on most of his correspondence.

During the twenties and thirties Carey's was easily the second (for years it was the first) most powerful general publishing firm in America. Older by thirty-two years than its leading rival, the Harpers of New York, it had developed the Southern Atlantic, Pennsylvania, and Ohio Valley market so extensively by the time of Cooper's arrival in 1826 that in terms of geographical coverage its distributive facilities were unmatched. It was probably not only business experience, astuteness, capital, and salesmen like Parson Weems that kept the company going in an era when publishing firms were short-lived, but also a strong family bond of the kind that cemented the house of Harper for three-quarters of a century.

Until about 1844 the Careys and their partners were easily the most distinguished literary publishers in the United States, and their influence on the course of literary history is incalculable. Even in the eighteenth century Mathew Carey had made a name in literary circles by editing and publishing the first successful literary magazine, the *American Museum*, whose contributors included the best writers of the nineties; and he had edited and published some of the best early anthologies of American verse. But poetry was not his forte, and it was probably true, as Poe remarked bitterly in 1829, that the Careys had always declined to publish the work of American poets at their own risk. In drama they were not specialists like Longworth of New York, but between 1807 and 1819 they brought out at least seven plays by American dramatists, including four volumes of a projected set of Dunlap's works.

Their great strength was a native fiction. By 1850 they had published 237 works of fiction by American authors, their closest rival being the Harpers with 188. Inasmuch as their list included the complete works of Irving, Cooper, and Kennedy, and some of the work of Mrs. Rowson, John Neal, Simms, Sedgwick, and Bird, to say nothing of short stories by Poe, their house may be said to have been the center of fiction production in the twenties and thirties. Add to this record their ownership of one of the leading critical journals of the twenties—the *American Quarterly Review*—(jealous New Yorkers said that the Careys now had a critical organ like John Murray, with an editor hired to puff their own publications), and their pioneer editing of one of the earliest and certainly the greatest literary annual—the *Atlantic Souvenir*, and one does not wonder that in their heyday they were courted by most American authors. The rumor that in 1836 they paid $30,000 to native writers was probably no exaggeration.

When one looks at their fiction record closely, however, a historical truth emerges. Before 1820 they published only two American novels; in the next decade, thirty-four (almost triple

the output of their closest competitor); in the next decade, 142—
which was tops in the trade. Their sudden expansion into large-
scale American literary publishing after 1820 was due mainly to
one fact: their early recognition of the commercial value of the
work of Scott, Byron, and their contemporaries, and their speed,
skill, and resourcefulness in exploiting that work in America.
They recognized the gold mine as early as 1817 (the year of the
founding of Harpers, who were to be their successors in the
field), and by 1822 they had put John Miller on salary to buy
early copies of Scott's novels. By 1832 they had published at
least eleven first American editions of Scott, and for a while they
led the American trade in printing Dickens. In 1825 the Harpers
guaranteed a Boston correspondent that they could win out in
the competition for a new British work against any firm in the
country except the Careys.

But though the Philadelphians were pioneers in a trade which
was to become almost lethal to native authorship, and though
they declined to deal in unprofitable native poetry, their standards were not exclusively commercial. In the twenties they were
attracting and seeking Americans whose names would add prestige to the firm's list, and like all good publishers (but like few
publishers of their time) they experienced professional pleasure
in linking their name with that of a distinguished author on a
title page. They were sure of Cooper's distinction when they
read *The Spy,* but, adhering to the ethics of their trade, they
had kept their hands off Wiley's author. During their bargaining
for *The Last of the Mohicans,* they wrote Cooper, "when an
author makes an arrangement with us, he is never disposed to
leave us. We have had within six months, applications from
seven authors, all of reputation, who are disgusted with their
publishers."

This statement represents the dawn of the modern author-
publisher relationship in America—a relation based on the conviction that there is no monetary or legal substitute for mutual
confidence. For seventeen years the Careys patiently demon-

strated to Cooper that they were doing everything a publisher could possibly do for an author, that they valued their association with him, but that they must be guided not only by his interests but their own, and by intelligent trade practice. Their surviving letters to him are models of candor, tact, sympathy, firmness, and humorous indulgence.

They needed all of these qualities, for Cooper was something of a spoiled child. Accustomed during his years with Wiley to taking the lion's share of the profit of his books, and to being his own judge of their salability, he insisted on extraordinary prerogatives in his dealings with the Careys. His novels had to be accepted, sight unseen, on the basis of a bare description of theme and scene, and he had to be guaranteed a flat sum for the right to publish the unseen book for a stated period. Sometimes, when a book failed, they got a rebate from him or a reduction on the price of the next book, but always the entire risk was theirs.

By the end of the twenties the pattern of profit and loss on Cooper's books had·become clear to them, and they revealed it to him. Paying him $5,000 per book, they lost money if the first year's sales were less than five thousand, broke even if they were 5,500 and made a reasonable profit if they reached six thousand. After the first year each book joined the Cooper sets, which were printed from the original plates and sold at trade sales at reduced rates. Up to 1829, they told him, only *The Red Rover*, which sold 6,500 copies, had shown them a clear profit. They considered that sale as "fixing the utmost limits to which the sale of a popular book can be pushed. It required great popularity to sell so many, and we cannot always calculate upon such a number." Unfortunately, no records of the size of the later and cheaper reprintings survive; we have thus lost a valuable index to the growth of Cooper's reading public.

The firm professed no great faith in the longevity of his books. When they took a new novel, they bought the right to reprint it for from two to four years. Old copyrights they bought for periods of up to fourteen years for only $500 apiece. Apparently the reprints sold poorly, for they wrote him in 1829, "The sale of books in this country is only for a few days or weeks, and then they pass away, almost as if they had never been." This conviction may have been a reflection of the old religious prejudice against fiction, long considered ephemeral diversion rather than a branch of "polite" literature. The fact that they let Cooper's copyrights get out of their hands suggests that they did not suspect that his novels would become classics.

The rest of the Carey-Cooper story, covering as it does Cooper's political decade (the thirties), and the cheap-book war, is one long diminuendo. The Careys published his travel books reluctantly, steadily reduced their payments for propaganda novels, and in 1843 ceased to be his publishers.

Looking back over the years of the Carey-Cooper connection, one sees Cooper's professional interests coming into conflict with what might be called, in one sense, his intellectual integrity, and in another, a wrong-headed obsession. For ten years, from 1830 to 1839, Cooper wrote no book that was not political, propagandistic, or controversial. Nothing that he wrote in that decade ranked, or ranks, with the general public as a Cooper classic. Yet it was the period when he revealed himself as a vigorous and interesting intellect. To his publishers it was a fascinating but painful spectacle.

The Careys had been fairly shrewd interpreters of the public taste for Cooper's novels. They knew in advance when a sea or frontier story would be a hit, and they predicted rightly that the heavily propagandized stories would not be popular. Yet they were not infallible in their judgment of the public. They had a low opinion of the salability of *Notions of the Americans,* and correctly estimated that the first sales would be about 2,500; but they published seven more editions before they were through with it. One understands their persistence in trying to hold him to his tried-and-true themes, but one regrets that Carey and

Bentley both firmly vetoed his plan to write a tale "in which ships would be the only actors." In 1841 he actually began the story with "all ships and no men. It is an experiment certainly, but so was the Pilot." Like most publishers, they liked only those experiments which succeeded. Cooper himself had taken the risk on all his early and successful experiments.

Looking back over the record, one sees Cooper in his pre-authorial days playing at avocations—seamanship and farming—as if no deep necessity lay behind any of them. Writing *Precaution* was also avocational, but the experience gave him an itch that kept him scratching the rest of his life. Almost overnight the gentleman-amateur became a professional, defying the myth, inherited from the Renaissance but then current in America, that the gentleman may write, but not for money. But the code of gentleman determined the character of the professional writer. That code required that he be completely independent, that he be beholden to nobody. Cooper's lifelong attitude was not that he wanted to sell something, but that he had something that publishers wanted to buy, and that the public might buy it from the publishers if they chose. Accordingly, he considered criticism of his books an impertinence; never let himself get into a position where a publisher could reject his manuscript after reading it or pay him according to actual sales; and declared that a writer is not indebted to the public which buys books. Thus, even within the system of democratic patronage of literature, Cooper refused to be patronized. His readers seemed not to care. Confounding critics and publishers alike, they made his best novels into classics simply by continuing to buy them.

1. This paper is based, for the most part, on unpublished Cooper correspondence at Yale University, records and correspondence of the Carey firm, now deposited in the Pennsylvania Historical Society, and the correspondence of Richard Bentley, in the British Museum and elsewhere.

CHAPTER SIX

Poe: Journalism and the Theory of Poetry

THE SUBTITLE of *Eureka* is "A Prose Poem." In his Preface Poe states that it is for dreamers; that it is an "Art-Product"—a "Romance"; and, finally and flatly, that it is a "Poem."

It is not a poem at all. It is not even a prose poem, as some of Poe's tales are. Edward Davidson ably demonstrates that it is "a central statement" of the symbolist theory that "art is man's one instrument for making some order out of the infinitude of empirical formlessness."[1] True: in *Eureka* Poe makes order of a kind, but it is not a poem's kind.

I am not concerned with the worth of *Eureka* as an essay (as Poe properly calls it in a second subtitle), but rather with how it became possible for him so to change his conception of the poem that he could put his lyrics and this work of "scientific detail"[2] (as he also described it) in the same genre-category. The reasons are complicated. I limit myself here to those that have to do with professional influences and pressures—those that transformed a natural lyricist into the author of a treatise on the universe.

I suggest that at least by the middle of the 1840's Poe became impatient of the limitations of the lyric, and even a little contemptuous of it, and came to realize that he could not afford to put his professional energies and talents into it. His alienation from formal verse increased as he committed himself to journalism as represented by the monthly magazine. The essential characteristic of the general monthly magazine was variety. In offering a widely varied fare of amusement and information, editors were responding, in part, to the American public's admiration of expertise—of specialized knowledge of disciplines, of how things work or are done. Through magazine writing and editing (perhaps especially through reviewing a wide variety of books), Poe discovered the versatility of his own mind,[3] and came to think of the magazine, rather than the book, as the appropriate expression of American culture. At the same time, he came to feel the need of a literary form of broader scope than the lyric and the tale—one in which both imagination and erudition could be allowed free play. In part, his wish to create such a form was a reflection of the nineteenth-century poet's desire to find a modern equivalent of the epic. *Eureka*—a mixture of philosophy, religion, mathematics, physics, and scientific theory in general, all serving as a vehicle of his private vision of the universe—was Poe's attempt to make a modern epic. Its modernness, in part, consisted of his effort to journalize scholarship, to make knowledge and theory diverting. Pathetically, he believed his "poem" (which had a slow sale of 750 copies) would be immensely popular.

In his last years Poe had two obsessions, and they were related. One was with the *idea* of *Eureka*, the theme of which was, to him, so "solemn," "august," "comprehensive," and "difficult" that it awed him into "humility." The other was a determination to establish what he envisioned as the ideal monthly magazine (which he entitled, first, "The Penn Magazine," later, "The Stylus"). The latter was the more important to him: he hoped to put his earnings from the book, and from lectures on it, into the magazine.

2

His magazine project, like his tales and poems, was dream work, inspired by revulsion against the realities of American journalism.

In spite of his reputation as editor of magazines (the legend of his success as editor needs careful re-examination), it is a question whether Poe was suited for the commercial magazine world at all. Harper and Brothers—shrewd, thoroughly business-minded, and certainly one of the foremost publishers of fiction—thought his magazine tales "too learned and mystical. They would be understood and relished only by a very few—not by the multitude. The numbers of readers in this country capable of appreciating and enjoying such writings . . . is very small indeed."[4] Poe's reputation as editor is based largely on his management of *Graham's*, but the owner, George R. Graham, one of the most astute magazine publishers of the 1840's, wrote after Poe's death: "The character of Poe's mind was of such an order, as not to be very widely in demand. The class of educated mind which he could readily and profitably address, was small—the channels through which he could do so at all, were few. . . . "[5] In introducing Poe's "For Annie" to *Home Journal* readers under the heading "Odd Poem," N. P. Willis, the most successful of magazinists, made the interesting suggestion that "money . . . could not be better laid out for the honor of this period of American literature—neither by the government, by a society, nor by an individual—than in giving Edgar Poe a competent annuity, on condition that he should . . . never dilute his thoughts for the magazines, and never publish anything till it had been written a year."[6]

These judgments came from both the book world and the magazine world, which were by no means identical. Poe's professional fate to a certain extent was determined by the position he took in the squeeze between the book and magazine economies in the 1840's, when publishers' rivalry in the reprinting of foreign works was at its height. During most of the first ten years of his writing life (1827–37) Poe was essentially book-minded—that is, he thought in terms of the permanence of the book as opposed to the transience of the periodical. The prestige of the book was infinitely greater than that of the periodical, a fact that most

American writers were keenly aware of, and one that determined the form and the tone of much that they wrote.

Of course, there was no clear physical distinction between the two kinds of artifacts, and works published as pamphlets (Poe's *Tamerlane*, for example) belonged to neither. Periodicals took forms as different as the daily newspaper and the booklike annual, and between these were the weekly, the monthly, and the quarterly. The longer the interval between issues, the greater the prestige of the periodical. But by the 1830's the book and the magazine were borrowing each other's characteristics: some books were issued in paperbound parts, periodically, and some of the worst of these looked as bad as the weeklies.

Yet despite the blurring of distinctions, the book maintained its superior status in the minds of writers and readers, and was imitated by those magazine publishers who were ambitious of prestige. The best magazines boasted fresh, unbroken type, good paper, wide margins, and finely tooled illustrations. Burton, the owner of the *Gentleman's Magazine*, wrote Poe that competition was forcing him toward book standards: "expensive plates, thicker paper, and better printing than my antagonists."[7]

In a letter of 1844 to Charles Anthon, Poe made an extraordinary statement: "Thus I have written no books. . . . "[8] Since by that date he had published three collections of verse, a two-volume collection of tales, a romance, and a textbook, the statement invites speculation. Some curious phrases in his book reviews are relevant: "absolutely bound volumes" and "absolute book." Sometimes he used them invidiously. "As the author of many *books* [Poe's italics], of several absolutely bound volumes in the ordinary 'novel' form of auld lang syne, Miss [Catharine Maria] Sedgwick has a certain adventitious hold upon the attention of the public, a species of tenure that has nothing to do with literature proper. . . . " He would not allow the hard covers of her works "to bias . . . critical judgment."[9] In his "Literati" papers he rarely neglected to state whether a writer's magazine work had been collected or to comment on the format and typography of such collections. When he favored a writer's work, its book publication was evidence of its quality; when he did not, the hard binding occasioned a sneer that such trash should be so honored. Thus a complimentary article on Willis refers to the "handsome edition of his poems . . . with portrait." But of Longfellow he wrote that the "country is disgraced by the evident toadyism which would award to his social position and influence, to his fine paper and large type, to his morocco binding and gilt edges, to his flattering portrait of himself, and to the illustrations of his poems . . . that amount of indiscriminate approbation which neither could nor would have been given to the poems themselves."[10] The point is sharpened by the circumstance that in 1839, long before the publication of the elegant, illustrated edition of Longfellow referred to, Poe had begged the publishers of his *Tales of the Grotesque and Arabesque* to print a few copies on fine paper. They refused because Poe could not afford to pay for the luxury.[11]

If "absolutely bound" means simply hard binding, Poe's *Tamerlane* (1827, forty pages, 12¼ cents) was not a book. But *Al Aaraaf* (1829, seventy-two pages) was in boards, and *Poems* (1831, 124 pages) in cloth.[12] (Purchasers complained of the bad printing of the latter.) Poe probably paid for the printing of all three, and could not afford attractive bookmaking.[13] Certainly, "The Prose Romances of Edgar Allan Poe, Number One," issued by a Philadelphia publisher of cheap books in 1843 as part of a "Uniform Serial Edition" at 12½ cents per miserably printed number, did not qualify as a book. Even at this price and in this format (halfway between book and magazine), there were few purchasers. There is no reference to this title in Poe's correspondence, but in his review of Sedgwick he said that the binding of her works gave her "a very decided advantage . . . over her more modern rivals [who are condemned] to the external insignificance of the yellow-backed pamphleteering." Graham had this circumstance in mind when he said in the article on Poe previously quoted that the "tendency to cheapen every literary work to the lowest point of beggarly flimsiness in price and profit" made "even the well-disposed" reader recoil from works so repulsively presented.

What of the *Tales* of 1840 and *The Narrative of Arthur Gordon Pym*, which were hardbound? (Indeed, the two-volume *Tales* was in the same format as Sedgwick's early novels.) We must now fall back on possible meanings of "absolute book." If the phrase refers to some standard of form or unity, or to serious-ness of content, he may have excluded *Pym* because, loose and episodic, it had none of the unity he strove for in his tales and expected in good novels. In a sense, he wrote *Pym* to order, and in a hurry. In June, 1836, the Harpers told him that "Readers . . . have a . . . strong preference for . . . a single connected story," occupying a "whole volume or a number of volumes."[14] Within six months of that date Poe began to serialize his first and only "novel." In the whole of his correspondence, the only word about it is that it is a "silly book." Obviously he wished it to be forgotten.

His unwillingness to let the 1840 *Tales* qualify as a book is harder to explain. From the early thirties he had wished to pre-sent his tales in a framework, which, he may have thought, would have given them book status as far as organization was concerned. The tales were to be recited by members of a club, and each tale was to be followed by a critical discussion. In 1836 he proposed a volume of three hundred pages, one-quarter of which would consist of connective tissue between tales. His claim that the tales were "originally written to illustrate a large work 'On the Imaginative Faculties,' "[15] if it is true at all, probably represented the all but universal tendency at that time to disguise fiction as something else more respectable—to give it dignity by asso-ciating it with history or philosophy or psychology or something equally "useful."

In his Preface to the *Tales*, Poe said, rather evasively, "I may have written with an eye to this republication in volume form, and may therefore have desired to preserve a certain unity of design. This is, indeed, the fact." The word "fact" must refer to "desired," for the collection has no design whatever. The publishers apparently rejected the critical interludes, and Poe, to fill up the customary two volumes, simply gathered together all the stories he had written, including eight late ones which had nothing to do with the "club" pattern.

3

Sometime between 1839 and 1842, Poe's conception of book unity changed. During the latter year he drew up a plan for a new two-volume edition of his tales to be entitled *Phantasy-Pieces*. All twenty-five of the 1840 *Tales* were to be included, together with ten uncollected ones. The significant feature of the new collection was to be the order of the pieces, a matter he pointed up in the margin of the Table of Contents: "To Printer—In printing the Tales preserve the order of the Table of Contents."[16] The "order" is simply that of variety. The first five tales, for example, are, successively, a detective story, a burlesque, an adventure tale, a satire, and a speculative dialogue on death.

The principle of variety is again emphasized in the 1844 letter to Anthon: "Unless the journalist collects his various articles he is liable to be grossly misconceived & misjudged [by those] who see . . . only a paper here & there, by accident. . . . He loses, too, whatever merit may be his due on the score of *versatility*—a point which can only be estimated by collection of his various articles in volume form and altogether." And again, in 1846: the 1845 tales, selected by E. A. Duyckinck for the publisher, did not succeed in "*representing* my mind in its various phases. . . . In writing these Tales one by one . . . I have kept the book-unity always in mind—that is, each has been composed with reference to its effect as part of *a whole*. In this view, one of my chief aims has been the widest diversity of subject, thought,

& especially *tone* & manner of handling. Were all my tales now before me in a large volume [their merit] would be the wide *diversity and* variety."[17]

The implication here is that the unity of the whole derives from the totality of the mind of the writer in all its diversity, a conception which certainly owes something to Poe's commitment to journalism. Yet Poe perceived that by its very nature magazine writing encouraged ephemerality and courted oblivion. Only the book offered the possibility of recognition and of a passport to posterity. On the other hand, he was convinced that the "energetic, busy spirit of the age [tends] wholly to the Magazine literature—to the curt, the terse, the well-timed, and the readily diffused, in preference to the old forms of the verbose and ponderous & the inaccessible." If Anthon would persuade Harpers to publish his *Phantasy-Pieces,* the groundwork would be laid for public acceptance of his ideal monthly, which would attract the "best intellect and education of the land, . . . the true and permanent readers."[18]

He would invest his magazine with the physical dignity of well-printed books[19]—clear new type, hand-press work, good paper, wide margins, French stitching (so that "the book" would lie fully open), thick covers, and woodcuts in the style of the best illustrated European books. It would acquire "caste" through contributions by men of wealth and status—Nicholas Biddle, Judge Conrad, Judge Upshur—and President Tyler's son! He would escape the domination of commercial publishers by seeking private capital, and of eastern critical cliques by getting subscribers in the South and West, where the influence of the cliques was slight. He would address the "aristocracy of talent" in America. His estimates of the circulation of such a serious journal ran as high as 100,000—at a time when the maximum circulation of *Godey's* was 40,000.

In Poe's more euphoric moods his dream took the form of a crazy conspiracy. His magazine would "control" American literature. The editors would be a "coalition" of a dozen influential men of letters; their names would be kept secret to protect them from the commercial press; the "elite" of our writers would "combine" secretly; new candidates for the staff would be subject to exclusion by blackball; and the profits would easily provide an income of $5,000 a year for each member, even if the circulation were only 20,000.[20] Toward the end of his life the dream became megalomania. In 1848 he wrote Mrs. Whitman, the middle-aged widow and poetess to whom he was briefly engaged: "It would be a glorious triumph, Helen, for *us*—for *you & me*. I dare not trust my schemes to a letter. . . . Would it not be 'glorious' . . . to establish, in America, the sole unquestionable aristocracy —that of intellect— . . . to lead & to control it? All this I *can* do . . . if you bid me—and aid me."[21]

Yet Poe put some real thought as well as wishful thinking into his project. One of the commonest phrases in his criticism is "the many and the few," and his use of it is almost always condescending to the many. Nevertheless, though he defined the mass as "the uneducated," "those who read little," and "the obtuse in intellect," he further divided these groups into two classes—"men who can think but who dislike thinking" and "men who either have not been presented with the materials for thought, or who have no brains with which to 'work up' the material."[22] Perhaps his dream of a large audience was sustained by the hope that some of the mass could be trained to like to think, and that some others would be hospitable to the materials for thought. This possibility seems to be confirmed in his statement that "the career of true taste is onward—and now moves more vigorously onward than ever."[23] His contempt for the mass is further mitigated in his Hawthorne review of 1847, where he refers to "the few who belong properly to books, and to whom books perhaps do not quite so properly belong. . . . The few . . . through a certain warping of the taste, which long pondering upon books as books never fails to induce, . . . are prone to think the public not right rather than an educated author wrong. But the simple truth is that the writer who aims at impressing the people is *always* wrong when he fails in forcing that people to receive the impression."[24]

The point of view expressed here is obviously that of an editor (or publisher) rather than an author. In the next sentence he turns author again and relieves Hawthorne (whose genius he generously admits and demonstrates) of the charge of failure because Hawthorne does not aim to impress "the people," who are, indeed, incapable of comprehending him. The passage is but another example of the doubleness of Poe's mind; yet, in the later years, Poe thought more and more like an editor and less and less like an author. Not only are his later works more calculated attempts to catch a wide audience than his earlier ones, but he repeatedly defends authors who, like Dickens and Bulwer, deliberately write for the many as well as for the few.

The defense becomes offensive when he says that Charles Fenno Hoffman's ability "to use the tools of the rabble when necessary without soiling or roughening the hands with their employment" is an "unerring test of the . . . natural aristocrat."[25] But he makes his point more objectively when he argues (in discussing Dickens) that "the writer of fiction, who looks most sagaciously to his own interest, [will] combine all votes by intermingling with his loftier efforts such amount of less ethereal matter as will give general currency to his composition." Indeed, "the skill with which an author addresses the lower taste of the populace is often a source of pleasure . . . to a taste higher and more refined."[26]

Thus, though Poe thought all his life of the mass audience as "rabble," he tended increasingly to dwell on the "skill" which succeeds in "uniting all the suffrages," and, inferentially, he came to believe that such skill is superior to that which is appreciated only by the few. This belief must have entered into his hopes for the *Stylus*, which he was most certainly thinking of when he said of Duyckinck's magazine, *Arcturus,* that it was a "little *too good* to enjoy extensive popularity," though "a *better* journal might have been far more acceptable to the public."[27]

4

Most of Poe's thinking about the potentialities of magazine literature had to do with prose, but his attitude toward poetry and the audience for it changed radically, too, as he became more deeply committed to an elevated journalism.

His early books of verse and his letters of the time contain a standard set of postures, many of which he borrowed from the elite tradition in England. Expecting to become, through inheritance, a man of independent means, he would address the cultivated few, ignore the rabble, and wait for fame. The postures are complicated and often conflicting. (1) One does not write for publication, and if one prints, it is for one's peers. *Tamerlane* was "of course not intended for publication," and the 1831 volume was "printed . . . for private circulation." (2) The gentleman is not "busy" or ambitious, and poetry is a product of "hours of idleness." "I am and have been from my childhood an idler," and thus it cannot be said that "I left a calling for this idle trade." (The "idler" pose was a commonplace among writers of the early nineteenth century.) (3) Maturity has nothing to do with the poetic gift. He wrote *Al Aaraaf,* he claimed, when he was ten, most of the other early pieces before he was fifteen. (4) Learning has little to do with the imagination, and poetry is not subject to intellectual analysis. Yet the gentleman-poet is erudite, and he assumes that his peers will understand his arcane allusions and his quotations from foreign languages. (5) The poet is indifferent to popular opinion. "I would be as much ashamed of the world's good opinion as proud of your own." (6) The poet is a rare, exalted creator, with gifts denied to ordinary mortals, and a poem

cannot be judged except by poets. If Shakespeare is praised by
the many, it is because the world has accepted the opinions
of a "few gifted individuals, who kneel around the summit,
beholding, face to face, the master spirit who stands upon the
pinnacle." Artists, he wrote in 1836, are the "gifted ministers to
those exalted emotions which link us with the mysteries of
Heaven," and are infinitely superior to the "vermin" who "crawl
around the altar of Mammon."[28]

Some of these attitudes recur in the Preface to *The Raven and
Other Poems* (1845). The poems are "trifles," collected and
republished to restore the correct text. They are not in accord
"with my own taste" or "very creditable to myself," or "of much
value to the public." He denies that he has ever made "any
serious effort" in poetry. Yet he insists that he holds it in too
great reverence to write it "with an eye to the paltry compen-
sations, or . . . commendations of mankind." Three years earlier
he had written a friend that the "higher order of poetry . . .
always will be, in this country, unsaleable,"[29] but publicly he
argued that the public had an appetite for verse, that we are a
"poetical people," and that our practical, utilitarian talents and
the love of poetry are not incompatible.[30]

It is difficult to make sense of all this (especially if we put all
the statements in chronological order), but it is likely that the
success of "The Raven" with the general reader made him revise
his concepts of the nature of verse and begin to consider the
possibility of "suiting at once the popular and the critical taste"
in verse as well as in prose. Though he could, in his lecture on
"The Poetic Principle" in 1848, repeat his 1842 statement that
poetry is a "wild effort to reach the Beauty above," there is little
recognition of the "wild" in his published criticism of verse after
1845. Rather, he tends to play down the "romantic" order of
poetry, to defend the "accuracies and elegancies of style" which
were associated with Pope, to admit that he had underrated the
value of Bryant's polish, and to argue the necessity of "reconciling

genius with artistic skill." "Nine tenths" of prosody "appertain
to the mathematics; and the whole is included within the limits
of the commonest common-sense."[31] "The Raven," he claimed
in "The Philosophy of Composition," was composed "with the
precision and rigid consequence of a mathematical problem."

This celebration of the role of precision, logic, mathematics,
and common sense in poetry, this denigration of "fine frenzy,"
"ecstatic intuition," and "accident," was in part a journalist's
attempt at a rapprochement with the common reader to whom
he had once denied any capacity for the understanding of
poetry. Poe was investing the poet with qualities that the reader
admired, and divesting him of those that set him apart from
the non-literary person.

His major effort to narrow the gap between poet and reader
was his analysis of "The Raven" in "The Philosophy of Composition" (which, we must remember, was published in *Graham's,*
the most popular of middle-class magazines). This essay caters
to the American appetite for the "inside story" of how something is done, and makes the reader feel that he can do it too.
In a sense, it deflates the romantic poet, who, Poe was sure,
would shudder at this "peep behind the scenes," at this exposure
of the backstage gadgets which constitute the "properties of the
literary *histrio.*"

The poetic "laws" which Poe stresses in this essay are those
most readily comprehended by the common reader. The insistence
on brevity, on a poem's suitability for a reading at a "single
sitting," Poe supports with the practical argument that in this
land without leisure or repose two sittings would allow "the affairs
of the world [to] interfere." His dicta that "melancholy is . . .
the most legitimate of all the poetical tones" and that "the death
of a beautiful woman is, unquestionably, the most poetical topic
in the world," especially if a "bereaved lover" is involved, must
have been acceptable to the sentimental reader. His argument for
the "intrinsic value" of the refrain is based on the "universality
of its employment" (he had kept "steadily in view the design of

rendering ['The Raven'] *universally appreciable"*). The "thirst
for self-torture" was an idea readily grasped by the consumers of
misery-novels. And, finally, he recognizes the popular desire for
an explicit and useful meaning in his admission that the last
stanza disposes the reader "to seek a moral."

To what extent Poe persuaded himself that his essay could
serve as a blueprint for the making of true poetry is questionable.
We cannot trust entirely his statement to a friend that " 'The
Raven' has had a great 'run' . . . —but I wrote it for the express
purpose of running—just as I did the 'Gold-Bug' . . . [but] the
bird beat the bug . . . all hollow."[32] Yet this private statement
is echoed in the essay itself: " . . . Irrelevant to the poem *per se*
[is] the circumstance—or say the necessity—which in the first
place gave rise to the intention of composing *a* poem [is there
significance in the italic?] that should suit at once the popular
and the critical taste."

If he believed that he had found a formula for writing poems
both good and popular, why did he not use it more often in
the last years of his life? He attempted to do so once more,
in "Ulalume" (1847), a poem so mechanically constructed, so
similar to "The Raven" in theme and tone, and so closely in
accord with the general prescription offered in "The Philosophy
of Composition" that one wonders why it has been such a
riddle to commentators, and why it is considered "private" and
obscure. Poe obviously planned a popular poem, and carefully
"promoted" it as such. The original title was journalistic: "To
———— ———— ————. Ulalume: A Ballad." He first published it anonymously; got a friend to reprint it, again anonymously, but with
a prefatory puff and the query, "Who is the author?"; planted
it twice again, with his name; and read it into a public lecture.
Five printings yielded much publicity but few dollars. Perhaps
this was why he wrote no more "Ravens."

After the 1831 *Poems* he wrote few lyrics—a total of twenty-
eight in eighteen years—and the public was rather indifferent to
most of those he produced. We tend to be impressed by the num-

ber of reprintings[33] of the individual poems—"The Raven," 11; "The Haunted Palace," 10; "To One in Paradise," 8; "Sonnet— To Science," 8; "The Coliseum," 7. Of fifty-one poems, twenty-eight were reprinted more than three times. But these figures include reprintings in his own four collections (some poems were printed in all four). Moreover, three-fifths of the reprintings were in periodicals with which Poe had a close connection, editorial or other, and some were reprinted at his request in magazines edited or controlled by friends. Most of the reappearances, therefore, do not represent a genuine response to public demand, and he was rarely paid for them. Even first printings were not highly valued by editors: when he was paid, his rates were among the lowest offered to poets who were paid at all.

Yet the necessity to be a poet remained, and he never quite gave up hope that he would be generally accepted as one. *Eureka* was an attempt to realize that hope: he predicted the need of a first edition of 50,000 copies. It was his last and most dismally unsuccessful effort to "suit at once the popular and the critical taste."

1. *Poe, A Critical Study* (Cambridge, Mass., 1957), p. 252.

2. John Ward Ostrom (ed.), *The Letters of Edgar Allan Poe* (Cambridge, Mass., 1948), II, 366.

3. The long list of subjects in which Poe was, or pretended to be, an expert includes modern foreign languages, Oriental linguistics, classical culture, Egyptology, physics, astronomy, mathematics, philosophy, logic, phrenology, seamanship, landscaping, music, painting, cryptography, and duelling.

4. Arthur Hobson Quinn, *Edgar Allan Poe* (New York, 1941), p. 251.

5. Quinn, *Poe*, p. 664.

6. Killis Campbell (ed.), *The Poems of Edgar Allan Poe* (Boston, 1917), p. 288.

7. Quinn, *Poe*, p. 278.

8. *Letters*, I, 270.

9. Edmund Clarence Stedman and George Edward Woodberry (eds.), *The Works of Edgar Allan Poe* (New York, 1903), VIII, 120; hereafter cited as *Works*.

10. "Sarah Margaret Fuller," *Works*, VIII, 76.

11. George Edward Woodberry, *The Life of Edgar Allan Poe* (Boston, 1909), II, 376.

12. "Second Edition" on the title page of this work was either a common false claim, or it means that *Poems* was to be considered a second edition of *Al Aaraaf*. Poe said that *Tamerlane* had been withdrawn from circulation. He wrote Lowell, July 2, 1844 (*Letters*, I, 258) : "I have [not preserved] copies of any of my volumes of poems—nor was either worthy of preservation," as if he had produced not three but two volumes of verse.

13. Jacob Blanck to the writer, May 16, 1960: "Many [small collections of verse in the 1820's] were issued as pamphlets; many in printed boards; . . . it is generally agreed that board binding was meant only as protection of the sheets until the sheets were put into permanent custom binding. But plenty of these slim productions were issued in cloth . . . frequently highly decorated and surely meant to be permanent."

14. Quinn, *Poe*, p. 251.

15. *Letters*, I, 103.

16. Quinn, *Poe*, pp. 336–40.

17. *Letters*, II, 328–29.

18. *Letters*, I, 268.

19. Lowell's *The Pioneer*, 1843, was said to have been physically an imitation of "the page, the type, the width of the columns of Chapman's and Moxon's pamphlet editions of the British poets." See Sculley Bradley's Preface to the facsimile of *The Pioneer* (New York, 1947), p. xi.

20. *Letters*, I, 247, 265–66.

21. *Letters*, II, 410. "Aid" apparently refers to the Whitman family property, which Poe hoped to use to finance the *Stylus*. Within a month after the engagement he was obliged to sign papers which put the property out of his reach. See Quinn, *Poe*, pp. 582–83, and *Letters*, II, 420–21.

22. "Henry Cockton's *Stanley Thorn*," *Works*, VII, 97.

23. "Lever's *Charles O'Malley*," *Works*, VII, 78.

24. "Hawthorne's *Tales*," *Works*, VII, 26–27.

25. "Charles Fenno Hoffman," *Works*, VIII, 126–27.

26. "Lever's *Charles O'Malley*," *Works*, VII, 67.

27. "Evert A. Duyckinck," *Works*, VIII, 59.

28. Jay B. Hubbell, *The South in American Literature* (Durham, N. C., 1954), p. 539.

29. *Letters*, I, 216.

30. "Mr. Griswold and the Poets," *Works*, VIII, 150.

31. These statements are in the 1848 version of "The Rationale of Verse" (*Works*, VI, 47), not in the version of 1843 (*The Pioneer*).

32. *Letters*, I, 287.

33. The figures are based on a rough count of listings in Campbell, *Poems*.

CHAPTER SEVEN

The Popularization of Poetry

CIVILIZED SOCIETY, in a very real sense, lives off poetry, but it rarely allows poets to do so. It respects poetry more than it respects poets. It boasts of its old or dead ones, quotes them, learns them by heart, buys mountains of anthologies, insists that poetry be taught in schools and colleges, and practices amateur versification on the sly. But it requires poets to subsidize themselves, sneers at their reputed "temperament," their "impracticality," their poverty; imputes to them a feeling of superiority to ordinary mortals. "Good-old-days" sentimentalists claim that this did not use to be true—that poetry in the eighteenth and nineteenth centuries had an audience and a prestige that has since disappeared. This is not so. It would be difficult to prove that there is any appreciable difference in the public status of poets then and now. Normal parents and relatives in the nineteenth century were as dismayed as our own to hear a potentially "useful" future citizen express a predilection for verse-writing; and normal boys, who are always representative of society as a whole, then as now persecuted the sissy who presumed to rhyme and made him think of it as something un- or anti-social. The youthful poet has always been excommunicated. If he persists and becomes popular, he is admired and forgotten. If he persists and succeeds with himself and "the few," he is abused for unintelligibility—for exhibiting a social alienation for which society was originally responsible.

But poetry somehow manages to survive, and so do poets. Economically, they contrive to do this in one or more of three ways. Some subsidize their talent through another allied occupation—lecturing (Emerson, Bayard Taylor, Sandburg, Frost); journalism (Freneau, Bryant, Poe, MacLeish); teaching (Longfellow, Lowell, Lanier, Hillyer); theater (Boker, Moody). Some refuse to exploit their talent even thus indirectly, and work at something unconnected with literature—public office (Whitman, the later Melville, E. A. Robinson); business (Halleck, Stedman); farming (Frost). The lucky ones have independent incomes or some other form of security—Emily Dickinson, Amy Lowell.

The reason why some such subsidy is necessary—why no American poet has ever made a living from his work except, in a few cases, late in life, is very simple. It is because of its density, its lack of bulk. Poetry is poor professional stock, compared to novels, for example. Readers will not pay for it in proportion to the work, thought, imagination, tinkering, and time-consuming revision that go into it. This is especially true of lyric verse, the compactness of which makes it uneconomical as an article of sale. To see what this means in terms of cash, consider that the total lyric output of a Bryant or a Poe is encompassed in one thin volume which seems a scant two-dollars' worth even to the most passionate devotee. Consider also that when *Graham's Magazine* was paying a flat fifty dollars a poem to top-ranking authors in the late forties, the editor wrote Longfellow that in submitting sonnets at that price he was cheating, for fourteen lines did not fill up enough space for the money. Can there be a relation between this circumstance and the fact that Longfellow, who was an excellent sonneteer, wrote so little in this form and so much in space-consuming quatrains?*

It is perhaps partly for this reason that most of our successful poets have poured the bulk of their work, not into the lyric, but into longer forms. Narrative verse, for example, uses up less of a poet's energy and allows more prolixity because its rhetorical,

---

* Longfellow wrote some ninety sonnets.—ED.

stanzaic, and metrical frame does not require constant tense control of word and phrase. The story itself diverts attention from verbal detail, and the long-sustained set-rhythm, whether it be the dactylic hexameters of *Evangeline*, the trochaic tetrameters of *Hiawatha*, the iambic couplets of *Snow-Bound*, or the blank verse of Robinson's *Ben Jonson*, carries along the poet in a looser idiom than that of the lyric. Literary history usually overlooks this fact and emphasizes instead the poet's need to attempt large-scale projects which give him scope, or the American critic's silly demand that the poet write on a scale commensurate with the country and its ideals. Bryant recognized this pressure in 1833 when he wrote impatiently to Dana, "I will write a poem as long, and, I fear, as tedious, as heart could wish."

On the other hand, the long poem has one serious economic disadvantage: it is not suited to magazine publication. By contrast, the lyric is excellent "filler" not only because an editor must cover all his white space with type but because magazine-buyers, geared to brevity, read and run. Once magazines began to pay their contributors (increasingly and at higher rates after 1825), poets found that double publication of lyrics in magazine and book form brought double pay. The rise of the American magazine was, indeed, crucial in the development of American poetry. The periodical became the primary outlet for poets. As the competition of British literature made American books less and less profitable in the thirties and forties, our writers resorted more and more to the magazine. British quarterlies could and did compete with ours, but the weeklies and monthlies which printed poetry could not be imported successfully. As our magazines climbed out of their early localism and class appeal, journalists learned to attune them to the place, the time, and the general reader. Professional standards of editing and sound commercial management developed as rapidly as transportation made large national circulation possible. By the forties the poet was in a position to communicate directly with all literate levels of society in all populated regions. No truly popular American poetry could be produced until this phenomenon had occurred.

Poets and the new national magazines were godsends to each other, but some practical problems had to be solved before poets were willing to key much of their verse to the magazine level. Because magazine publishers and writers continued, well into the twenties, to assume that American literary property was not very valuable commercially, they neglected to take advantage of copyright laws. A writer who was paid twenty dollars for a poem was flattered to see it appropriated by scores of other magazines and newspapers. Such clipping built up his name and reputation. But too often the clippers misprinted his work, neglected to identify him with it, or even attributed it to someone else. Most editors did not mind being robbed because they were robbers too. But when in the forties magazines in the big literary centers found that they could fill their pages with original matter, and when their rate of pay was forced up by competition for the best popular poetry, the strongest of them began to copyright their contents. This did not put an end to petty filching by country periodicals, but it did enable the successful magazines to intimidate or punish their dishonest competitors. By the late forties protected magazines in New York and Philadelphia were paying Bryant, Longfellow, and Willis as much as fifty dollars a poem. But before the era of magazine copyright began, clipping had served a good purpose. It helped to popularize American poetry and to create a demand for it which Longfellow and Whittier later were to profit by handsomely.

There were limits, of course, to the usefulness of magazines as outlets for poets. In the forties a successful magazine would pay top prices only if it had a monopoly on the poet's work. Inasmuch as it could not use more than one or two poems by a single author in an issue, his income from magazines was limited—even at fifty dollars a poem—to a theoretical six hundred dollars a year. He rarely made even that because he could not count on producing even one poem a month which was of a kind and quality that would maintain his reputation and hold his readers.

Beyond the magazine audience were several others which the book trade learned to find and exploit for poets. A collection of verse previously printed in, and paid for by, magazines, and sold at from fifty to seventy-five cents, reached that rather small but important reader group that buys new poetry. When several such slim volumes were brought together and printed more compactly and cheaply as the "Works," at a dollar or two, they seemed a good buy to a large group who bought only the poetry of established and popular writers. If an edition of this was issued in paper covers, it found still more buyers. And still another so-called reader group were those who were willing to pay three to six dollars for an edition, elegantly bound and illustrated, for the parlor table.

But these were publishing developments of the fifties, when a group of poets had established themselves as "popular." The word requires some definition. Somewhere between the level of non-commercial poetry (that of Shelley and Whitman, for example), which rarely acquires monetary value during the author's lifetime, and the merely commercial rhymes of an Edgar Guest, which have little or no survival value, exists another level where a combination of technical competence and contemporaneity produces "respectable" verse in which the poet succeeds in communicating with his generation. And since readers are usually sentimental about poets who appealed to them in their youth, they are likely to stretch the longevity of such verse to three or four or more generations by exposing their children to it at home and in school and schoolbooks. Such poetry is not accounted "deathless" by critics, but it keeps on living until the cultural conditions and ideals which it reflected disappear. After that it may have an additional span of artificial life because it is perpetuated in school anthologies which have a historical rather than aesthetic basis. We call such poetry "professional" because it has an important if not primary relation to its writer's material well-being; and it has this relation because it is poetry that communicates, *in its time*, to a large portion of the reading population. By critical standards, popular poerty may be good, or bad, or neither. Ordinarily it is not conspicuously or radically experimental in form; it does not challenge the reader on grounds where he does not wish to be met; it is not intellectually daring or adventurous; it is not pervadingly cynical or pessimistic. More positively, it is, or seems to be, clear and lucid; its rhythms and rhyme patterns are unmistakable; its imagery and symbolism are exposed rather than hidden, functional rather than ends in themselves. Its subject matter, not its method or its devices, is its reason for existing. It need not be moralistic in purpose, but it must not be immoral or amoral. Such poetry may be shallow, or it may be so good that it continues to appeal long after the culture that produced it has passed. To be professionally successful, the poet who produces it must have a "manner" that is his own and is as readily recognizable as a brand name, and a "matter" or "matters" that can be exploited without seeming repetitiousness over a long period of time.

Poetry that was popular according to this definition arrived late in America—later than the popular novel, the short story, the essay, or the drama. At the end of the eighteenth century Freneau and Barlow, unlike most of the gentleman writers of their time, wanted a large audience because they felt they had something important to say to their country. But perhaps because the temper of their time was too stridently political, they were too earnestly argumentative, they failed to divert or excite the many who do not read literature for social significance.

Before the advent of magazines of national circulation in the thirties and forties, the only poet who seemed to have the qualifications for popularity was William Cullen Bryant. But though his *Poems* of 1821 contained characteristic verses, including "Thanatopsis," which he never surpassed, it took five years to sell only 270 copies of it.

CHAPTER EIGHT

Longfellow

B EFORE 1865 no American poet, not even Longfellow, was able to live comfortably or with any sense of security on his income from verse. Since 1865 a few poets have, in their old age, received a dependable, though never sufficient, income from the sale of their collected verse—verse which failed to support them at the time they wrote it. In the 1870's and 1880's the Osgood-Houghton, Mifflin firm paid Longfellow, Holmes, and Lowell flat annuities for the right to reprint their past works (the biggest was Longfellow's—$4,000—at a time when his income from his wife's estate was double that amount). Though these annuities might have supported the poets when they were young, they were in every case inadequate at the time received. The term "the poet's life," therefore, has never had a genuine economic dimension, like the term "physician's life." Lip service to the poet's place in culture cannot alter the fact that society will not support a poet at an economic level higher than mere subsistence, and rarely at that level until age has robbed him of creative energy.

The exclusion of the Edgar Guests, James Whitcomb Rileys, and Robert W. Services from this generalization calls for explanation and definition (Riley's royalties in 1903 when he was fifty-four were about $23,000). The general assumption in literary history and criticism is that there are only two kinds of poets: "genuine" poets like Emily Dickinson, and "popular" poets like Longfellow and Riley, a Riley being only a lesser Longfellow. Actually, a Riley is as different from Longfellow as from Dickinson. There are three kinds of poets, not two: private poets (Dickinson), public poets (Longfellow), and mass poets (Riley). The Rileys are excluded from this history because they are not artists but manufacturers—impersonal producers of a commodity. Riley catalogued his wares in much the same spirit that the modern "pic" magazine allots space to Sex, Babies, Nature, Sport, and Celebrities:

What We want, as I sense it, in the line
O' poetry is somepin' Yours and Mine—
Somepin' with live stock in it, and out-doors,
And old crick-bottoms, snags, and sycamores:
Putt weeds in—pizenvines, and underbresh,
As well as johnny-jump-ups, all so fresh
And sassy-like!—and groun'-squir'ls,—yes, and "We,"
As sayin' is,—"We, Us and Company!"

Putt in old Nature's sermonts,—them's the best,—
And 'casion'ly hang up a hornets' nest
'At boys 'at's run away from school can git
At handy-like—and let 'em tackle it!
Let us be wrought on, of a truth, to feel
Our proneness fer to hurt more than we heal,
In ministratin' to our vain delights—
Fergittin' even insec's has their rights!

No "Ladies' Amaranth," ner "Treasury" book—
Ner "Night Thoughts," nuther—ner no "Lally Rook"!
We want some poetry 'at's to Our taste,
Made out o' truck 'at's jes' a-goin' to waste
'Cause smart folks thinks it's altogether too
Outrageous common—'cept fer me and you!—
Which goes to argy, all sich poetry
Is 'bliged to rest its hopes on You and Me.

The "pic" magazine photographs its goods; Riley packages his in rhyme and dialect and comfortingly bad English. The important difference is a historical one: writing in 1893 before mass culture producers had acquired the self-confidence appropriate to big business, Riley flatters his customers by identifying himself with them, and guarantees that his product is 99 44/100 per cent free of privacies—unlike that of competitors Edward Young ("Night Thoughts"), Thomas Moore ("Lally Rook"), and F. T. Palgrave ("Treasury" book).

The mass poet, then, writes primarily to exploit a market, and he is on that account excluded from this history. The private and the public poet, in contrast, write primarily to meet a need within themselves, whether that need is for fame, or to teach and lead, or simply to discover and explore themselves. The private poet who makes little or no attempt to reach a public through print (Edward Taylor, Emily Dickinson) is also excluded, but any private poet who develops partly through the attempt to communicate is eligible. But our main concern here is with those writers the bulk of whose work is in verse form (unlike that of Emerson, Poe, and Thoreau) and whose character as men of letters has developed through a prolonged endeavor to reach a general audience rather than a coterie. He not only believes that the verse he writes to answer a need of his own meets a need of his readers, but hopes that there are enough readers to support him in verse-writing as a way of life.

Not all public poets are popular. There are as many degrees of success and failure among public poets as among private, and there are more "mute, inglorious Longfellows" than Miltons. For every Longfellow there are half a dozen Laniers and Tuckermans who were relative failures—that is, in their time. Equally variable is the survival value of public verse. Longfellow and Whittier still have readers after six or seven decades, but the poems of Thomas William Parsons and Richard Henry Stoddard died with them.

Very few public poets were financially successful. Up to 1845 no poet was read more eagerly than William Cullen Bryant. By 1842 *Graham's Magazine* was offering him (and Longfellow) $50 a poem, with a guarantee of one purchase a month, or a total of $600 a year, which was tops for the time and the country. But note the context of the offer: (1) To get the maximum magazine rate, he had to turn out poems at the editor's pace, not the poet's (he sent in only two a year). (2) To maintain the contract, he would have had to continue to produce the kind of poems that *Graham's* wanted. (3) The poems in *Graham's* were instantly reprinted, without payment, by half the magazines in the country.

In the late forties Bryant's collected works were selling at the rate of 1,700 a year, with royalties of $500 a year. He could thus count on $1,100 a year from verse. But by 1848 he was fifty-four years old; he was full-time editor and owner of a newspaper which netted $40,000 a year; and he had been forced into the editorship of this paper by the failure of his early poetry.

The verse of both the private and the public poet originates from the unique privacies of the poet as person. The private poet is concerned not only to preserve that uniqueness but to intensify it through the writing of verse—even at the cost of being rejected for unintelligibility. But the public poet progressively subordinates or submerges his uniqueness. For reasons which are the province of the psychiatrist-sociologist, his sense of separateness is less strong than his social sense. And though his urge to be a moral leader may be shared by the private poet, his wish to be a *spokesman* is not. A writer may through his works be a leader in his old age and after he is dead, but he can be a spokesman only in his time. Representativeness *in his time,* then, is the differentiating quality of the public poet, and it is the quality that makes the fundamental difference between his verse and that of the private poet. For to be a spokesman he must speak in a vocabulary and syntax familiar to his audience in his time, and though these poets have a personal style, as two conversing neighbors may have two different styles, each is completely intelligible to his audience. The private poet, by contrast, creates a vocabulary which the world must *learn* as it learns a new language—as it learned, ultimately, but not contemporaneously, the language of Keats, Shelley, Emerson, and Whitman.

In the realm of ideas, the minds of the public and the private poet function with a basic difference. Man's natural condition is a state of conflict between assumptions he inherits from the past (through his parents, his teachers, his minister, and his books) and acquires from the special facts of his immediate and changing environment, and of both of these with what he feels as a unique individual at war with both the past and his environment. Most men simply live with these conflicts rather than try to resolve them because resolution is, emotionally and intellectually, a painful process. And because he speaks for himself only, his resolution is rarely acceptable to any but the very few—few in any age—who get nourishment from the poetic process in itself without reference to specific conclusions.

But the public poet either preserves the conflicts or tries to argue them out in terms the public understands (symbols, slogans). If in preserving conflicts he seems usually to be unaware of them, it is because he takes it for granted that such conflicts are as legitimate in poetry as in people.

For example: The famous public poem "Thanatopsis" is made up of three layers of ideas about the relation between Nature and Morality, deriving from three different areas of Bryant's education. The first comes from current Romantic nature-sentimentalism: Nature sympathizes with those who respond to her. The second came from his readings in Classical stoicism: Nature quite indifferently absorbs everyone back into itself regardless of "response" and without promise of rebirth. The third comes from Christian theology: Live right and you won't mind being absorbed, because (by implication) living right will make a difference in what happens to you after absorption.

If these ideas are not completely contradictory, they are at least unconnected. But since Bryant revised the poem several times long after he came to maturity, and since there is no one unifying image but three separate ones, we can assume that defects in its logic are a result not of oversight but of an attitude toward poetry. This attitude is that poetry is not thought but feeling—the kind of feeling, moreover, that helps us to forget the conflicts among our unanalyzed assumptions and beliefs and even to believe that they make sense.

It is precisely this principle that operates in perhaps the most universally known poem in all history—"A Psalm of Life." A poem full of socially sanctioned, though almost totally unrelated, assertions about Life, Death, and Work, it nevertheless worked like a shot of adrenalin on multitudes who had reason to wonder why they bothered to get up in the morning.

The public poet preserves the conflicts of past and present and of both of these with himself, and his public feels at home with him not in spite of the conflicts but because he preserves them. For example: an "official" assumption of Longfellow's society was that Protestantism, a product of progress and an ally of American enterprise and Manifest Destiny, was superior to all other religions, Christian, non-Christian, and pagan. When Longfellow's Kavanagh, having in the course of his Jesuit training become acquainted with Protestant doctrine, chooses to become a Protestant minister, his choice is in accord with the official doctrine. Yet Longfellow images this act as but "passing from one chapel to another in a vast cathedral." The symbol derives from an inherited system of thinking, known as the "great chain of being," which was "official" among the liberals of eighteenth-century Europe, but inconsistent with the nineteenth-century American conception of progress. In the "chain" all entities, including religions, have their place in the divine scheme of things, and all are "equal" to the extent that they perform a needed function: they are subordinate not to each other but only to the divine plan.

Now Kavanagh, from the point of view of contemporary American assumptions, does not pass from one "equal" chapel to another: he moves into the cathedral itself. Having made his decision, he cannot believe that the chapel he left is as good as the one he enters, for Longfellow expressly states that his Protestantism retains the good and rejects the bad of Catholicism. It is therefore superior to Catholicism, and higher up on the historical ladder of progress.

There is, then, a disparity between Kavanagh's act and the figure used to describe it, and Longfellow allows it to stand, apparently without recognizing it as such. Compare this episode with Emerson's essentially private poem, "The Problem." Here, too, Catholicism is rejected after its attractions are admitted. But all other religions, including Protestantism, are rejected, too, because they require a passive submission to a divine sovereignty inconsonant with the individual's share in divinity. In effect, Emerson is denying the official doctrine of institutional progress, in spite of the pain of excluding himself from institutions which have, he recognizes, produced the bibles and the litanies of the race.

Bryant produced poetry in such moments as were "spare" in the life of a New York editor. Longfellow, as professor, had far more free time; and as retired professor after 1854 he was our first full-time poet. But the financial yield of his work was only relatively greater than Bryant's. The record is as follows:

SOURCES OF LONGFELLOW'S INCOME

	Year	Books	Magazines	Total	Harvard Salary
First book of verse	1839				
	1840	$ 173.00	$ 46.00	$ 219.00	$1,800.00
	1841	187.50	45.00	257.50	1,500.00
		25.00			
	1842	202.00	315.00	517.00	1,500.00
Marriage	1843	235.00	100.00	335.00	1,500.00
	1844	225.00	300.00	525.00	1,500.00

SOURCES OF LONGFELLOW'S INCOME—*Continued*

	Year	Books	Magazines	Total	Harvard Salary
First collection	1845	2,610.00	250.00	2,860.00	1,500.00
	1846	1,700.00	100.00	1,800.00	1,800.00
	1847	1,100.00		1,100.00	1,800.00
	1848	1,425.00	100.00	1,525.00	1,800.00
	1849	2,556.25	305.00	2,861.25	1,800.00
	1850	1,650.00	150.00	1,900.00	1,800.00
		100.00			
	1851	1,857.60		2,537.70	1,800.00
		680.10			
	1852	1,055.60	50.00	1,105.60	1,800.00
	1853	1,275.00	250.00	1,525.00	1,800.00
Resignation	1854	1,600.00	100.00	1,700.00	
Hiawatha	1855	3,475.00	200.00	3,675.00	
	1856	7,400.00		7,400.00	
	1857	2,450.00	100.00	2,550.00	
	1858	1,660.00	250.00	2,660.00	
		750.00			
	1859	1,767.00	50.00	1,817.00	
	1860	1,132.00	50.00	1,182.00	
	1861	874.50	50.00	924.50	
	1862	1,022.50	50.00	1,072.50	
	1863	1,131.00	250.00	1,381.00	
	1864	2,262.50	300.00	2,682.50	
		120.00			

A new contract in 1865 resulted in an average yield for the next ten years for collected editions of $3,284, and from 1875 to his death he got a flat payment of four thousand a year for all his old books. The only other poet who came even close to this record was Whittier. His income from books was negligible until he wrote *Snow-Bound.* From that year to 1879, though he sometimes had ten books and editions on the market, and though in 1868 and 1875 printings totaled 53,100 and 49,360, his income from books averaged only a little over $3,000 a year.

Longfellow's average, then, for his first quarter century as popular poet, during much of which time his audience was European as well as American, was $1,844.50. But even these figures do not tell the whole story. The public poet, though he usually has made his reputation by his lyrics, has, in effect, given his lyrics to the world free, and has derived the bulk of his income from, and diverted the bulk of his production into, non-lyrical literary activity. Almost without exception he has been a storyteller in verse, in fiction, or in drama—sometimes, as in Longfellow's case, in all three. A good 80 per cent of Longfellow's verse is in narrative form; and he wrote six poetic dramas and two "novels." Moreover, Longfellow's long narratives, like *Evangeline,* or connected short narratives, like *The Golden Legend,* had a longer life as separate volumes than the collections of lyrics. Not one of Longfellow's first six—and famous—collections of lyrics was reprinted separately after 1849. Absorbed into collections, they sold widely but not with proportionate returns for the author. But single narratives like *Evangeline* and *Hiawatha* continued their separate existence to the end of the author's life, *Hiawatha* yielding royalties of over $7,000 in its first ten years. It goes without saying that for the public poet, verse in story form is functional for his purpose. It is less obvious that the density of lyric verse makes it poor professional stock compared, for example, to novels, and that readers will not or cannot .pay for it in proportion to the work that goes into it. The entire work of an exclusively lyric (and private) poet like Emerson, Whitman, or Dickinson can be compressed into a package that is handed over the counter for a dollar or two. Not so the complete works of a Cooper, a Twain, or a James.

Unread and forgotten now, Longfellow's three fictional and semifictional books in his time were as widely read as his poetry. To 1864 the record of sales is:

Outre-Mer	6,060
Kavanagh	8,620
Hyperion	14,450

Compressed into a special edition of two volumes in 1857, they sold an additional 6,500 copies by 1864. The separate printings of the three works constituted 85 per cent of the printings of the seven separate volumes of verse which had been published up to 1849, the date of *Kavanagh*. For these separate volumes Longfellow's gross receipts for the prose exceeded that for the verse—$5,427 to $5,350. And comparing the best-sellers in the two groups, *Hyperion*'s sale of 14,450 is greater than *Evangeline*'s separate sale of 14,425 to the same date.

Aside from professional and economic significance, the figures tell us something about reader taste in the mid-nineteenth century. But for the cultural historian there is a more important lesson: Longfellow's readers knew him not only as poet but also as novelist. If we read him now as poet, we lack the perspective available to his contemporaries—for the prose works state explicitly aspects of Longfellow's mind that are implicit in, or entirely absent from, the verse.

It is characteristic of the public poet's gifts and bent that he has frequently been a translator of foreign poetry. Content rather than technique forming the attractions of his own original work, he has assumed the value of rendering the content of foreign works available to the general reader. We are again struck by the fact that although Emerson, Whitman, and Dickinson did little or no translating, the public poets have done much: Bryant —Homer; Longfellow—Dante; Taylor—Goethe. In another sense this activity has stemmed from the scholarly tradition with which the American poet allied himself. Thinking of himself as the heir of European culture, he has associated himself with it through his services in translating Continental classics. Similarly he has put much of his energy into the editing of the works of other poets, especially European (Longfellow, Bryant, Emerson). (Details on *Poems of Places*) *

The great bulk of American verse in the nineteenth century was, of course, public verse, and its producers included practically

---

* Thus in MS.—ED.

all poets except Poe, Emerson and his fellow Transcendentalists, Whitman, and Emily Dickinson. Yet the popularity of even public verse was an extremely slow growth, and until after 1870 only Bryant, Longfellow, and Whittier achieved "household" or "fireside" status. Compared to Emerson's annual average, for five years, of 300 copies of his 1847 collection, Bryant's and Longfellow's average of 1,500 and 2,000 in the same period was substantial. But Bayard Taylor, in spite of his enormous popularity as travel lecturer, had difficulty getting rid of even his domestic and travelogue verse in any quantity: *Poems of the Orient* (1855) sold 3,500 copies, and *Poems of Home and Travel* (1855), 1,625. In the decade of the 1860's his collected editions found only 6,000 buyers, and his long "serious" poems of the seventies were flat failures. Bret Harte, whose dialect poems came close to being mass poetry, made a good thing of his 1871 *Poems*—22,850 sales, $3,427 earnings—but his collected poems sold only about 6,000 in the seventies.

All American poets before Longfellow were public poets in method and intention, but none had succeeded in finding security in society as poet. The greatness of Longfellow's historical position is that he was the first poet to arrive at a clear understanding of his relation to society—indeed, to create a relationship by defining for himself his place in a world traditionally hostile to the living—or at least, to the young—poet.

Essential to that definition was Longfellow's sense of place in the social structure of his time. From the beginning he was exempt from the penury and the galling sense of social inferiority which, from Shakespeare's time on, had exacerbated the writer of humble origins in a world in which high culture was dominated by men of high social station. A boy whose paternal grandfather was a state senator; whose maternal grandfather was squire of 10,000 frontier acres in Maine, himself a distinguished Revolutionary War general and a representative to Congress from

Maine; whose father was a Harvard graduate and a lawmaker for both his state and his nation—such a boy knew he "belonged" not only to the present but to the American past. The present provided for him the amenities taken for granted by an educated and comfortably situated, though not wealthy, family—graceful and comfortable living, private schools, foreign travel, and college. A boy from such a background, like any Adams or Channing or Emerson, knew in that day some sort of public leadership was expected of him, and he dutifully considered being a leader as lawyer or minister. When Longfellow chose instead to be a leader as teacher and poet, both he and his family were satisfied that he was fulfilling his social obligation, as well as making a living.

Essential also is the fact that with no expectation of inheriting family wealth, Longfellow learned that his place was among the vast majority of the human race who must make their own livings. For twenty-five years after he joined the faculty of Bowdoin, Longfellow worked for a salary and knew the salaried worker's frustrations and dissatisfactions. This self-reliance was not psychologically affected by his marriage into the wealthy Appleton family in 1843. He continued to teach for eleven years after his marriage, and in only one of these years was his wife's income larger than his earnings. And when he resigned his professorship in 1854, his reputation was so firmly established that he knew he could survive if necessary, though only on a subsistence level, on his income as professional writer.

Whether as professor or as beneficiary of Appleton stocks, Longfellow was financially secure, but this security fostered rather than inhibited his career as public poet. Public poets, like private ones, sometimes write from hunger, but Longfellow's independence from his craft provided the most important material security of all: the knowledge that he need not yield to the pressures of the literary market place in order to survive. To this security we may charge not only his serene indifference to popular fads in verse but his inalterable determination to write an epic (*Christus*) which could not possibly attract a wide audience.

Once he was established, these securities were bulwarks, but it was in getting established that he had to meet the central problem: not whether he could be an American poet but whether the literary life was possible in America at all. In 1824, a year or two before Irving gave up belles-lettres for history, Representative Longfellow wrote his son from Washington that the literary career he desired must be very "pleasant" for the man who could afford it. "But there is not wealth & munificence enough in this country to afford . . . patronage to merely literary men." The words *pleasant* and *merely* might have been (and were) a warning of the universal condescension of the man of action to the artist; and the assumption of a relation between wealth and literary creation echoed a traditional British cultural attitude. But all that Longfellow was asking for, or thinking of, at the moment was the opportunity to study history, "polite literature," and foreign languages for a year or two after he got out of college. Unknowingly, but perhaps instinctively, he was setting a course which by-passed the trap into which Irving had fallen and Poe was about to fall: the illusion that creative writing was professionally possible in the 1820's except in the field of the novel.

The literary life was possible, but only in terms of the traditional European concept of scholarship. Even as his father penned the letter, a group of young Americans were establishing an American tradition of scholarship as a branch of literary and humane learning inseparable from the learning of Europe. George Ticknor, now professor of modern languages at Harvard and later historian of Spanish literature, George Bancroft, future historian of America, and Joseph Cogswell, our first scholarly librarian, had served their apprenticeship by studying in Germany; and it was from these men that Longfellow got letters of introduction to European scholars and to Irving in Spain, who, in 1826, made his crucial shift from Geoffrey Crayon to historian. Out of two strains of American cultural experience now came a new combination. Irving had tested the life of the gentleman-amateur writing for the diversion of himself and his audience, and had given it up as degrading and financially precarious. Ticknor, on the basis of a private income, had solved the problem of the gentleman-scholar by basing his studies solidly and safely on European scholarly methods, and had become the first professor of modern languages at Harvard. Longfellow now spent three years abroad collecting notes for essays like any Geoffrey Crayon, but also learning languages and literatures in preparation for a professorship of modern languages at Bowdoin. For years the Irving in him remained in tension with the Ticknor. Bowdoin and later Harvard exploited him as teacher of elementary French and German, and until 1829 funneled his major energies into the writing of language textbooks, translating foreign works, and preparing scholarly articles for sober quarterlies. But the temptation to be an Irving continued, and finally blossomed weakly in a sketch-book imitation called *Outre-Mer* (1835).

Absurd as this jumble of a book is, it is one of three prose works that are indispensable guides to the inner life of a writer whose letters and journals are almost completely unrewarding. (Looking back on his journal—which was little more than an engagement book and weather almanac—at the end of 1853, Longfellow wrote in it, "How brief this chronicle is, even of my outward life. And of my inner life, not a word. If one were only sure that one's Journal would never be seen by anyone. . . . ") The inner life is in the prose works, disguised, but transparent to anyone ready to put them into the context of the American public writer's development.

Outre-Mer suggests that the writer-reader relationship in America had remained static since Irving had explored it in *Bracebridge Hall* and *Tales of a Traveller* over a decade earlier. Here is Irving's nervousness about public scorn for the imaginative writer. The anonymous first-person speaker begins by begging the "Worthy and Gentle Reader's" indulgence; is persistently conscious that the reader is "busy" and the author "trivial"; thanks the reader for wasting his valuable time; and ends by feeling sorry for himself and for the little book which the "busy world" will so soon forget. There is the same dodging behind concentric nests of narrators: the "I" becomes a "Pilgrim," who reports an antiquarian's retelling of a story he "found" in an old "manuscript," and even these poor strategies are destroyed by authorial intrusions. Stories alternate with on-the-spot travel notes, or with lectures that smell of the Bowdoin classroom rather than of the sweaty Pilgrim.

The most promising note in this jumble seems to be completely irrelevant: a book review by Longfellow of Sidney's *Defense of Poetry*, lifted out of the *North American Review* for 1832. But as Sidney's essay is the first attempt in English history to make an outright plea for the validity of imaginative literature as such, the review is a pathetic revelation of the American poet struggling to be born. Throughout it throbs the awareness that the busy public thinks of poetry as "effeminate nonsense" or dangerous moonshine injurious to the life of action, and of the "vocation of the poet" as beneath the contempt of "active" men. But implicit also are the defenses upon which Longfellow was to build his own career as poet. Poets *have been* men of action—useful men, and Longfellow was to be the *useful* citizen in the career of teacher which he had just begun. And poetry *is* useful, not only in its adherence to the "truth of nature," but as instruction in the history of foreign nations.

Longfellow was here already laying the foundations of American public poetry: a poetry, in part, of the past, about which this country without a past must be forever curious; a poetry about Europe ("Holy Land," the Pilgrim calls it) which for the American had the fascination that the concept of parents has for an orphan. American poetry was also to be a story-poetry.

Aware of the world's contempt for the mere story-writer, the Pilgrim insists that the world still loves stories, and that this is an age (the new age of Scott and Cooper, one must remember) "more willing to be pleased" than the preceding one. And public poetry is also to find its major audience among young people, especially young girls, who were that portion of the public most endowed with leisure. The Pilgrim sees "in this fair company" the "listening ear of youth," and he consecrates to "gentlewomen" the love-stuff, and the nature descriptions in his book—the "sweet embracements . . . mongst hills and rivers." (From Selden, but meaning of Selden changes in this context.)

He was still, in 1835, not poet but scholar, and was to remain so for five more years: between 1824 and 1838 he averaged little over two original poems a year. But in 1838-39 he made the decision which deflected him from scholarship to verse, and the shift is exhibited in his novel *Hyperion* (1839). *Hyperion*, like *The Sorrows of Young Werther*, was a piece of private therapy. The world (in 1839 and a century later) would have been spared a lot of silly speculation about the relation of the book to the author's love life if *Hyperion* had been recognized as primarily the spiritual autobiography of a man in the process of becoming a professional poet. Longfellow may indeed have been still sorrowing over the death of his first wife and mooning about the girl who was to become his second. But it is a part-time heroine who appears for the first time in the twenty-first chapter of a book, and stays for only seven out of thirty-six. Mary Ashburton has a function, but it is not the one biographical key-holers think it is.

Hyperion is a campaign by a man who wants to be a poet to make the poet respectable. (It may be historical convention, but writers choose those conventions which serve their private purposes.) Superficially Longfellow appears to be following the tradition of the pseudonymous stand-in, for though the work was published anonymously, the first-person narrator is readily

identified with the "hero." But in the course of writing, Longfellow made a significant change in the name of the hero—from
Hyperion to Paul Flemming. *Hyperion* remained as title to serve
as guide to the nature of the hero, but the hero's name is the
name of a man, not an apologetic symbol-tag like "Knickerbocker" or "Crayon" or "Pilgrim." Henceforth in American
fiction the American artist was to be presented as a man, not
as a cute label. Even the anonymity of the book was a gentle-
manly gesture rather than a concealment, for, far from striving
to keep the authorship secret, Longfellow talked freely about it
to his friends, and in the text itself declared that the writer spoke
"from these scholastic shades . . . this beautiful Cambridge."

Though "the reader" is addressed from time to time, and
though he is early and strategically made a partner (a description
"would make this chapter too long," and "This evening my style
flows not at all"), no prologue or epilogue begs his indulgence.
Indeed, he is put on the defensive in the very first sentence by
being told that he is a "fool" if he asks the author to define a
"Poet." Gone is the craven admission of the Pilgrim that the
world thinks the writer effeminate. Paul Flemming is described
in aggressively masculine terms: he resembles Harold the Fair-
Hair of Norway, as presented in the Icelandic *Death-Song of
Regner Hairy-Breeches* who got into mischief with maidens and
"handsome widows."

Movement in the book is provided through a travelogue of
Central Europe, and scenes, scenery, and historical background
motivate the crucial dialogues between Flemming and the Baron
of Hohenfels. In arguments that have more edge than anything
else Longfellow wrote in his life, the two defend the life of the
scholar, the poet, the musician, the artist. Next to the *Newgate
Calendar*, they agree, "the most sickening chapter in the History
of Man" is the "Biography of Authors." Just before the young
Viking buries himself in "dusty old books" for the winter, they
chide the world for deriding the dedicated scholar, and assert

that the "secret studies of an author" are the "sunken piers on which [rests] the bridge of his fame." Indirectly they draw the reader into an attitude of respect for art by dialogues (which are disguised classroom lectures) on German artists and thinkers, illustrated by translations from their verse, and by relating magnificent scenes and historic names to literary works.

Most important of all, however, is a line of argument by Flemming that suggests why Longfellow never provoked the hostility of the general reader. Every defense of the artist's and scholar's way of life and work is accompanied by a defense of the public's prejudices. A plea for scholars is followed by an attack on the evils of excessive scholarly seclusion from the world of men, and a caricature of a scholar who wants to "die with a proof-sheet in [his] hand." Sorrow for the "calamities of authors" is balanced by the admission that many of them have "false and exaggerated ideas of poetry and the poetic character," disdain "common sense," and wrongfully "keep aloof from their fellow men." Goethe is great—and very much like Ben Franklin— but too sensual: his *Elective Affinities* is "monstrous" and his "sinful Magdalens" and "rampant Fauns" remind one of Pompeii. France is quaint, but modern French writers are obscene. The Baron (whose European toleration for the immoral and the non-Christian gives Flemming the opportunity to speak for American orthodoxy) recites the whole of Suckling's "Why So Pale and Wan," but is rebuked for quoting from a "licentious age." A lecture on the "New Philosophy" of Fichte and Schubert is followed by a bull session that sounds like an attack on the New Criticism: the new thought is old stuff dressed up in jargon; at best it is "pleasant speculation" that "leads to no important result"—like a western road, it peters out in a "squirrel track."

Finally, in this book, Longfellow commits himself to an art attractive to the woman of his day. Mary Ashburton may have been Fanny Appleton (as the rhythm of the two names suggests), but in her seven chapters she is a target less for Flemming's love than for his poetry. She is the new American woman, more likely to be trained in academies in numbers exceeding those of men, in courses more closely related to the arts than to the practical sciences. She has time to read and travel, and she has been trained to emote. Mary is a sketcher, and can illustrate Flemming's ballads. She can talk fluently, and listen even more fluently. Flemming pours out to her his theories of nature and art (which are Longfellow's, of course) with an abandon not equaled in his talks with his male companions. When, after hearing his translation of a German lyric, "she turned away to hide her tears," she was behaving like the sympathetic audience that Longfellow was soon to be honestly proud to reach.

Mary's tears were a sociological fact, not the dream of a verse-writing Walter Mitty. While Longfellow was still writing *Hyperion,* the news that his "Footsteps of Angels" made a colleague's wife "cry like a child" led him to confide to his journal, "I want no more favorable criticism than this." Soon after this poem appeared in *Voices of the Night,* Mrs. Harrison Gray Otis reported that a friend's little girl could recite the whole of "The Reaper and the Flowers" and had asked that it be "mixed with" her bedtime prayer. Mrs. Otis' German maid had her own copy, and read nothing else.

But he wanted a male audience too. Paul Flemming had a "passion for ballads," and as a boy had known the German *Boy's Wonder-Horn* by heart. Early in 1840, Longfellow announced that he had "broken ground in a new field," the *"National Ballad"* being a "virgin soil here in New England. . . . I am going to have this printed on a sheet and sold like *Varses* with a coarse picture on it. I desire a new sensation, and a new set of critics." Professor Felton said, "I wouldn't," but Hawthorne was "tickled to death with the idea," and wanted to distribute copies to skippers at the customhouse and report their reactions. The ballad was "The Wreck of the Hesperus," and though it was not printed as a broadside, it did appear in a crude "mammoth newspaper," a new mass medium of the time. "I have a great notion of *working upon people's feelings*," was the way he summed up this new impulse.

Here at Harvard in 1840 two ancient conflicting traditions of verse-making were come to confluence in an American poet: that of the balladmonger and that of the scholarly gentleman sonneteer of the coterie. Since 1838 he had been yearning to be heard by the man in the street. Even the popular middle-class magazines like the New York *Knickerbocker* and the *Ladies' Companion*, which accepted his work readily enough, had too small an audience to satisfy him in this mood, and he not only trafficked with the new mammoth weekly newspapers of 1839, which claimed circulations of up to 35,000, but considered competing with them with a paper of his own. Increasingly irked by elementary language teaching, he tried again and again to arrange for public lectures packed with his own and translated foreign poetry. At the peak of his restlessness in 1839, he considered deserting the college for Grub Street [to devote himself "wholly to literature"], took careful note of the incomes of professional Grub Streeters like Willis and Ingraham, and planned popular novels, dramas, narrative poems, and more volumes of *Hyperion*. From Willis came the tempting advice that he was "not quite merchant enough" with his poems.

For a brief moment in 1839–40, but never again afterward, it would seem, Longfellow was a victim of the cultural confusion which for another decade was to deny the would-be professional writer a clear sense of his place in his society. There are signs that he vacillated between taking his poetry, and himself as poet, too seriously and not seriously enough. The impulse to reach the common man through broadside balladry was balanced by regret that his youthful aspiration "to build/Some tower of song with lofty parapet" was dimming. During the applause— and the gossip—that followed the publication of *Hyperion* and *Voices* in 1839, he began to enjoy the public's dramatization of

him as the "artist type." A friend's sister was convulsed to find
him at a social gathering wearing a wig—"a compound of red,
black, brown, long and straight, hanging over face and eyes,"
and the friend himself enjoyed teasing Longfellow about the
young ladies who imagined him to be "tall, thin, emaciated, with
melancholy eyes." Surely Longfellow was laughing at this earlier
version of himself when in 1848 in *Kavanagh* he portrayed the
Poet Dandy, H. Adolphus Hawkins who sported loud English
waistcoats, whose "shiny hair went off to the left in a superb
sweep, like the hand-rail of a bannister," who was publicly love-
sick but in private life was "by no means the censorious and
moody person some of his writings might imply."

And in Longfellow himself the gentleman successfully battled
the balladmonger. In spite of the demand for his verse he wrote
few poems, and none "to order"; poetry was still a sacred and
private pursuit—"a chaste wife," as he put it, "not a Messalina
to be debauched in the public street." If the hawkers of the
vulgar *New World* were able to sell "The Wreck of the Hesperus"
to the groundling, the *New World* was clearly dealing with Longfellow on his terms, not theirs, when it printed such a sedate and
conventional rendering of classical mythology as "Endymion."

Nothing better illustrates Longfellow's professional schizo-
phrenia between 1838 and 1846 than the typography and format
of his works. At the very moment that "Hesperus" was appearing
on the New York newsstands in the wretchedly printed, 12½
cent *New World, Voices of the Night,* containing a scant two
dozen lyrics, elegantly printed on fine paper in Cambridge, was
selling in Boston bookstores for seventy-five cents. This and
successive volumes throughout the forties were also available in
expensive large-paper editions, copies of which Longfellow presented to the ladies and gentlemen of the Boston-Cambridge
coterie. But in 1845 Longfellow paid for double-column plates
of *Voices,* and from these one of Boston's mass-audience publishers printed at least one edition in pamphlet form, on poor

paper, at 12½ cents. In the same year he allowed a Philadelphia publisher to bring out his collected poems, sumptuously illustrated with steel plates, at from $3.50 to $7.00 a copy, but within six months he paid for double-columned plates of these poems which Harpers contracted to use for a fifty-cent paper-covered pamphlet. For almost five years these editions, at the two extremes of price, were the only available "complete poems" of Longfellow. And for five years Longfellow struggled to discover where he belonged between the two economic extremes of buyers that these editions represented.

Even as he vacillated in the years before his marriage in 1843, the cultural-economic situation was experiencing drastic change. Not only were the cheap mass-circulation papers, which had tempted Longfellow with their "common" readers, killing each other off as they lowered their prices in lethal competition; they were lowering their quality to catch new buyers who, barely literate, cared nothing for writers blessed by respectable British patronage. In these papers Dickens' novels were being displaced by anonymous *Mysteries of New York*—or Boston or Philadelphia or Baltimore; and it was only a matter of time before even Professor Longfellow's name would cease to make a poem on "Endymion" palatable to an audience that preferred Mrs. Sigourney on the death of Little Annie. The fifteen dollars a poem they paid him was probably as poor business as the fifty dollars paid him a few years later by *Graham's* was good, for *Graham's* was patronized by readers of truly middle-class incomes and educations. The periodicals, in other words, were seeking and finding their proper cultural levels.

In sum, between 1839 and 1845 Longfellow learned that he had an audience—an audience that included all levels except the two extremes—the story-paper readers at the very bottom and the intellectuals (the Transcendentalists) at the top.

But it would be 1845 before any of the periodicals were financially safe. The depression dragged on—fatally for many periodical and book publishers—through the early forties. Half the book publishers in the country failed, among them the publishers of *Hyperion*, a potential best-seller, and of Longfellow's early collections of poems. In the copyright confusion, American novels that had sold for two dollars were driven down to fifty cents, and a poem sold to *Graham's* was reprinted without permission or payment by scores or hundreds of country papers.

Longfellow's literary score during these years speaks for the entire profession. From 1840 to 1844, when he became nationally known, when he had four books in print, and when the sales of *Voices* (at seventy-five cents) were a phenomenal 5,300 copies, his income from literature was this:

Year	Books	Periodicals	Total
1840	$173.00	$ 46.00	$219.00
1841	212.50	45.00	257.50
1842	202.00	315.00	517.00
1843	235.00	100.00	335.00
1844	225.00	300.00	525.00

With a Harvard salary of $1,500 it is no wonder that he held on to his academic job, irksome though it was. The sheer drudgery of it had been reduced by the hiring of an instructor to help drill 115 students in elementary French, but "dry research into dusty books" and the dutiful writing of scholarly articles for the *North American Review* had become drudgery too: "I had rather write Psalms." But he could not eat Psalms.

His double status as professor to the few and writer of Psalms to the many posed a problem. In the non-literary world he felt secure enough, for socially there were no insurmountable barriers between Cambridge and Beacon Street. If, in his wooing of Miss Appleton, Beacon Street was a little standoffish at first, it was probably because he was a "widower and an outsider from Maine." When he wrote her father in 1853 that he contemplated resigning his professorship, Appleton replied, "So far as I am concerned your connection with the College is a pleasing circumstance, but your resigning it will give me no 'uneasiness' should you think it expedient to do so." The wording suggests there is a possibility that some other in Appleton's set thought differently, but with the Appletons on his side, why should Longfellow care?

What his general public thought of his professorship is another matter. Probably that public was as mixed on the subject as it is now. His vocation was no secret in the East, where literary commentators frequently referred to him (sometimes flatteringly, sometimes pejoratively) as "Professor" Longfellow, but in his works he avoided reference to his specific academic status. "Poet" and "Scholar" are common symbols in both his verse and prose, but not "Professor"; and it is significant that in his last autobiographic prose work, *Kavanagh,* he appears as "schoolmaster" to small children, a role that could set up no social barrier between him and the common reader.

In *Tales of a Wayside Inn* the narrators with whom Longfellow can be identified are Poet, Scholar, Theologian, Musician—but there is no Professor. In "The Birds of Killingworth" (narrated by the Poet) the "hero" is master of an academy but he is called "Preceptor," a title that suggests the role of teacher but not intellectual. None of his references to the university world of the * * * there are many clerks but no "doctors." And in his summing up in "Morituri Salutamus," a Bowdoin anniversary poem delivered to an audience fully conscious of his professorial career, the symbolic figure is a medieval "clerk"—i.e., student.

But it is of the essence, in his handling of his problem of status, that in his writings he not only did not conceal but exploited his professorial erudition. His three prose works are loaded with classroom commentary, his poetry is packed with learned, if popularized, allusion to foreign history, myth, and geography; and his translations were evidence that he knew half a dozen European languages. Learning was the traditionally accepted, and popularly respected, avocation of the gentlemen; learning as paid vocation was a dubious cultural status.

<Tradition was one thing, but performance was another. Readers probably enjoyed his glamorization of Art and Scholarship and delighted in his contempt for aesthetes and intellectuals in *Hyperion*; but the mass of his readers saw only his verse, and it was his verse itself that had to be the medium of his campaign to make the Poet socially as respectable with the practical citizen as Poetry. In *Hyperion* his sense of the hostility of the world to the Poet is intense. In most of the poems before 1838 it is implicit. These are in the Romantic "I-me-my" mode of the alien talking to himself or to the solitary "thou" who hears among the deaf; they are full of divisive references to "gifted Bards" and "Poets" who are described rather too explicitly as seeing and understanding more than the common man. In "Excelsior" the separation of Poet and Man is plain. As he himself explained it, but not in the poem, the "youth," speaking in an "unknown tongue," is a "man of genius" resisting the lures of ordinary citizenry in the "rough, cold paths of the world—where the peasants cannot understand him."

But by 1841 he was beginning to get a hearing from the American equivalent of the "Peasant," and to feel that the Peasant was not the real enemy of the Poet. Again and again in verse of the early forties, and later, he dwelt on the fact that in medieval and Renaissance Europe the "master singers" were laborers and sang for the people. When the crude mammoth newspapers began to beg for his poems, he began to feel that he might be exempt from the nineteenth century's separation of Poet and Public, and that he need not be limited to the frustratingly small and (abnormally) exclusive audience of the Romantics.>

In "Carillon" (1845), though the chimes (rhymes) scatter "downward" and "in vain," it is because of work and weariness that common men fail to hear. In "Walter von der Vogelweid" (1845), the birds ("poets of the air") are starved out as "unwelcome guests" not by the people but by the "portly abbot." In "Pegasus in Pound" (1845), conspicuously placed as the proem to an anthology, it is the town officials who fail to feed the poet's horse, but the people themselves gladly drink from the fountain the horse leaves behind. The point is clear in a poem almost twenty years later: In "The Birds of Killingworth," the materialistic farmers kill off the "poets of the air" under pressure from a trio (satirized in as contentious a tone as Longfellow ever summoned up) labeled the Squire, the Parson, and the Deacon. The impassioned Poet-Preceptor tries in vain to stop the slaughter, but he gets to "another audience out of reach,/ Who had no voice nor vote . . . But in the papers read his little speech." These "made him conscious . . . He still was victor, vanquished in their cause." It is of some interest that he equates the unholy trio with Plato, who, "anticipating the Reviewers,/ From his Republic banished without pity/ The Poets." Clearly, the enemies of poetry were not the people but their leaders— [critics and materialists].

When the fifty-cent edition of his poems was eagerly accepted by the Harper Brothers (then noted for their wholly business-like and unsentimental attitude toward literature), and as eagerly bought by the farmers in the western market, which the Harpers controlled, Longfellow was even more certain that the people would read poetry. The instant success of *Evangeline*, both as a separate (6,050 copies the first two years) in 1847 and as an addition to the Harper pamphlet (1849), confirmed him.

His feeling that the public was not only drinking from the fountain but admiring the horse is expressed in the "Dedication" of *The Seaside and the Fireside* (1850). In intensely personal and direct address, a multiple "you" replacing the lone "sleepless wight" who hears the poet in the dedicatory poem of *The Belfry of Bruges* only four years earlier, Longfellow speaks to multitudinous friends whom he will never see, but who have flooded him with fan letters, who consider his books "household treasures," and at whose warm firesides he is "no unwelcome guest" but has a "place reserved among the rest," as one sought and invited. Only ten years earlier in *Hyperion* he had said that the American artist "must wait"—must resist the public pressure which tempts the writer to scrabble for fame and popularity, but instead let the public come to him for what he has to give. If the implication of the "Dedication"—namely, that *one* poet, at least, has conquered the immemorial hostility to Poets and made the people beat a path to his door—sounds a little smug, it is justified: Longfellow had found a common ground. What was that ground?

It was, first of all, the recognition that central in his life and in the life of the average citizen were the unpleasant realities of frustration, failure, weariness, deprival, and death. This "realism" forms the solid base—but not the superstructure—of Longfellow's standing as a public poet in his time. By a process of abstraction the modern historian, by focusing on the incredible economic expansion and the widening democratic liberties of Longfellow's and Emerson's time, has fastened on it a label which is best summed up in a favorite word of V. L. Parrington (one of the busiest of abstractionists)—"ebullience." But a citizen of 1849, living from day to day, probably did not feel ebullient much of the time. He knew that there was room for everybody out West, that the new railroads would stimulate business, that he would find a new free school system no matter where he went. But he also knew, if he was a laborer, that he worked twelve hours a day; that he might be released from fatigue by the loss of his job next week; that his business, if he was a shopkeeper, probably would fail, for in those days bankruptcy sooner or later was the rule rather than the exception. If he was rich, he might cease to be so in the constant flux of American fortunes. No matter who he was, he could expect, in those days of a still appalling death rate, that he would lose one or some or all of his children, his wife, his brother, his friend. As for the opportunities of social democracy, consider Hawthorne's testimony in 1851:

In this republican country, amid the fluctuating waves of our
social life, somebody is always at the drowning-point. The tragedy
is enacted with as continual a repetition as that of a popular drama
on a holiday, and, nevertheless, is felt as deeply, perhaps, as when
a hereditary noble sinks below his order. More deeply; since, with
us, rank is the grosser substance of wealth and a splendid establishment, and has no spiritual existence after the death of these,
but dies hopelessly along with them.

It is irrelevant that Longfellow himself never experienced
economic disaster. The point is that as a worker in the classroom
and at the writing desk, and as a family man, he understood
the weariness, frustration, dissatisfaction, and loss that loomed
so large in the lives of other men. Whoever thinks of him as a
Pollyanna has failed to stay with his verse long enough to feel
the emotional weights in his vocabulary. The endlessly reiterated
words are "care," "weariness," "sorrow," "burden," "fear," "toil,"
and "defeat" in contexts relating them to a man's work and a
man's family. The prevailing weather is cold, dark, rainy, dreary,
chill, damp. A sentimentalist about childhood, he nevertheless,
in "To a Child," made his central image a portal beyond which
are realms of "darkness blank and drear"; and though his dove-
like girl in "Maidenhood" has visions of "fields Elysian," he sees
floating over her the falcon-shadow of "sorrow, wrong, and
ruth." His "sentimentalized" Europe has fewer sweet villages and
carillons than bloody battles, bigotry, wretched serfs, shipwrecks,
and murder, and in his vision of the South there are none of the
happy cabins and Uncle Toms of cheap northern fiction, only
the viciousness and suffering of slavery. A poet like Thoreau
could understand but imperfectly the "mass of men" who "lead
lives of quiet desperation," because he had learned to do without
what they thought they had to have; but a Longfellow, like the
average citizen, needing *things*, needing family, [emotionally]
dependent upon friends, needing some sort of recognized public
status, could speak freely of the "weight of care,/ That crushes

into dumb despair,/ One half the human race," which is "Steeped to the lips in misery,/ Longing and yet afraid to die." If, along with the dark imagery, there is also a recurrent use of words like "comfort," "balm," "cheer," and "sooth," it was because he felt that the need for comfort was great.

But the comfort he offers is anything but coddling. The youth in "Excelsior," said Longfellow in explication, perishes "without having achieved the perfection he longed for," and we are "comforted" only by the assurance that in the freezing air is the promise of immortality. <One by-product of his years at Harvard was that he did not like his work and thereby was able to share (at least in his role as teacher) in the fate of most men.> In "The Goblet of Life," published in a prosperous middle-class magazine, and one of the poems on which he made his early reputation, the bitter herb fennel, which serves as central image, restores vision and renews strength, but only to the end that the overwhelming miseries of life are rendered endurable until death brings relief.

It will not do to dispose of these dark tones as the product of a literary convention, for they are less pronounced in Longfellow's juvenilia of the 1820's, when he, like Bryant and Poe, was indulging in stylish Romantic melancholy, than they are in *Michael Angelo*, which he was writing at the time of his death in 1882. They were a product of experience—and of the perception that that kind of experience is man's fate. And they are part and parcel of that substratum of American "ebullience" which made our poets, from Bryant and Poe to Whitman and Dickinson (all indeed, * * * mass faith) sharers in Emerson's bitter outcry, "Nothing is left now but death. We look to that with a grim satisfaction, saying there at least is reality that will not dodge us."

It was his identification with the many that gave this member of the American elite the psychic security as public poet which he achieved by 1849. The climax of the argument in the "Dedication" to *The Seaside and the Fireside* is that he has made friends with his readers because he has "the same hopes, and fears, and aspirations."

And his readers exempted him from the common suspiciousness of the Poet partly because of the persistent reassurance in his verse that the Poet is not a creature set apart from other men but a working citizen subject to the same responsibilities and hazards as everyone else. "Nuremberg" reminds us of a time and place when (supposedly) Art enjoyed a universal acceptance rather than a class status because a Hans Sachs or a Dürer or a cathedral stonemason walked among his fellow men as a physical laborer; but even in those days, Longfellow perceived, the alienating misconception was taking shape. In *Michael Angelo* a condescending cardinal tells a painter that he reveres him as a man "Who lives in an ideal world, apart/ From all the rude collisions of our life,/ In a calm atmosphere," to which the painter replies, "If you knew the life/ Of artists as I know it, you might think/ Far otherwise." The poet was even more suspect because the pen was lighter than the brush and the chisel. Hence Longfellow's persistent equation of the job of writing with "toil," one of the most recurrent words in his vocabulary, and with toil that ends more often in frustration and defeat than in satisfaction. In "To a Child" he speaks of the struggle "with imperious thought,/ Until the overburdened brain,/ Weary with labor, faint with pain . . . retain/ Only its motion, not its power." Nine years later in "Epimetheus" he asked whether "each noble aspiration" must "Come at last to this conclusion,/ Jarring discord, wild confusion,/ Lassitude, renunciation," and whether a Dante "By defeat and exile maddened" or a Milton "By affliction touched and saddened" must have felt that "All this toil for human culture" was futile.* For forty years Longfellow kept reminding men that he, the Poet, shared with them "the long

---

* The reference to Milton and Dante is in "Prometheus."—ED.

pedigree of toil"—even more explicitly, that "I, who so much with book and pen/ Have toiled among my fellow-men,/ Am weary. . . . "

Yet identification has its limits—even for a public poet. Longfellow was intensely aware that, after all, he was not a storekeeper or a land agent but a poet, and that what he had to sell had always been in demand but seldom paid for. The buyer of Longfellow's works may not have been aware of it, but he was buying poems that advertised poets and poetry; and Longfellow was one of the greatest of all promoters of the arts. Ninety per cent of all the poems he ever wrote contained some favorable reference to poetry, poets, artists, art, scholars, or literature. Bards are sublime, grand, immortal; singers are sweet; songs are beautiful; art is wondrous; books are household treasures. Hans Sachs is remembered after kaisers are forgotten. Michael Angelo is impudent to cardinals. John Alden, the scholar, wins out over Miles Standish, the man of action.

Poetry is identified with the natural and familiar, with great organic processes of nature, rather than with the exotic and the intellectual. Birds are poems, flowers are poems, children are poems, as are seaweed, horses, the wind, and hearth-fire. In *Evangeline* it is *the forest* that sings the tradition; in "Daylight and Moonlight" it is *the night* that interprets a poem unintelligible by day. Poetry is identified with the practical arts: poems are bells, towers, bridges, even strands of rope; poets are architects and sculptors.

But if such devices gave status to poets and poetry, it was, of course, his subject matter and his announced aims as writer that mark him as public poet. Primary and paradoxical is the fact that though the poet's subject, essentially and necessarily, is himself, Longfellow as public poet had to disguise himself. In the 1820's such verse as he wrote was as unabashedly in the first person singular as Wordsworth's, but from 1838 to 1845 when he was trying to find out who he was, the pronominal structure of his poems was as confused as his mind. The new poems in *Voices* range through the entire scale of I-you-they-we (sometimes, as in the "Psalm," all three in one poem). Only in "Flowers" does his future stand-in, the Poet, appear. In the 1841 volume, *third*-person poems like "Hesperus" prevail not only in number but in position, but *you*'s are next most frequent. Only two poems are flatly in the "I" mode, and in one of these he stops complaining long enough to tell himself, "Thy fate is the common fate of all." By the fifth volume in 1845 the second- and third-person emphasis is general, and in the few poems where the "I" is not almost completely sterilized, it is again mitigated by the "common fate" theme.

After 1845 the basic style is that of the third person of narrative verse, with the Poet or Scholar or Artist—or even Nature—as the obvious spokesman for Longfellow, or an I-you structure so depersonalized that even in the direct address to the reader, in prologue or epilogue (such as "Weariness" in *Birds of Passage*), the weariness of "I" is expressly an official and vicarious fatigue for you and me. As he grew older, he tended on the one hand to restrict the "I" to sonnets, where the personal statement is authorized and formalized by sonnet traditions reaching back to Petrarch and Shakespeare, and to literally "public" poems like "Morituri Salutamus" where he was expected to speak in his proper person; or, on the other hand, to shift the "I" to speakers in poetic dramas, where a St. John or a Michael Angelo stands in for him as Religious Thinker or Public Artist.

But of course the management of ego was not much of a problem to a man who mourned that he could not get it even into his private journals, and whose private letters are the most barren of all literary letters in the nineteenth century; who excluded from his published works even such partial privacies as his regret that he had produced no great work at the age of forty-two ("Mezzo Cammin") and his memory of the death of his wife ("The Cross of Snow"). He could share with others his

feeling about his children by making them Children (compare
"The Children's Hour" with Emerson's "Threnody"), or about
his friends, who are always the object of his Friendship.*

In the work of such a man "I" is far less significant than
"you"—the pronoun which recurs with a frequency in direct
proportion to the growth of his sense of public representativeness—as to his increasing certainty, based not only on the
reception of his poems but on his tremendous fan mail, that *his*
values, *his* brand of spiritual therapy, *his* kind of self-consolation,
were of universal as well as private efficacy. The world had, in
1838, "listened in on" the "Psalm," a poem so personal, he said
later, that "I kept it some time in manuscript, unwilling to show
it to anyone." We are entitled to be skeptical about such a
statement concerning a poem, which is dominated by the pro-
nouns *we, our, us,* and the plural *you,* which seems about as
personal as a statue of General Lee on horseback; but it must
be understood that a man capable of choosing, as the vehicle of
a statement that seemed private to him, a form as public, as
institutional, as the "psalm" or hymn, was by nature and nurture
a social and institutional personality rather than an island unto
himself. Longfellow (like most of us, to be sure) thought of
himself as made up of two personalities—citizen and unique
individual, breadwinner and star-gazer, drudge and dreamer,
moody animal and disciplined soul. When it became clear to
him that his readers identified themselves not only with the
drudge-citizen-breadwinner (which was to be expected) but with
the unique, dreaming soul which he had thought alien to the
world, the instinctive, unconscious use of the plural *you* of the
"Psalm" became the conscious, strategic *you* of the orator, the
leader, the one teaching and speaking for the many.

---

* This paragraph was written before the publication of Andrew Hilen's *The
Letters of Henry Wadsworth Longfellow* (Cambridge, Mass., 1966).—ED.

Teaching is of the essence in all Longfellow's verse after the "Psalm," and everything that he taught for the next forty-odd years is implicit in the "Psalm." If teaching of a sort is a function of all poetry, including the private, the great prerequisite of teaching in public poetry is that truths be lifted out of the complexity in which they generate and reduced to explicit and *separable* statement. The teachings in the "Psalm" and all later work center on one central "truth": the necessity and the value of *acceptance*—acceptance of life's labors and sorrows. What makes acceptance preferable to suicide is faith in two unprovables: the value and satisfaction inherent in *work,* carefully done, for its own sake; and immortality. And the two are one. Although he sometimes presents immortality as the comfort of reunion of the bereaved with the dead, his major emphasis on the concept is that it promises permanent physical *rest* as the sequel to *work.*

Austere as this program sounds, it does not exclude as values the pleasures of life: the pleasures of friendship, of family life, of nature, of the arts, are endlessly reiterated and set in balance against the sorrows. And, indeed, the assertion that there *is* a balance constitutes some of the comfort or balm he advertised his poetry as offering. The concept of balance pervades his verse, not only in the form of innumerable pairs of verbal opposites (sorrow-delight, toil-rest, soothe-affright), but in larger units like the *Tales of a Wayside Inn,* where the Theologian, for example, atones for his story of the vicious religious fanatic, Torquemada, by telling of a kindly monk in "The Legend Beautiful."

Yet even as he asserts the balance, he denies it by putting his thumb on the wrong side of the scale. The "Psalm" argues the balance concept not only through verbal pairs like "enjoyment-sorrow" but through prosody—each end-stopped line and couplet balanced against the next; but how can enjoyment be in balance when seven out of eight stanzas mention or imply death? The summing-up stanza in "Haunted Houses" is:

Our little lives are kept in equipoise
By opposite attractions and desires;
The struggle of the instinct that enjoys,
And the more noble instinct that aspires.

But there can be no equipoise when one instinct is "more noble"
than the other, particularly when we note that from "Excelsior"
to *Christus* aspiration is associated with frustration and death.
In *Wayside*, where dark tales are literally and specifically alter-
nated with light ones, the firmness and authority of his story of
Charlemagne's terrifying power is in sharp contrast with the
feebleness of his anecdote of Charlemagne as a kindly, forgiving
monarch. A poet whose first three collections of verse were
dominated by themes of death and loss and sorrow, and whose
last ten years were devoted to four poetic dramas of tragic subject
and tone, may have thought balance but certainly did not feel it.
<When we look at the record of the middle years, the fifties
and sixties, we are tempted to wonder whether such relatively
cheerful performances as *Hiawatha* and *Miles Standish* were not
the result of audience pressure. Certain it is that these "happy"
books sold better and faster than the sadder ones:

Happy

Hiawatha—50,771 / 13 years, average: 4,000 minus
Miles Standish—29,424 / 7 years, average: 4,000 plus

Sad

Evangeline—28,005 / 22 years, average: 1,300
Golden Legend—9,848 / 13 years, average: 757
But—*New England Tragedies*—15,500 / 1 year
Christus—5,980 / 2 years (6 different editions), average: 2990

Balanced

Wayside—22,000 / 2 years, average: 11,000

Moreover, after *Wayside*, when he stuck to his tragic vein, the sales of his individual volumes declined drastically. Yet these figures can be accounted for by so many complicated trade factors that they cannot be taken too seriously as a guide to reader taste or Longfellow's response to it; and above all, by the time he died the great majority of his sales were in the field of collected editions, and we have no way of knowing what these readers preferred. But a man who could shift from the cheerful and popular themes of *Hiawatha* and *Miles Standish*, to the evenly divided sunshine and shadow of *Wayside*, to tragic poetry, was obviously not responding to audience pressure.>

Balance, then, no doubt served his doctrine of acceptance and resignation, but though repeatedly asserted, it is rarely demonstrated convincingly. His exploitation of it was probably never questioned by his readers because it was in accord with the "Common Sense" which they thought they learned by observing the simplest laws of nature, but which had actually been drilled into them by a culture still dominated by eighteenth-century rationalism and Newtonian physics. <And if the disparity between the assertion of balance and the demonstrated imbalance of the story-poems and dramas was not apparent, it was because most readers did not suspect (as they do not now) that poetry should have a logic of its own.>

Longfellow's persistence in clinging to an inherited way of thinking without questioning closely its relevance to his own society was a cause at once of his immediate success and his long-run failure. For his public, like himself, clung the more determinedly to the rural-mercantile eighteenth-century frame of thought even as the facts of the new urban machine world were making that kind of thought irrelevant. So it was that his readers welcomed verse in which there were towns and villages but not cities except those attached to the adjectives "crowded" and "hot"; in which there were no factory workers, no businessmen, no salesmen, no staple-crop farmers, no slaves (after 1842)—only blacksmiths, cobblers, and other holdovers from the images of an agrarian-handicraft economy; no railroads (except the one in *Kavanagh* that destroys the rural quiet of the town).

It was perhaps a stroke of luck for this public poet that he got no satisfaction out of his vocation, teaching, and equated it with drudgery and exasperation; for he was living in a world which increasingly hated its work, in which machines were rendering the making of things meaningless for the maker, in which farming was less and less the source of a well-rounded subsistence and more and more a struggle with the market, banks, and railroads, and in which Arthur Miller Salesmanship not only increased but took the forms of Barnum, Bonner, and Beecher in the fields of amusement, publishing, and religion. In such a world he could urge that action, that work, is an end in itself, an anodyne, and ignore the question of lasting results. And thus it is that though his blacksmith begins and finishes something each day, the reward mentioned is not a perfect horseshoe but rest for the aching back; that the *Hesperus* skipper's resistless will to act is favorably presented, though it leads to nothing but pointless sacrifice of life; that in the "Psalm" we are to "Trust no Future," which in context means that we are to act without hope of meaningful results.

This doctrine of submission was, of course, in accord with both the Christian principle of endurance for the sake of the hereafter, and with that still widely taught doctrine of the preceding century, the static "chain of being," which counseled that each individual take satisfaction in his predestined place in the chain. As Longfellow put it in "The Builders," where we are urged to do our work well, whatever it is:

> Nothing useless is, or low;
> Each thing in its place is best;
> And what seems but idle show
> Strengthens and supports the rest.

But in so far as Longfellow identified himself with Art rather than with the world of gainful and futile employment, he had to take a different view of *results*. Not only had the labor of the Artist historically and continuingly eventuated in results of value to others, but the Artist had always achieved an Immortality that amounted to something more than the pleasures of not working and of reunion. Longfellow's poems are full of the assumption that the Artist was in this respect a man apart. But of what comfort was this to his non-artist audience? To be sure, Longfellow draws the non-artist into the general area of promise of results and immortality by vaguely attaching the world of Art to the world of Action without even demonstrating the existence of non-artistic activity. In the "Psalm" we are told, after being exhorted to Action, that great men have left footprints; but since the prints are immediately described as giving "heart" to a shipwrecked brother, it is pretty obvious that the prints are those of a poet like Longfellow. The blacksmith's work at the forge is equated with "burning deeds" as well as thoughts; but in Longfellow's work as a whole he denies fame to the deeds of the "Councils and Kaisers" of Hans Sachs's day, and denies dignity to "active" Miles Standishes while granting it to scholarly John Aldens. True it is that again and again he looks longingly back to a day when physical work, action, and Art were tied together; when cobblers sang; when cathedral masons "wrought with greatest care,/ Each minute and unseen part"; but the total impression his verse gives is that, since the Renaissance, all work except that of the Artist has gone into the market place and thus lost its meaning. When he declared himself, directly and personally, in "Morituri Salutamus," at the age of sixty-eight, he dichotomized the "scholar and the world" and made the latter the equivalent of

> The market-place, the eager love of gain,
> Whose aim is vanity, and whose end is pain!

But even as the world of Art and thought was becoming
established in Longfellow's mind as the only world in which
work has intrinsic value, and even as the world was convincing
him that his art was valued, a change was taking place in his
thinking about his purpose and his future as poet. The change
almost resulted in his ceasing to be a popular poet, as far as
new works were concerned, in the last fifteen years of his life.

To understand what happened, we must go back to the Longfellow of 1849, who, with the success of *Evangeline* singing in his
ears and happily convinced that his work was getting results,
acknowledged in his "Dedication" that his long wait for acceptance had come to an end. This Longfellow is revealed in *Kavanagh* (1849), the most literally autobiographic work he ever wrote.
Though a really bad novel (too obviously, he was "using up"
material he did not wish to waste), it sold almost as well (about
6,500 the first eighteen months) as *The Scarlet Letter*, which
appeared a year later. It had all the "balance" that Hawthorne's
book lacked. In it one girl loses, the other wins. One man is
a dreamer, the other a doer. Humor (one comic male, one comic
female) is balanced with pathos (one frustrated woman, one
frustrated man), "realism" with "romance."

Though "the names have been changed to protect the innocent," it is perfectly plain that the author distributed his personal
history and his professional problems and his trials and errors
among the male characters. Churchill, the would-be author, is by
fate a harassed schoolmaster and the father of five, his aspiration
to write frustrated by pupils, domestic life, and the intrusions
of other matters.

The frustrated Churchill is Longfellow's picture of the self he
outgrew in the 1840's: dedicated to Art, but producing only
scraps; trusting to be inspired by books which only drew him
into sterile dream and reverie, so that "while he mused the fire
burned in other brains"; expending his imagination on the
strange and exotic, and missing the significance of the newer and

familiar life; attributing to domestic care and an irksome profession the failure that was in himself, lacking, as he did, the "all-subduing will . . . the fixed purpose that sways and bends all circumstances to its uses."

Kavanagh, though a preacher, is presented as a leader, a public mentor, definitely the poetic and scholarly type, and endowed with European learning, his sermons full of European story. Himself endowed with family estates in Maine, he marries the daughter of a wealthy and influential person, and moves into their mansion, goes to Europe with his wife for one year, and stays three. A minor character, Hiram Hawkins, the poet-dandy, is a caricature of the Europeanized Longfellow of 1838.

Kavanagh, like Longfellow, combines the culture of Catholic Europe with the psychology of Protestant America that Longfellow saw himself as becoming. The scion of an ancient European Catholic family, he was nurtured on the Lives of the Saints and educated in a Jesuit College in Canada. But after his mother's death, Reason (the search for intellectual and spiritual truth) leads him away from that "august faith" of "crystalline turrets" and "dark, terrible dungeons," and he becomes a Protestant, bringing with him "all he had found in [Catholicism] that was holy and pure and of good report," "its zeal, its self-devotion, its heavenly aspirations, its human sympathies, its endless deeds of charity," but "not its bigotry, and fanaticism and intolerance." As Protestant clergyman he is in sharp contrast with his orthodox, fundamentalist predecessor. He affirms and consoles, and in his tower study meditates "the great design and purpose of his life, the removal of all prejudice, and uncharitableness, and persecution, and the union of all sects into one church universal." His life is one of "active charity and willing service." And above all, he is the leader with the will (unlike Churchill) to make his dream prevail. Though "suspicions of his orthodoxy" spring up in "many weak but worthy minds," and though he realized the danger that he "might advance too far, and leave his congregation behind him," he courageously attacks their prejudices and succeeds in drawing "the main current of opinion" with him. This was the history of Unitarianism.

Before the year 1849 was out, Longfellow began to write the book that Churchill would never get around to but which had been in Churchill-Longfellow's mind since 1842. Longfellow would cease to be a mere writer of lyrics and become a Dante, a Milton. He would be the architect of a "tower of song," an epic work of theme and profoundness which would find in the story of man's treatment of his gods, and religious institutions' brutal treatment of man, a fit expression for "the trouble and wrath of life, for its sorrow and mystery." At the same time, his epic would be an apologia, a justification of his preoccupation with Europe, for which he was being constantly blasted by "isolationist" critics, whom, in turn, he had attacked in Chapter XX of *Kavanagh* (a chapter often reprinted but never seen in this its proper context). For here at last would be proof that the American cannot understand his religious condition unless he understands the European past which was Longfellow's major poetic stock.

This was a large order for a poet who had been devoted to simplicities rather than complexities, and he never filled it. *Christus: A Mystery*, which came out in 1872, contained only three parts of the story, loosely connected: Christianity in the Holy Land, the Middle Ages, and Colonial America. It was a flat failure. In spite of Longfellow's reputation, and in spite of the publisher's expert marketing of it in six different editions to suit every pocketbook, less than six thousand were printed, and no one knows how long it took to sell these. Yet two parts of it, published earlier and separately, were moderately successful— *The Golden Legend* (1851), 9,848 copies in 13 years, and *The New England Tragedies* (1868), 15,500, the sales of which stopped in one year.

Why had this "great design and purpose" of his literary life come to so little? For one thing, *Christus* is cast in one of the least popular of all literary forms, poetic drama; to a stage-loving public it was not drama at all; and to many of his poetry fans, the long stretches of blank verse, lacking the definite rhythms and rhymes of his characteristic verse, were not poetry. And some readers might have been warned off by a word which they had never before seen on his title pages but which appeared twice on this one: *tragedy*.

But we are more concerned with the intrinsic failure of the book and the "great design" from which it came. For this failure we must look into his thinking on the problem of progress in the totality of his work. Inseparable from his project was the problem of progress. Material progress he simply ignored, but ethical progress he tried to cope with. In general, Longfellow's historical assumptions were those of his generation: paganism, no matter what its virtues, was inferior to Catholicism, no matter what its faults; Catholicism, no matter what its strength, was inferior to Protestantism, no matter what its weaknesses; and a "religion of humanity" must eventually displace doctrinaire Protestantism.

He had no trouble with the first phase of this formula. The Jew, though better than the Pagan, is excluded from the march of progress because, unlike the Christian, he looks backward in time even as he reads backward in his books ("The Jewish Cemetery at Newport"). The pagan Indian can hardly be allowed to waste the soil of his hunting grounds while "downtrodden millions [of Christians] starve in the garrets of Europe" ("To the Driving Cloud"). The old Norse gods perished because their "law of force" was challenged by the meek Christ's "law of love." But at this point the formula began to fail him. For his tales of Christianity are dominated not by a meek Christ triumphant but by a suffering Christ who is worshiped by greedy and venal monks, vicious Torquemadas, and witch-hunting Justice Hathornes and Cotton Mathers. Theological bickering is exhibited as equally corruptive in the scholastics and Martin Luther of *The Golden Legend,* and Cotton Mather of *The New England Tragedies*; and the Theologian of *Wayside*, speaking presumably in the year 1861 in Massachusetts, hears a preacher

ranting about hell-fire, and asks, "Must it be Calvin or Methodist? Must it be Athanasian creeds, Or holy water, books and
beads?" True, there were meek, pious Moravians and Quakers,
and in a little village in Maine an enlightened Unitarian named
Kavanagh made some headway with his "weak but worthy"
brethren, who had sponsored his fundamentalist predecessor; but
of these Longfellow never wrote anything but anecdotes: they
never found a place in his epic. The measure of his naïveté as a
historical thinker, of his inability to reconcile his knowledge of
history with his inherited convictions, is perfectly reflected in
his desire to add a third drama to his two *New England Tragedies*—the scene to be laid among the Moravians of Bethlehem—
in order to "harmonize the discord of the *New England Tragedies*, and thus give a not unfitting close to the work." He would
thus, apparently, have tacked a happy ending to what was
obviously a tragic history, and "balanced" the blight of Protestant fanaticism against the piety of a forgotten religious community. This is as far as he would let himself think toward the
triumphant "Charity" of "the Present."

Religious and ethical progress, then, was something that Longfellow "thought," but he could not believe in it sufficiently to
make it operate in an extended, unified work of art. <And it is
possible that as he got deeper into his study of religious history
after 1849, he gradually ceased even to think it. For a decade or
so after he began, he took side trips off his main road to write
popular poems like *Hiawatha* and *Miles Standish*, in which sunshine and shadow were more or less balanced. *Hiawatha* might
have been contributory to his epic, but at its end, in looking to
the future, he somewhat less than candidly depicted the Indian
as happy to be dispossessed by Christians. In *Wayside* (1863)
where he used many by-products of *Christus*, the balance between
good and evil is so mechanical (even statistical, if one counts
the happy and the sad stories) that the effort to find equipoise
seems desperate. The middle sixties were dominated by his
translation of *The Divine Comedy*, the mood of which per-

meated *Christus.*> His verse thereafter, both lyric and narrative, is overwhelmingly poetry of death and despair, two words which appear in the last lines of his last work, *Michael Angelo*, who as he works on his figure of the dead Christ says,

> . . . What darkness of despair!
> So near to death, and yet so far from God.

But *Christus* was a failure not only of intellect but of art itself. That Longfellow thought and felt in terms of parts rather than wholes is plain. The fate of *Christus* is implicit in the very symbols he found in pledging himself to the "loftier strain" in 1849: the "broken melodies" which had breathed through his soul would, he hoped, "unite themselves into a symphony." <Of course, melodies do not unite themselves into symphonies any more than stones unite themselves into a cathedral. And his> Even more common than the song-symphony in his art-imagery is a block-tower allusion. From 1846, in "The Builders," to 1872 to the " * * * " of *Michael Angelo*, he saw the poet as a builder surrounded by blocks and filled with yearning to build a tower with them. The block is always primary: "Each minute and unseen part" must be wrought with care, "for the gods see everywhere." But the tower is never described. The image functions with pathetic if unconscious candor in *Michael Angelo* where he described what he had been doing all his life:

> Men build their houses from the masonry
>   Of ruined tombs; . . .
> So from old chronicles, where sleep in dust
>   Names that once filled the world with trumpet tones,
>   I build this verse; and flowers of song have thrust
> Their roots among the loose disjointed stones,
>   Which to this end I fashion as I must.
>   Quickened are they that touch the Prophet's bones.

But of course "loose disjointed stones" no more unite themselves into a house than melodies unite themselves into a symphony. "These fragments I have shored against my ruins," says Eliot in 1922 at the end of *The Waste Land*. But Longfellow in the midst of the Gilded Age, to which he firmly closed his eyes, held on to the illusion that it was the past rather than he that was in ruins, and that he could build without a blueprint.

The failure of religious institutions—the failure, therefore, of progress itself—is clearly implied, though never expressly stated, in the work culminating in *Christus*. Longfellow, the public poet, had ceased to believe in one of the major tenets of the public [faith], a tenet which in 1849 he thought he shared with the people and made the subject of an epic on which his final and permanent reputation would rest securely. The people probably never noticed his defection. They received the parts of *Christus* respectfully, if languidly. It took thirteen years to sell 10,000 copies of *The Golden Legend*; about 15,000 copies each of *The New England Tragedies* and *The Divine Tragedy* (part I of *Christus*) were printed, but the sale of both seems to have stopped in about a year. When the whole appeared as *Christus* (1871), the publishers desperately tried to get rid of a total printing of 6,000 in six different editions to suit every pocket-book. Even this record was a tribute to his reputation rather than to *Christus*, and Longfellow seemed to know it. They kept right on reading what he considered his lesser works in all editions, in ever-increasing quantities. By 1869, over one-third of a million copies of his works had been sold, and in the early seventies his collected works were selling about 15,000 a year, at one time in six different editions. The rest of the world was busy with translations that eventually numbered 708 in twenty-four different languages.

His pleasure must have been wry indeed to see a new and expensive edition of a single poem—"The Building of the Ship"

—selling at the rate of 2,000 a year in the seventies when *Christus* was being received in respectful silence, and such somber poetic dramas as *The Masque of Pandora* and *Judas Maccabæus* barely got a hearing, for this affirmative lyric with a happy ending had come out in 1849, in the year he embarked on *Christus*; and perhaps equally wry to see "The Hanging of the Crane," a "family" poem based on an idea he had tried to give away to another poet, eagerly bought on the newsstands in the biggest lower-class family story-paper in America—Bonner's *New York Ledger*.

And while his works were flooding the world in the seventies, his new productions became gloomier and permeated with the smell of death and frustrated aspiration. Except for a bitter picture of a corrupt and luxurious papal regime in Michael Angelo's Rome, after 1873 the history of religion as subject matter drops out of his verse. The prevailing preoccupation of the last nine years is Art, and faith in Art as a way of life displaces the old faith in mankind's collective religious aspiration. It is a bitter faith, stripped even of the pretense that the despair of the artist is "balanced" by any reward but the drive to create which keeps him alive. Great art, if it is achieved, is immortal, but the artist himself can never know whether his great effort will be failure.

One persistent note in this late verse of the most famous of all living poets was disillusionment with fame. Again and again, the "plaudits of the crowd" are named vanity. This poet who has been praised for the wrong things finds that the "fame of his poems is his, and not his," and when he (as St. Francis) feeds the birds "With manna of celestial words," he "knows not if they understand." Nothing avails but work. "Have faith in nothing but in industry," Michael Angelo tells Benvenuto, "And work right on through censure and applause, Or else abandon Art." Gone is the assertion of the early poems that the artist's "toil" is like that of everyone else. For there can be no "common ground" in the new conviction that creative work is the "divine Insanity of noble minds," a "malaria of mind," a "fever to accomplish some great work that will not let us sleep."

There is a significance hard to define in the fact that Longfellow turned to the subject of the Great Artist in the same year that he began *Christus*. In 1850, when he began *The Golden Legend,* he also wrote a part of Act III, Scene IV of *Michael Angelo,* which takes place in the Coliseum. To Michael it is a marvel of art, "the rose of Rome." To Cavalieri the rose smells of "a people/ Whose pleasure was the pain of dying men," and suggests that Michael's work is nobler than that of the Coliseum builders because "its end and aim are nobler." Michael sees no connection between the beauty of the structure and the use to which it was put: he is obsessed with the superiority of Roman artists to himself, a pupil, not a master, and can only hope that he can learn. A parallel is here. Longfellow, who so often in talking of the immortals saw himself as a "humbler poet," stirs himself to great effort by seeing in the humility of Michael Angelo a replica of his own, and justifies his derivativeness (for which he was often attacked), by seeing in Michael Angelo a smiliar dependence on predecessors. In the "Dedication," which anticipates the finale of *The Waste Land*'s "These fragments I have shored against my ruins," Longfellow writes, "Men build their houses from the masonry/ Of ruined tombs. . . ./ So from old chronicles, where sleep in dust/ Names that once filled the world with trumpet tones,/ I build this verse. . . ./ Quickened are they that touch the Prophet's bones." And in *Michael Angelo*'s world, Longfellow sought "Shanti."

The voice of Cavalieri, arguing in effect the superiority of the Christian Michael Angelo to the pagan architects, is probably the voice of Longfellow contemplating *Christus* in 1850. But so, too, is the voice of Michael the Artist arguing the irrelevance of religious partisanship in art and later bitterly resenting the critics who find him "wanting/ In piety and religion, in proportion/ As

I profess perfection in my art." Although religion is Michael
Angelo's patron, it offers as many vexations and obtuse inter-
ferences as Longfellow's patron, the public. The external framework of the play is designed to reveal the Renaissance world
of art as a vital world in which, although some artists sell out
to their patrons, and others are talented playboys, the representative man is Michael Angelo, despairing over his failures, com-
batting misunderstanding, ignoring applause, and creating simply
because he has to create. Tortured by aspirations in art he thinks
beyond his ability, his great work, St. Peter's, unfinished after
decades of labor, and under attack by critics, he asks the unarti-
culated question of all Longfellow's later poems:

> How will men speak of me when I am gone,
> When all this colorless, sad life is ended,
> And I am dust? They will remember only
> The wrinkled forehead, the marred countenance,
> The rudeness of my speech, and my rough manners,
> And never dream that underneath them all
> There was a woman's heart of tenderness.
> They will not know the secret of my life,
> Locked up in silence, or but vaguely hinted
> In uncouth rhymes, that may perchance survive
> Some little space in memories of men!
> Each one performs his life-work, and then leaves it;
> Those that come after him will estimate
> His influence on the age in which he lived.

Michael Angelo and the writer of "Morituri Salutamus" are one.
The old poet, cheering himself with thoughts of Sophocles,
Chaucer, and Goethe writing masterpieces in old age (though too
honest to think that old age is anything but old age—"not
strength, but weakness," "some living sparks . . ./ Enough to

warm, but not enough to burn"), will not write an *Oedipus* or a *Canterbury Tales*, "But other something, would we but begin."

At the end of the line, the world's most successful poet, and the first American professional poet, was paying the penalty private poets do not pay. The man who at the age of thirty-two had declared he had a notion to work on the public's feelings, who in 1850 might have said with greater justifications than Goethe,

> What were I without thee
> O my friend the public?
> All my impressions monologues
> Silent all my joys [sorrows].

who had attempted, as his major opus, a theme which he could not finish on the socially acceptable terms in which he had hopefully begun it—was, at the age of seventy, not enjoying the peace of the poet whose work had been a means of finding himself, but was baffled by a public still reading *Hiawatha* while it ignored his major opus; was disillusioned about the acceptance he had enjoyed; was still querulous about critics, and wondering about his rating with posterity—in other words, was worrying about what readers thought of him. [American Poet must wait— wait for what? Acceptance.]

Side by side, the scores of poems about and references to writers who "made it"; the statements that "making it" in your time is no good; the wish to die.

CHAPTER NINE

Longfellow's Income from His Writings, 1840–1852*

I PRESENT in this report a few of the results of a study of manuscript materials in the Craigie House in Cambridge of which almost no use has been made heretofore. The materials consist of: (1) An Account Book in which Longfellow listed, among other things, his receipts from writing and teaching for the years 1840–52. Details herein include usually the title, price, and place of publication of each poem he was paid for; payments for each printing of books; his salary from Harvard; and, after 1843, his wife's income. (2) A list of editions of each of his works to 1864, indicating the date and the number of copies of each printing. (3) A number of contracts, copyright documents, and bills for stereotyping; and lists of the number and value of stereotype plates acquired between 1845 and 1852. (4) Letters from publishers and editors to Longfellow.

When it is carefully integrated, this information offers a fairly complete story of the business aspects of Longfellow's literary career in America[1] for the period stated. I have reconstructed that story partly in the belief that it adds significantly to our knowledge and understanding of a poet whose reputation has suffered not because we know too much about him but too little. The traditional portrait, almost unmodified until recent years, lacks humanizing nuance and three-dimensional solidity. But I am still more interested in the facts for the evidence they give of Longfellow's importance in the history of professional authorship. It is no small matter that he was the first American writer to make a living from poetry—that by shrewd, aggressive, and intelligent management of the business of writing, he raised the commercial value of verse and thereby helped other American poets to get out of the garret.

The period covered by the Account Book begins the month after the publication of *Voices of the Night*; it ends a year after the appearance of *The Golden Legend* and two years before Longfellow resigned from Harvard. It is the period of the *Ballads, Poems on Slavery, The Spanish Student, The Belfry of Bruges, Evangeline, Kavanagh*, and *The Seaside and the Fireside*; of three anthologies; and of three collected editions. It represents, therefore, the era of Longfellow's life when he established his reputation and popularity as a poet; and inasmuch as he published fourteen books in these thirteen years, it was also one of his most productive periods. Anyone who tries to write while he carries a full-time job can appreciate what has never been fully recognized—that the gentle Longfellow was a phenomenally industrious worker. Fortunately we need not break the story off short at 1852, for Longfellow's list of editions enables us to construct the publishing history of these books to the year 1864, by which time, apparently, most of his old separate publications in their original form had been taken off the market.[2] It is thus possible to determine the total sale of many of his works during their whole existence, and to offer comparative statistics concerning them.

Two warnings concerning the interpretation of these facts are in order. The first is that one must not assume that Longfellow's accounts are entirely correct or complete. One's private bookkeeping rarely is. I have discovered a few minor omissions, and one amusing error: in the year 1849 there is a mistake of $1,000 in Longfellow's addition of his receipts—$1,000 too little—which shows that he was getting on pretty well in 1849. Moreover, the year-by-year accounts are slightly misleading because they record income only, not outgo. There is no indication of the important fact that up to 1852 Longfellow paid out about $2,600 for stereotype plates, an expenditure which, as I shall show, added greatly to his prosperity.

My second warning concerns the muddy problem of comparative cost of living. Let us assume, unscientifically, like most economists, that money in the 1840's had three times the buying power it had in the 1930's. On that scale, Longfellow's income of $2,019 for 1840 was equal to $6,000 today, and better than that of a congressman in 1840, who earned $8.00 a day when he worked. By this standard Longfellow's rate of $15 or $20 a poem in 1840–41 was not so poor as it sounds. It would have been poor enough had he been forced to grind out poems at this rate to pay his rent. But, as we shall see, Longfellow never let himself be blown about by book-trade winds. Once he began to take himself seriously as a poet with an audience, he became a first-rate sailor.

The total bulk of a poet's work is usually small compared to that of the prose writer, and the problem of the poet who wants to make a living is how to sell the same poem as many times as possible. Ordinarily, in the nineteenth century, his resources in this respect were three: (1) single publication in a newspaper, magazine, or annual; (2) collection in a small volume; (3) reassembly of small volumes in a "collected" edition. Longfellow learned exactly how to use each of these methods; in fact, it is doubtful whether any other poet of the century was so resourceful in bringing his work before the public in so many forms and on so many price levels.

Concerning the first of these, a glance at the facts shows that Longfellow did not remain one of the miserable brotherhood of "magazinists" very long. Though contributions to magazines brought in almost half his literary income from 1840 to 1844, they counted for less than 10 per cent of his total literary income for the whole period. During the thirteen years he averaged only three paid contributions a year.

The accounts illustrate graphically the sudden and startling rise in magazine rates for authors in 1842, for though in 1840–41 poems brought him $15 or $20, in two years he moved permanently into the $50 level. This increase in the pay scale has rightly been attributed chiefly to George Graham; but the correspondence shows that Longfellow helped to bring this scale into effect by putting pressure on the publisher.[3] The most interesting fact about the situation is that Graham paid these high prices only for a monopoly of an author's work, and that this was his way of protecting himself against the unethical Mr. Godey.[4] From 1843 to 1848 Longfellow's paid contributions appeared in *Graham's* only;[5] and it is likely that he was one of the first American authors to try this early form of the modern contract for exclusive rights to an author's name.

Inasmuch as Longfellow never gave even Graham as many contributions as the latter was willing to pay for, it is apparent that he realized that book publication was, or could be made, more lucrative than magazine work, and that to be salable a volume of poems must be made up partly of previously unprinted pieces. Concerning this second form of publication, it should be stated at once that Longfellow did not merely follow established techniques; he helped to create new ones. In the 1830's he had tried the old unsatisfactory plans of flat payment for copyright, and sharing profit with the publisher; and it was on this latter plan that he was obliged to begin his relations with John Owen when he published *Voices of the Night* in 1839. For Owen's first five printings of *Voices* and first four printings of the *Ballads*, Longfellow's half share of the profits was six or seven cents a copy, or an average of 8 per cent on a retail price of seventy-five cents. But as soon as these books had proved successful, he somehow persuaded his publisher to revise the contracts,[6] so that beginning in 1842 and 1843 he received for *Voices* and the *Ballads* ten cents a copy—which was a royalty of 13⅓ per cent —a high rate for poetry in those days—and these. He made the same arrangement for *The Spanish Student* in 1843 and *The Waif* in 1844.

On June 18, 1845, he took an important step: he bought from Owen the plates of his five books, crediting himself in the Account Book with $400 for royalties due, with the explanation, "Received payment in stereotype plates." [7] In 1845 and 1846 he ordered stereotypes of his old prose works, *Outre-Mer* and *Hyperion*. From then until at least 1865 Longfellow paid for and owned the plates of all of his books (except *Poets and Poetry of Europe* and the Philadelphia illustrated edition), and sold to publishers the right to print from them. Let us see what effect this had on his rate of profit.

From Owen he had received, when the publisher owned the plates, first 8 per cent, then 13⅓ per cent. After 1845, when he owned his own plates, he received, on eight books on which the facts can be clearly determined, gross rates of from 20 per cent to 27½ per cent—an average of 23½ per cent—on the retail price. But of course his real royalty depended upon two factors —the cost of the plates of a book, and the volume of its sale. Thus, for example, the *Estray* of 1846 yielded him a gross royalty of 26⅔ per cent; but as the plates cost him almost $100 and only 1,000 copies were printed, his real royalty was only 13⅓ per cent. Now, the plates of *Evangeline* also cost $100; but as the book had a sale of 13,425 in seventeen years, his gross royalty of 26⅔ per cent (twenty cents a copy) was a real royalty of 25.6 per cent. His net average royalty for all eight books was 18¼ per cent.

The moral, of course, is that if a mid-nineteenth-century author of some reputation had a little capital and the sense to invest it in stereotype plates, he could get 18¼ per cent rather than the traditional ten. Moreover, as Prescott, who also used this system, pointed out, it provided perfect insurance against the vagaries of publishers' bookkeeping. Longfellow could not be cheated. When Ticknor needed more books, he had to ask Longfellow to send an order to Metcalf to print so many copies, and payment for these became due when the volumes were printed, not when they were sold. There were variations on this method, of course, most of them inferior. Longfellow's first arrangement with Harpers for the cheap edition called for the delivery of the completed book, manufactured at Longfellow's cost, the publisher taking a commission for sales. This was Emerson's system for many years. Longfellow wisely avoided it, perhaps because it would have deprived his publisher of incentive. His own method not only brought him author's pay but made him a publisher's partner who shared in some of the profits of book manufacture. It is worth noting that, from the business point of view, his two most troublesome books were the *Poets and Poetry of Europe* and the illustrated edition, both published by Carey and Hart in Philadelphia in 1845. The publishers owned the plates of these, and he and they quarrelled frequently over control and management of copyright. Finally, not the least of the advantages of his method was that he could choose his own printer and thus control more effectively the typography of his books.

The sales record of the eight volumes of original verse produced in this period is interesting, if not surprising. From smallest to largest, their sales, or rather, their printings, to 1864 were as follows:

Poems on Slavery	1,750
(not including the Anti-Slavery Association reprint)	
The Spanish Student	1,850
The Belfry of Bruges	2,050
Ballads	2,940
The Seaside and the Fireside	5,000
Voices of the Night	7,000
(not including Redding's pamphlet edition) [8]	
The Golden Legend	8,968
Evangeline	14,425
(this is only one-third the sale of *Hiawatha*)	

If Longfellow's records of receipts and printings are not misleading, one can generalize to the effect that long narratives, like
Evangeline, or connected short narratives, like *The Golden
Legend,* had a longer life as individual volumes than the other
works. Excepting *The Seaside,* which was absorbed into the
collected edition after one printing, not one of the first six volumes
listed above was reprinted or brought Longfellow any royalties
after 1848. It is true that a Ticknor advertisement lists all of
them (except *Poems on Slavery*) for sale as of October, 1856, but
it is likely that Ticknor, who apparently bought Owen's stock
when the latter failed late in 1846, was, in 1856, trying to get
rid of all of his separate Longfellow titles before he published his
"Blue and Gold" collected editions.

One of these volumes deserves a digressive paragraph. Ordinarily *Poems on Slavery* is dismissed with the slighting comment that Longfellow left it out of the Philadelphia edition of
1845. In the Account Book there is only one entry for this work:
"Poems on Slavery, oo.oo." I interpret this to mean that Longfellow refused to profit by a work which he intended to be his
contribution to a cause; and the integrity of his motive is further
vindicated by the fact that he permitted the New England Anti-
Slavery Tract Association to reprint it, without compensation to
him, [9] in a region where its distribution could do the most damage
to his reputation. Longfellow could be quietly stubborn about his
convictions as his unprinted letters concerning these poems show.
The figures for the three prose works, to 1864, are as follows:

Outre-Mer 6,060
Kavanagh 8,620
Hyperion 14,450

The surprising fact here is that the total printings of the prose
works was 85 per cent of that of the seven separate volumes of
original verse published in the same period (that is, up to 1849,

the date of *Kavanagh*). Comparing the best-sellers of the two groups, *Hyperion*'s 14,450 is greater than *Evangeline*'s 14,425. Even more interesting, Longfellow's gross receipts for the prose exceeded that for the verse group—$5,427 to $5,350.[10] Obviously Longfellow was better known as a prose writer in his time than one would suppose.

The third form of publication—the collected edition—was, of course, the most important financially. Longfellow's first three collections—the illustrated edition of 1845, the cheap edition of 1846, and the Ticknor and Fields two-volume edition of 1850— brought him almost double the returns of the individual volumes which they embraced, even though the sales of the collected editions were somewhat smaller. Experience early showed Longfellow that the technique of this form was worth watching. On the one hand, several levels of market could be reached by variations of price; on the other hand, each collection could be strategically outmoded through the publication of new separate volumes of verse and the inclusion of these in new collected editions. Longfellow's first venture, the de luxe illustrated edition at $3.50, was brought out on the initiative of the publishers, Carey and Hart; but the fifty-cent, paper-covered Harper collection of 1846 was Longfellow's idea. Carey and Hart unreasonably tried to block this edition, and gave up only after they turned the question over to Little and Brown for arbitration. In a way, the cheap edition was like a neat recovery of a fumble. In 1845, feeling that it was time to tap the cheaper market for *Voices of the Night,* Longfellow brought out a twelve and one-half cent, double-columned, paper-covered edition through Redding of Boston. Inasmuch as the plates for this cost him $72 and he received only $60, he was a loser. But not for long. After selling the idea of a cheap collected edition to Harpers, Longfellow thriftily built the plates of the Harper edition around those of the cheap edition of *Voices.* Early in 1849 he freshened up the collection commercially by adding to it new double-column plates of *Evangeline,* raising the retail price from fifty to sixty-two cents.

The whole operation cost him about $340 for plates, but his net royalty for total Harper sales of 6,000 averaged 16 per cent.

He could not, of course, continue very long to expand the cheap edition by these methods. Harpers had even hesitated to accept his proposal to add *Evangeline* to their edition on the ground that if they increased the price to seventy-five cents, as Longfellow apparently had suggested, they would drive his buyers into the bound book market.[11] After the publication of *The Seaside and the Fireside,* Longfellow decided to bring out his first regular trade edition—the two-dollar, two-volume collection of 1850; but since by this date it was generally agreed that Boston was the best market for poetry, Ticknor, Reed, and Fields got the contract. The plates of this edition cost him $625; but with sales of almost 20,000 by 1864, his net royalty was a fat 18½ per cent. This edition was, in turn, outdated and surpassed in sales by the Blue and Gold edition of 1856, which, at $1.75, had a sale of 40,000 by 1864.

It might be assumed, from consideration of the question of royalty percentages in general, that as Longfellow's work grew in popularity, his revenues increased in proportion. Not so. Longfellow reached his peak in royalty rates in 1846–49, when Ticknor paid him, for *Evangeline, The Seaside and the Fireside,* and for editions of some of the older volumes which he had taken over from Owen, a gross rate of 26⅔ per cent. In the case of *Evangeline,* as I have said, this meant a net of 25.6 per cent—perhaps an all-time high for any poet.

The gross rates began to slip—as follows:

1849	*Kavanagh*	20 per cent
1851	*Golden Legend*	20 per cent
1855	*Hiawatha*	15 per cent
1856	"Blue and Gold" *Poems*	10 per cent

By 1871, 10 per cent, net, was his regular royalty.

I have only guesses to offer for this phenomenon. One is that Longfellow's greatest relative prosperity came betwen the two great depressions of 1837 and 1857. Following the pattern of business history in general, publishing went through a great expansive period in the late forties and early fifties, and when the boom began to wane, publishing, always the first to suffer, had to contract. Ticknor and Fields did so in time; Phillips Sampson and Company (for example)—publishers of Emerson, Prescott, Holmes, and the *Atlantic Monthly*—did not. They collapsed in 1859, letting their mantle fall on their more wary rivals, Ticknor and Fields. I think it may be possible to show eventually that America's great literary activity in the fifties was directly related to this economic situation.

Returning now to the Account Book for a final glance, I should like to explore a natural but unwarranted assumption concerning Longfellow. Everyone knows that he married the daughter of a great industrialist in 1843; it is less generally known that he had no private invested funds. He worked for every cent he got; indeed, in later years, he paid to the rest of the family what he had borrowed from his father when he was young. Now, those familiar with the most elementary facts concerning Longfellow know that he did not lie back among pillows and mint juleps after he married the "heiress." They may even know that he continued to work hard at his two professions for eleven years thereafter. But more particular facts may be welcome even to the initiated. In the four years before his marriage, 1840–43, Longfellow's average yearly income, all of it derived from teaching and writing, was $1,917. In the nine years following his marriage, his yearly average was $3,536. The literary record is even more interesting, especially when one remembers the remark by Henry James's writer in "The Lesson of the Master," that marriage and children are an "incentive to damnation, artistically speaking." Longfellow's damnation was spectacular in that it skyrocketed his income from writings alone from $335 in 1843 to $2,860 in 1845; and his average, from writings alone, from that year to 1852 was almost $2,000. To clinch the subject, let it be known that during the first ten years of marriage, only once was his wife's income larger than his; and that in three of those years his income from writings alone was larger than hers from investments.

One may draw one's own conclusions from these facts and figures. I think it would be hard to deny that Longfellow helped to make the literary profession respectable by making it profitable, as had long been the case in England. It was harder, after his example, for fathers like his own to discourage their sons from entering the literary profession because it was not self-supporting. It would be unfair, I think, to attribute his financial success wholly to the almost universal readability of his work. That success was not handed to him on a silver platter: he worked hard for it and he used his head to solve his professional problems. One gets the impression, as one goes through the records and correspondence, that Longfellow took an extraordinarily active part in the publication of his own works[12] at a time when commercial publishing in this country was not yet fully developed, and that he helped explore the potentialities of new reader markets. His success suggests that the lack of international copyright was not necessarily an insuperable obstacle to the development of American literature.

---

*The author wishes to thank Mr. H. W. L. Dana for generous assistance in the preparation of this paper.

1. Longfellow's publishing arrangements in England have been investigated by Clarence Gohdes. See his "Longfellow and His Authorized British Publishers" in *PMLA*, LV (December, 1940), 1165–79. My materials reveal receipts of $25.00 in 1841 from Richard Bentley for contributions to Bentley's *Miscellany*; $100.00 in September, 1850, for an English illustrated edition of *Evangeline* (500 copies); $480.10 on December 13, 1851, for a London edition of *The Golden Legend*; and $200.00 on December 15, 1851, for a London edition of *Poems,* illustrated.

2. W. D. Ticknor's death in 1864, and the appearance of a variety of collected

editions in the next few years, suggest a complete rearrangement of Longfellow's contracts by James T. Fields, the surviving partner, at about this time.

3. On December 23, 1841, Graham offered Longfellow $30.00 a poem. On January 20, 1842, he wrote: "When I mentioned $30 I intended it on poems only, and as I have purchased at $20, I thought I was liberal." (Letters in the Craigie House.)

4. Graham to Longfellow, May 24, 1844: "I find it is time for me to protect my own interests. I have been paying high prices, and have fixed these prices permanently—for the articles of our best writers, and have agreed to take them *regularly*—not *once or twice* a year. Mr. Godey gets an article from some writer who has been sustained by me, and makes constant use of his name among his contributors. I shall stop that. He must have his set and I will have mine. And when I am deserted I shall cut the name from my list. This rule I shall apply to all, whose articles I *bind myself* to take regularly. I must have the obligation as strong on the other side." (Craigie House.)

5. This statement does not apply to annuals and gift books, which were not in competition with magazines. The Account Book shows that these also paid $50.00 and that Longfellow contributed to them fairly regularly.

6. The revised contract for *Voices*, dated February 8, 1842, is at the Craigie House; for the *Ballads*, same date, at the Morgan Library. The Accounts show that the latter did not go into effect until 1843.

7. The details of this transaction are not entirely clear. The full entry in the Account Book is as follows:

Voices XI	500	Received
Ballads IX	500	payment in
Spanish Student		stereotype $400
Poems on Slavery		plates
Waif IV	500	

It is confirmed by a receipt (at the Craigie House) dated June 18, 1845, and signed by Owen, for $400 in payment for the plates of the five works. But at the Yale Library there is an authorization, signed by Longfellow on the same date, for Owen to print from Longfellow's plates of *Voices, Ballads, The Spanish Student*, and *The Waif*, all in 16mo format, to the number of 2,667 copies. At fifteen cents a copy, this comes to almost exactly $400. Since the authorization does not include *Poems on Slavery*, these printings were to be made from only four of the works. Yet Longfellow does not record any further printings by Owen beyond those specifically mentioned in the Account Book (*Voices* XI, *Ballads* IX, and *Waif* IV), a total of only 1,500. It is possible that Owen's bankruptcy in 1846 (documents in the Registry of Deeds, Middlesex County, show that his property was assigned January 12, 1847, as of December 23, 1846) prevented his reimbursing himself in full for the plates. But the publication by Ticknor of an edition of *The Waif* in November, 1846 (for which he paid Longfellow) leaves that explanation open to question.

8. Published in Boston, 1845. A statement by Longfellow, dated July 7, 1846, in a notebook marked "Gleanings" (Craigie House) indicates that between 1,000 and 2,000 of this edition were printed.

9. In the foreword to one of these pamphlets there is an acknowledgment of "the magnanimous generosity with which the distinguished author has contributed [the slavery poems] to our series."

10. These figures cover sums actually paid to Longfellow. Colman, the bankrupt publisher of the first edition of *Hyperion*, seems to have paid only $272 out of a total of $500 due. See "Longfellow's Letters to Samuel Ward," *Putnam's Monthly*, III (December, 1907), 304.

11. Harper Brothers to Longfellow, November 28, 1848 (Craigie House).

12. Scattered documents and letters at the Craigie House show that Longfellow kept himself informed on the manufacturing costs of his various works.

James T. Fields and the Beginnings of Book Promotion, 1840–1855

I N RECENT YEARS much has been written concerning the efflorescence of American literature about the middle of the nineteenth century. Mr. Matthiessen has ably discussed the tone, the quality, and the aesthetic psychology of American romantic literature, and Mr. Brooks has revealed the New England writers as products of a regional culture and as points in the curve of a culture-cycle. But the genius or talent of a newly emergent group of writers is one thing; the transformation of genius into books which provide a living for the geniuses is quite another—and on this subject we have little information. No great art can flourish unless it has an audience and unless artists can live on it: in other words, to be born and to survive, it must have patronage. Up to the eighteenth century that patronage was predominantly royal or aristocratic. From about 1700 on it has been increasingly public, or popular, or democratic—in a word, commercial. The transition from the one kind of patronage to the other was long and chaotic; but the fifteen years which are described in these pages represent the end, in America, of that transition. The last five years of it are those of the first full flowering of American literature.

I propose to describe some of the means by which literary art was put on a basis of effective democratic patronage. If a slight odor of venality hovers over some of these proceedings, let us remember that flowers do not bloom luxuriantly without fertilizer. On the other hand, if these revelations seem a little appalling to the aesthete, it is because literary historians have failed, on the whole, to recognize the fact that literature is, from one point of view, a form of business enterprise. Writers must eat, and the improvement in their diet since 1800 (in America, at least) is to be accounted for, to an appreciable extent, by improvements in the manufacture and marketing of their books. Considered in historical perspective, the business methods of early publishers, as described in this paper, were neither better nor worse than those of other respectable merchants and manufacturers; and if competition among them engendered abuses, time and experience have supplied correctives.

In 1840 the general problem of the American publisher was that of all manufacturers: mass production and distribution. For the book manufacturer, accelerated competition called for speeding up and reducing the cost of printing processes by means of improved machinery; greater production created a need for wider markets; and expanding markets called for new sales and distributive techniques.

The result of all this was a kind of business revolution. Up to about 1835 American publishing was predominantly local: most cities and towns in the Atlantic states produced their own books; and almost all publishers were primarily retail booksellers. When a bookseller printed a work whose interest transcended local boundaries, he sold sheets to booksellers in other towns who bound them up for distribution in their own neighborhoods. Thus a book sometimes appeared with the imprints of half a dozen booksellers, in as many towns. Some publishers simplified this cumbersome system by assigning the market of a book in a whole area to one large retailer who distributed it at a discount to smaller stores.[1]

The South and West were not so easily served in the days before transportation had developed considerably, but New York and Philadelphia had natural geographic advantages which allowed such houses as Harpers in New York and the Carey-Lea-Blanchard dynasty in Philadelphia to monopolize the book business out to the receding frontier. That is a major reason, perhaps, why New York and Philadelphia were more important literary centers up to 1850 than Boston: they controlled a wider market area. We are still too ignorant of publishing history to make such pronouncements with absolute certainty, but when the subject has been explored, it is possible that the tendency to discuss literary history in terms of geographical "schools" of writers—of inscrutable "flowerings" of genius in New York or Boston or Chicago—will have to give way to more realistic analysis. Consider, for example, that much of New England's famous flowering went on in Philadelphia and New York. For one thing, before the founding of the *Atlantic Monthly* in 1857, most of the paid contributions of Boston authors appeared in periodicals published in other cities. For another, most of the New England writers who reached professional maturity before 1840—Bryant, Dana, Willis, Prescott, Sparks, Bancroft—did much or most of their book publishing outside of Boston. Even the better known men—Longfellow, Whittier, Lowell, and Hawthorne—published some of their early work in New York or Philadelphia. The fact is that Boston publishers came dangerously close to missing out on the New England renaissance. A case in point is Longfellow, who, having experimented with publishers, committed himself to a Boston firm only in 1847. Before that date he brought out five of his most remunerative books through New York and Philadelphia houses. When *Evangeline* was ready in 1847, Ticknor had to offer a higher royalty than Harpers to get it—higher, probably, than had ever been given for poetry in Boston. Except for Holmes and Emerson, the other major writers turned permanently to Boston publishers even later—Whittier and Lowell in 1849, Hawthorne in 1850. In other words, New England literary activity did not achieve its remarkable unity and homogeneity until the middle of the century, and its pre-eminence in literary publishing was not assured until the *Atlantic* was founded. As late as 1866, Bayard Taylor made this interesting statement to Aldrich: "If it were not for the damnable want of unity among our authors, we should have had Ticknor and Fields in Broadway by this time. Even now, it is the best place for them, if they would but see it."[2]

Much of the credit for making Boston the center of literary activity, however belatedly, must go to the firm of Ticknor and Fields, ancestor of Houghton, Mifflin Company, and it is likely (although, again, further investigation is needed) that this enterprising house won the business of New England writers by developing a national market for their books. Without belittling the business sagacity of William D. Ticknor, it can be shown that James T. Fields's special talents enabled the company to sell its publications in quantity all over the country despite the geographical disadvantages of Boston and the jealousy of other literary centers. Fields had a gift for what is now called "promotion"; in his own time it was a new but rapidly developing brand of American business enterprise which was shared by his contemporaries, P. T. Barnum, Henry Ward Beecher, James Gordon Bennett, George R. Graham, and Robert Bonner. Fields was a more subtle promoter than some of these, but he was no less successful.

Having begun as a clerk in the firm of Allen and Ticknor in 1832, Fields beca .e Ticknor's junior partner in 1843 and a full partner in 1854. A student of the early history of the firm quotes an authority to the effect that when Fields was made junior partner, to him "was delegated the responsibility for the literary and social c ntacts of the firm."[3] While it is true that Fields was corresponding with Whittier and Longfellow as early as 1840, it is unlikely that his real value to the firm in 1843 is accurately indicated by the phrase "literary and social contacts," unless its author had his tongue in his cheek. In view of the condition of book publicity at that time, it is far more likely that his real usefulness lay in his relations with men, not then well known, who had access to the book columns of newspapers and magazines—

his old friend E. P. Whipple, Epes Sargent, Park Benjamin, H. T. Tuckerman, and Rufus Griswold. In the absence of the systematized publicity techniques which today we take for granted, these men were indispensable links between publishers and the periodicals in which books were noticed and reviewed. At their worst they were logrollers and parasites; at their best they were useful agents of the literary profession which in the 1840's was struggling to be born. Inasmuch as their activities were necessarily anonymous, their methods must be reconstructed from such of their correspondence as has survived. At any rate, it was Fields's job to deal with these gentry, and with editors.

The situation which Fields faced in 1843 was somewhat as follows. Book reviewing in the newspapers was completely haphazard. There were no literary editors, no signed reviews. Reviews were, for the most part, short notices, laudatory if the publisher advertised or had influence, libelous if someone on the staff, or some favored outsider, disliked the author or the publisher.[4] Newspapermen were overworked and underpaid. As late as 1849, so conscientious a critic as George Ripley of the *New York Tribune* complained that he not only wrote all of the book notices but had charge of city news as well, and that he had to work night and day to earn his salary,[5] which was ten dollars a week. It is unlikely that less able and erudite men had time to read books and prepare notices, and under such conditions, countless small venalities on the part of publishers and newspapermen alike were inevitable.

Magazines were hardly subject to corruption through advertising, since few printed any. The publisher's approach to periodicals, and to newspapers as well, was through review copies. These made up the bulk of his advertising expense. Publishers' accountings to authors in the forties show that from 150 to 250 copies of a promising new work were sent to editors, constituting as much as 10 per cent of a first printing. Inasmuch as there were, in 1840, over 1,500 American magazines and newspapers,[6] it was easy for a publisher to incur the displeasure of an editor who had the power to hurt him, by not sending him books or by sending him the wrong ones. Horace Greeley wrote Griswold in 1840, "I shall walk right into your Philadelphia publishers [Carey and Hart] very brisk, if they don't behave themselves. They have sent me three or four of their ordinary rye-and-Indian novels this week, and *not* Mrs. Norton's poems, which you know the New Yorker has done as much to sell as any other paper."[7]

To the impecunious employees and owners of the shaky periodicals of that day, editorial copies were an object of some consideration, particularly if the publications were expensive. In 1845 H. J. Raymond, later editor of the *New York Times,* told Griswold that if he could get Lindsay and Blakiston, Philadelphia publishers, to send him one of the twenty-five-dollar copies of Wilkes's book on exploring, he would write six or ten articles for it in the *New York Courier.* "I will very gladly write extended notices of any books of which they send *me* a copy." But if they were sent to the editor, who regularly discharged his obligations by copying reviews from other papers, Raymond would write "only such notices as are matters of course."[8] In view of these facts, it is a little naïve for a biographer to boast, as George Ticknor did of Prescott's *Conquest of Mexico* (1843), that a book had drawn 130 good newspaper notices.[9] This work was a six-dollar set, and Harpers was not likely to waste money again on any editor who failed to acknowledge it properly.

How publishers arranged for the writing of acceptable notices is an interesting matter. One common method was to ask the author's friends to write or to place reviews in home-town newspapers where they had influence. Thus Hawthorne reviewed Longfellow and Melville in the *Salem Advertiser.* George S. Hillard, who acted as literary attorney for his friends Hawthorne, Longfellow, and Francis Lieber, had strong influence on the *Boston Courier,* of which he became part owner in 1856,[10] and in its columns appeared reviews of Prescott's *Mexico* by friend C. C. Felton, and of various Ticknor and Fields authors by Whipple, who knew most of the Boston writers. When Harpers published R. H. Dana's *Two Years before the Mast* in 1840, they wrote him that they were sending copies to the principal editors of Boston, of which they enclosed a list of twelve, and added, "We shall feel obliged if you can exert a favorable influence on the 'notices'; which we have no doubt is the case, both by your intimacy with the editors and by local feeling, aside from the intrinsic merit of the book."[11] When Ticknor and Fields published Boker's *Plays and Poems* in 1856, the author sent them a list of twenty friends in half a dozen cities, who, he said, would review his book, and he promised to distribute copies in the right places in Philadelphia.[12]

But usually reviews came to editors in a less roundabout way. The *Charleston Courier* asserted in 1856 that review copies were usually accompanied by several prepared notices which the editor was tactfully invited to use if they would save him trouble,[13] and there is no lack of evidence that this system was used in the early forties and that editors took advantage of it. Such prepared notices were procured by publishers from various sources. Sometimes junior members of the firm wrote them and passed them on to editorial friends. The notices were then clipped and sent to other editors along with review copies. Fields wrote Bayard Taylor in 1849, "If you do not care to use this article of mine for the Tribune, it may serve your tired brain some purpose elsewhere. No one need know that I wrote it, if you please."[14] H. C. Baird, of Hart and Baird, performed similar services for his company,[15] and it is possible that Frederick Saunders, an employee of Harpers,[16] and Francis Underwood, of Phillips, Sampson and Company, did the same sort of work.

More often, it is likely, publishers made use of a group of hack writers who served as agents for authors, or publishers, or magazines—sometimes all three, as in the case of the ubiquitous and versatile Mr. Griswold, whose anthologies had made him a kind of patron of publicity. An analysis of Griswold's letters shows that in the space of seventeen years (1839–56) he functioned in various business capacities for at least thirteen book publishers, twelve magazines, eight newspapers, and seven authors. It is no wonder that in 1843, when sixteen-year-old Charles Eliot Norton took a trip to New York, Longfellow asked Griswold to show him around. "I want him to look a little in the Literary *machinery* at work around him—the Editors' chambers, and publishers' dens, and the *whereabouts* of penny-a-liners."[17] During most of the decade Griswold seems to have been a paid publicity and author-contact man for Carey and Hart and their successors. Horace Greeley said so rather crudely when he wrote Griswold in 1847 that he had arranged for him to contribute a literary column to the *New York Advertiser.* "You understand what is wanted. A column not of puffs of your books, nor Carey's, nor anybody's, but of stuff that will cause the paper to be read and preserved"[18]—high-toned language from a man who, in 1840, had asked Griswold to get a notice into the *Philadelphia Ledger,* with the admonition, "pay for it rather than not get a good one."[19] The same note is struck in a letter from Carey and Hart to Griswold: the publishers said that they would get his review of one of their books into the *Philadelphia North American* "even if we have to pay for it."[20] In 1847 they instructed their agent to get Park Benjamin to reprint, along with an advertisement of one of their books, a review to be clipped from the *Richmond Times.*[21]

But Griswold had too much energy to confine his work to Carey and Hart. His friendship with Fields, which went back to 1841, was on the "Dear James"–"Dear Rufus" level and sufficiently close for Griswold to invite Fields to be his best man at his third wedding, in 1852. Their professional intimacy is no less obvious, for on July 10, 1843, Griswold wrote him, "Did you see what a puff I gave Tennyson [then being published by Ticknor] in the Sat Eve Post? . . . You must send a copy to that paper and one to me, which shall be duly acknowledged. I puff your books, you know, without any regard to their quality."[22] For these services, and later ones,[23] Fields seemed to have paid in kind rather than in cash. In 1842 he got J. S. Dwight to "do the amiable" for Griswold's *Poets* in the *Christian Examiner*,[24] and he himself probably reviewed his friend's *Female Poets of America* in *Graham's Magazine* in March, 1849.[25] An attempt earlier that year was less fortunate. He reported to Griswold on January 17, 1849, that his article on the *Female Poets* in the *Boston Atlas* "was altered and revised by an individual who was usurping the Editorial chair during [the editors'] absence. I was mortified and maddened. . . . To print it castrated and non-sensed, with 'an admirer' tacked on to the end was an insult I resented I assure you." But, he added comfortingly, "I have written an article . . . for Parley's Pic-Nic, which goes into all our families here, and will also be printed in the Bee with a circulation of some 5000."[26] Still another revelation of the sufferings of publishers in their dealings with newspapers appears in a letter of November 12, 1855. "I have only today learned the real reason why my notice [of the sixth edition of Griswold's *Poets*] has not appeared in the Transcript. It seems the Correspondent of the Transcript itself, is an American Poet who does not like yr. notice of him, and so Haskell [the editor] has been instructed by him to be chary of praise in noticing the new Ed." Fields assured Griswold that he had approached Haskell and that the latter "knows he will offend me if he says ought disparaging to you."[27]

Other letters show that Griswold probably ground out notices for Harpers,[28] who hired him to edit, on salary, an encyclopedia of biography;[29] for T. B. Peterson, the Philadelphia pirate, who wrote him furtively on January 7, 1850, "I would like you to get a good notice of [Peterson's twenty-five-cent edition of Anne Brontë's *Agnes Gray*] in the Tribune and any other papers in New York you can, *all of them if possible,* and you can send your Bill to me for your trouble. . . . Tear this up and let *no* one see it";[30] for George W. Childs, also of Philadelphia;[31] and for Herman Hooker of New York.[32]

Griswold's status is fairly clear, but that of Edwin Percy Whipple, who had real standing as a critic, is much less so. There is no evidence to back up Van Wyck Brooks's assertion that Whipple was the chief reader for Ticknor and Fields. Though he did read one or two of Hawthorne's novels in manuscript, he more frequently read works in the form of proof, which suggests that he functioned as publicity man rather than as a reader. But there is no evidence that he was on Ticknor and Fields's payroll in this capacity either, and it is quite possible to charge off his long and valuable services to the house to his boyhood friendship with Fields and to his later intimacy with Fields's authors. If his reviews were almost invariably kindly, it would be much easier to prove that his criticism was naturally of the appreciative variety than that he was paid for his work.

Nevertheless, his criticism needs to be scrutinized from a new angle. He had, from the early forties, precisely the kind of contacts that publishers valued. His influence grew rapidly from 1842, when he appears to have written notices for the *Boston Times*,[33] to 1847, when he was Boston correspondent of the New York *Literary World*,[34] and when, though a modest man, he wrote Griswold, "The truth is, from my connection with literary organs, I enjoy a great deal of power, which would make me a dangerous gentleman to abuse."[35] This power made him an irresistible object of the celebrated charms of James Fields, who saw to it that Whipple met, and remained in permanent social relations with, as many Ticknor and Fields authors as possible. It is not surprising that these were the subject of a majority of Whipple's unsigned reviews in *Graham's* between 1849 and 1853. But Fields used him in other ways as well. When young Bayard Taylor was beginning his work on the *Tribune*, Fields wrote him congratulations on his new volume of poems, published

by Putnam, and said, " . . . look for my printed praises in some
one of our Boston papers before the week is out. I am determined
Whipple shall do you up brown and that you shall ride in a
shiny coach made from the profits of Boston copies sold in
our diggins."[36]

There is no room here to discuss Whipple's later work in the
Atlantic Monthly, the *Boston Transcript,* and the *Boston Globe,*
but it is apparent that much of his forty years of critical work
was the result of Fields's promotional activities. Whether his
development as a critical thinker was enhanced by this relationship is another question, but Fields must take some of the blame
for what Poe referred to as Whipple's "critical Boswellism."

Other informal methods which publishers used to build up
good will are well illustrated by Fields's doings. His recognition
of the importance, from the publisher's point of view, of breaking
down sectional animosities is reflected in the following note to
Taylor: "Did you see the other gossip of mine (in the Transcript) touching the literary men of New York? Was my mention
of you agreeable or otherwise?"[37] In return for such favors, he
was able to get publicity in New York, for Longfellow wrote in
his journal in the same year, "Fields has written for some New
York paper a sketch of 'what the Literary Men are doing in
Boston,' one of the gossiping articles, which I do not much
affect."[38] Just how much of this sort of thing he did is impossible
to say, but one can assume that he was not referring merely to
his ability as a poster hanger when he wrote Longfellow, in May,
1849, "No family of any respectability shall sleep unapprized of
the publication of K[avanagh] on Saturday night. By this hour
today New York is glittering with our new show cards. All Broadway at least is ornamented with the fact that Kavanagh is 'just
published.' "[39] And a little later, "I am off in the morning for
N. Y. where I hope to do a deed that will make a noise in our
Bk. of Debits."[40]

Another publicity method he developed was the publication in periodicals of selections from forthcoming books. He aimed to serve both publicity and good will when he asked Longfellow to send a chapter of *Kavanagh* to the *Literary World* for advance publication.[41] He gave the same writer exact instructions about the set-up of the "Dedication" to *The Seaside and the Fireside* in *Graham's*[42] and in the *Boston Transcript*, whose editor, Epes Sargent, Fields said, "is always kind to 'our house.'"[43] Perhaps the kindness was that of one partner to another, for the *Transcript's* owners, Dutton and Wentworth, sometimes published books in collaboration with Ticknor and Fields.

Still another Fields specialty was winning the friendship of critics in other cities before their ability was generally recognized and rewarded. How he got the backing of powerful George William Curtis, a Harpers man, is suggested by the fact that in 1854, when Curtis was an editor of *Putnam's* and had been newly appointed assistant for the Editor's Easy Chair in *Harper's Magazine*, Ticknor and Fields gave him a banquet in the company of Longfellow, Holmes, Whipple, and other literary lights.[44] It is possible to see a connection between this thoughtful gesture and a letter which Curtis wrote Fields not long afterward: "Will you let me see an early proof of Longfellow's poem . . . that I may make a notice for Putnam . . . [The publishers] promise to get in an article I have made upon Tennyson and Maud [a Ticknor publication]. There ought to be in the October number at least a 'book notice' of Hiawatha."[45]

Perhaps young Thomas Bailey Aldrich was amenable to Fields's blandishments because, as a reader for Derby and Jackson, and G. W. Carleton, he had the publisher's point of view. As junior literary critic of the *New York Evening Mirror* in 1855, he received copies of Fields's books with personal inscriptions, in return for which he sent such billets doux as the following: "I have access to every department of the 'Mirror' and if I can be of service to you in any way, please command me heart and pen."[46] In the same year he wrote from the office of the New York *Home Journal* that, as newly appointed subeditor, "I can do more for the books which you so considerately send me than hitherto."[47] Later, Aldrich was to edit two magazines published by the house.

Henry Mills Alden was still another critic and editor whose friendship Fields secured early. When Alden was a struggling hack writer in the early sixties, Fields, as editor of the *Atlantic*, accepted some of his articles and hired him to do book notices. But Alden's gratitude overflowed when Fields used his influence to procure for him the Lowell Institute Lectureship for 1863, which, as Alden wrote him, was "highly auspicious to myself and my future prospects as a worker and thinker on this earth."[48] This event paid off in both directions, for that same year Alden became managing editor of *Harper's Weekly*, where he was in a position to place reviews which he wrote of Ticknor and Fields books.

Rather more independent was Richard Grant White, critic on the staff of the *New York Courier*, who wrote in 1858 that if his projected weekly literary paper should come into being, "books and things will be talked about in it I hope in a way that you will like—that is unless Ticknor and Fields take to publishing very poor books."[49]

In their printed reminiscences James and Annie Fields have presented a picture of famous friendships with Hawthorne, Dickens, Trackeray, and other literary notables; but a reading of Fields's private correspondence shows that, from the point of view of the publisher, these connections were window dressing compared to the vital relationships which Fields built up in the world of critics, editors, and reviewers. In his almost pathetic effort to make himself remembered as a writer, lecturer, and patron of authors, he succeeded only in looking like a glorified autograph hunter. In doing so he concealed his real talent as a publisher, which was his amazing ability to secure the good will of young men who later turned out to be molders of public taste. The list is impressive: Whipple, Griswold, Aldrich, Lowell, Curtis, Alden, Taylor, White, not to mention "Grace Greenwood," whose occasional literary comments in her fluffy "columns" had the same kind of publicity value as the late Alexander Woollcott's book plugs.

Incidentally, it is worth noting at this point that in the light of the facts here presented, the numerous recent studies of the contemporary reputation of American writers are subject to careful scrutiny. To attempt to estimate Melville's reputation, for example, by counting up favorable reviews is simply naïve. Melville himself was well aware of the value of such evidence, for he had the far more realistic figures of Harper's accounting office to tell him how popular he was with readers.

The last chapter of this cheerful story is sour but prophetic. In 1855 a loud explosion blew up the cozy nest into which publishers and newspaper critics had settled, and, amusingly enough, it was a *faux pas* by the normally tactful Fields that ignited the fuse. But the dynamite was advertising.

Since the early forties the advertising of books in newspapers had increased enormously. A casual examination of some of the large metropolitan dailies in the middle fifties shows that books were one of the products most advertised, and that they were given relatively more space than in the modern newspaper. This was true also of reviews and notices. Moreover, it is evidence of the nationalization of publishing that many, frequently most, of the advertisements came from publishers in other cities. Needless to say, there was a perceptible relation between advertisements and reviews. The "Silent Bargain," as Bliss Perry called it, had become an institution.

On November 13, 1855, the *Boston Daily Evening Traveller* printed a notice of Longfellow's newly published *Hiawatha,* which, though respectful to the poet's reputation and ability, ended with this passage:

> We cannot but express a regret that our own pet national poet should not have selected as the theme of his muse something higher and better than the silly legends of the savage aborigines. His poem does not awaken one single sympathetic throb; it does not teach a single truth; and rendered into prose, Hiawatha would be a mass of the most childish nonsense that ever dropped from human pen. In verse it contains nothing so precious as the golden time which will be lost in reading it.

Three days later, the *Traveller* printed an article headed "Attempt to Coerce the Press." After stating their pride in the independence yet kindliness of their book notices, the editors printed the following letter, dated November 13, and signed by Ticknor and Fields:

> Dear Sirs—From the above extract from a notice of one of our publications in this evening's Traveller, we presume that your Editors care very little for our personal feelings as publishers or our friendly regard in any way. So marked and complete a depreciation of our book is, to say the least, uncalled for. You will please send in your bill of all charges against us, and in future we will not trouble you with our publications or the advertisements of them. You will please also stop the paper.

The editors' concluding comment was,

> They may deceive themselves if they hope to defeat criticism by withholding their publications from us. . . . We shall find no difficulty probably in procuring copies of such of their works as may be worthy of criticism.

Fields should have known better, of course, but he was not used to such treatment. In fact, he was downright spoiled. Evidently his friend Griswold had not told him that three years earlier the same scrappy editors had refused to reveal the authorship of an unfavorable notice of a book in which Griswold was interested.[50] On the other hand, it is unlikely that the *Traveller* had the belligerence of ten because its heart was pure. Its columns, from October 31 to November 13, show that Ticknor and Fields advertisements were few and small; in fact, they had been channelizing their ads a little too pointedly, for the bulk of their space was taken up by five insertions of a two-and-one-half-inch advertisement of *Hiawatha*. Certainly they made a poor showing in the counting-room, compared to Crosby, Nichols; Phillips, Sampson; Appleton; and Harpers.

The publishing world hastened to respond to the *Traveller's* deed. On December 1 the *American Publishers' Circular* countered with a rejoinder written by a man who turned out later to be one Mason, of Mason Brothers, New York publishers. The writer admitted, for the sake of argument, that publishers, anxious to get good notices, may take "objectionable means" to procure them:

> in other words, that they pay, directly or indirectly, a pecuniary consideration therefor. They have a right to expect able and impartial criticism. If then they seek to bribe the press . . . it is from necessity, not choice. . . . As a whole the press is not only susceptible to pecuniary influences in its book criticisms, but openly so; it is not only willing but anxious to be bribed. 'Give us advertisements and we will give you good notices' is a proposition made every day to publishers. . . . It is a common thing for an editor to refuse to notice a book at all, because it is not advertised in his columns. Again, critics occupying important positions are plainly seen to be influenced in their published opinions. . . . In some cases, the manner of doing the thing properly is simply to enclose five dollars to the critic without word or comment. In other cases, more delicacy must be used, and the critic may be salaried by the publisher as manuscript reader, or in some other capacity.

The juicy tidbit about critics salaried as publishers' readers referred, of course, to George Ripley of the *Tribune* and Harpers, and on December 12 Francis Underwood, of Phillips, Sampson and Company, spiced it up in the *Boston Atlas*, over the signature of "Upsilon."

> If [said Upsilon, cattily] the literary editor of a paper so able and widely known as the New York Tribune, were "salaried as manuscript reader" by one or more prominent publishers in that city, what value would the world at large attach to his judgment of books? . . . In such circumstances, impartiality is out of the question. The critic *must* remember the hand that feeds him. . . . It is time, if such be the case, that these disguises were stripped off, so that the confidence of readers and fair-dealing publishers may be no longer abused.

This was too much for the *Tribune*. Even before he had seen Upsilon's article, Greeley, who was a slightly soiled St. George, in view of his earlier proficiency as a logroller, growled, in the issue of December 12,

> We can say that [Mason Brothers] have made repeated efforts to control our columns for their own purposes, and have been repeatedly disappointed. Extensive advertising has failed to secure the admission of notices of their books prepared by their own writers, to obtain for them any more favorable reviews than their intrinsic merits would justify. Some of these disappointments have been the occasion of anger privately manifested.

Coming back to the subject of publishers' readers the next day, the *Tribune* put up a convincing defense of the hurt and bewildered Ripley, asserting that the jobs of reader and critic were compatible because "the fact that a gentleman has long been trusted in such capacity by any publishing house able to select and to pay for its literary employees, must therefore be highly favorable to the reputation of that gentleman for integrity, independence, and soundness of judgment."

On December 15 the *Tribune* turned its attention to Underwood, declaring that he had repeatedly sought the use of its columns; that just before his company published *Modern Pil-*

grims, a "stupid book," Underwood had visited the *Tribune* offices in a friendly way, and that he was now angry because the book had been thoroughly castigated. Underwood, the *Tribune* summed up amiably, is a "small and unclean insect." But "while our hand is engaged . . . we will also hang up another better-known person of the same class," who has encouraged the attitudes of Mason and Underwood—Rufus Griswold—"a person so notorious in this community that to trace a calumny to him suffices effectually to dispose of it."

A few days later (December 19) Underwood got revenge by printing in the *Atlas* specific details about Ripley: that he was paid $1,200 a year by Harpers, and $800 by J. C. Derby. Underwood's concluding statements have all the earmarks of culpability:

> Very few people go through the world without committing some folly or absurdity, or worse perhaps. And if nothing more can be urged against me than having once accepted a courtesy from a man who afterwards proved himself so little of a gentleman, [etc.].

As tempers cooled down somewhat, the belligerents became rather more philosophical and constructive in their discussion of what was, after all, a situation that needed cleaning up for the good of all concerned. The *Tribune* (December 26) got at one aspect of the problem by revealing that publishing had expanded so enormously that no paper had room for notices of all books; and it pointed out that already specialization had begun, in that the *Tribune* stressed works relating to "progressive ideas and popular reforms," the *Courier,* "elegant literature," the *Evangelist* and the *Independent,* theology. As to critics who held other jobs, the *Tribune* admitted that because newspaper work was poor pay, all employees had to fill in with other work.

As to the aftermath of the fracas, Longfellow apparently was shocked into silence by Fields's indiscretion, for no word of the event appears in his letters or private journals. Ripley, in a steaming letter to Theodore Parker, refused to be reconciled with the perfidious Underwood, whom he called the "sneakingest and nastiest of men."[51] Griswold, writing sadly to Fields, denied having given occasion for such "wanton and malevolent libel."[52] Fields, who had the sense to keep quiet after his initial blunder, suffered less than these bystanders, for Ticknor and Fields were hardly mentioned in the squabble. Fields's New York friendships now paid dividends, for Richard Grant White wrote him, "I sent you a paper in which I handled the matter you stirred up. . . . The other journals have followed my lead as you see: it will divert attention from you." Then, unable to resist the temptation, he nuzzled Mason's jibe into Fields's ribs: "I shall write quite a notice of [your edition of Browning] and very favorable; but none of your five dollar bribes if you please: I do nothing for less than fifty."[53]

In perspective, this tempest was a sign that though newspaper and book publishing had both become large industries by 1855, neither had faced realistically its relation to the other. Though publishers provided a sizable proportion of newspaper advertising, the papers had failed to realize the news value of competent and responsible book reporting. The publisher, on the other hand, having failed to develop publicity as a legitimate business technique, tried to keep up the pretense that reviews were the uninfluenced opinions of critics working in the interest of the public. The solution still lay far in the future. For the newspaper it was to depend upon the establishment of a regular literary department, under responsible management, with signed reviews, book-note columns, and lists of new publications. For the publisher it called for proper selection of advertising media, the newspaper to be used only for those works which had a general or topical appeal.

Able though Fields was, conditions were no longer such that one man could handle the multifarious needs of publicity by the personal approach. It is significant that after 1855 there is less and less evidence that Fields bothered with the writing and placing of reviews; he concentrated, instead, on building up the general reputation of his group of stars,[54] whose devotion to him is evidence that he had their interests at heart as well as those of his firm. By the time he retired in 1871, Ticknor and Fields publications had become the core of the American canon of classics. His later career, including his editorship of the *Atlantic*, still remains to be studied; but it is probably a good guess that if some of the New England writers enjoyed, in the latter part of the century, a reputation beyond their deserts, it was in part due to the behind-the-scenes activities of James T. Fields, public relations counsel.

1. Carey and Hart (Philadelphia) to Longfellow, November 28, 1845: "We have sold the entire market [for Longfellow's illustrated *Poems*] for Mass[achusetts] to Mesrs. Ticknor & Co." (MS, Craigie House).

2. March 16, 1866, MS, Harvard College Library.

3. Florence W. Newsome, "The Publishing and Literary Activities of the Predecessors of Ticknor and Fields, 1829–1849" (Master's thesis, Boston University, 1942), p. 53.

4. W. A. Jones, in *Arcturus*, I (February, 1941), 149: "A newspaper criticism is generally a puff or a libel."

5. Ripley to J. S. Dwight, July, 1849, MS, Boston Public Library.

6. F. L. Mott, *A History of American Magazines, 1741–1850* (Cambridge, Mass., 1938), p. 342.

7. W. M. Griswold, *Passages from the Correspondence . . . of Rufus W. Griswold* (Cambridge, 1898), p. 51.

8. *Ibid.*, p. 175. John R. Thompson of the *Southern Literary Messenger* asked Longfellow to intercede with Fields, who had apparently taken the *Messenger* off his editorial list because it did not do justice to his books. Fields wrote Longfellow (November, 1849, MS, Craigie House) that hereafter Thompson would receive good books for very poor notices. Griswold curried favor with Whipple by placing the *Boston Times* on Carey and Hart's editorial list (Griswold to Whipple, January 17, 1842, MS, Yale Library).

9. *Life of William Hickling Prescott* (Boston, 1864), p. 205.

10. Hillard to Lieber, January 6, 1860, MS, Huntington Library.

11. September 17, 1849, MS, Massachusetts Historical Society.

12. March 16, 1856, MS, Huntington Library.

13. January 9, 1856. Reprinted in the *American Publishers' Circular and Literary Gazette,* January 19, 1856.

14. April 10, 1849, MS, Huntington Library. In December, 1849, Fields asked Longfellow to send the editor of the *Boston Sentinel* a poem "to be headed by an article touching the new Bk. which I will write for him" (MS, Craigie House).

15. Baird, in a letter to Griswold, December 16, 1848, said he had written a notice of Griswold's *Poets* "which Mr. Hart thinks will do . . . I am just commencing, and require practice" (MS, Boston Public Library).

16. "He was for some time connected with the Harpers, as their literary critic, taster, and man-of-all-work in that department." (MS, annotated: "George Ripley thus refers to Saunders in his newspaper correspondence, 14 Dec. 1849"; Griswold Papers, Boston Public Library.)

17. April 13, 1843, MS, Harvard College Library.

18. Griswold, *Correspondence,* p. 223.

19. *Ibid.,* p. 50.

20. *Ibid.,* p. 233.

21. Hart to Griswold, November 10, 1847, MS, Boston Public Library.

22. MS, Huntington Library.

23. Griswold promised to review Whittier's *Margaret Smith's Journal* in return for a copy of the book (Griswold to Fields, undated MS, Huntington Library).

24. Fields to Griswold, May 6, 1842, MS, Boston Public Library.

25. Joy Bayless, *Rufus Wilmot Griswold* (1943), p. 154.

26. January 17, 1849, MS, Boston Public Library.

27. *Ibid.*

28. Harper Brothers to Griswold, June 11, 1841, and May 4, 1849, MSS, Boston Public Library.

29. MS contract dated February 18, 1847, Boston Public Library.

30. *Ibid.*

31. Childs to Griswold, October 23, 1856, and November 22, 1856, MSS, Boston Public Library.

32. Hooker to Griswold, January 6, 1855, MS, Boston Public Library.

33. Epes Sargent to Whipple, January 18, 1842, MS, Harvard College Library.

34. L. A. Peacock, "Edwin Percy Whipple" (Doctoral dissertation, Pennsylvania State College, 1942), pp. 42–46.

35. Griswold, *Correspondence,* p. 224.

36. December 26, 1848, MS, Huntington Library.

37. April 10, 1849, MS, Huntington Library.

38. MS journal, April 18, 1849, Craigie House.

39. *Ibid.*

40. *Ibid.,* December, 1849.

41. *Ibid.,* March, 1849. Fields gave Whittier similar instructions (May 1, 1857, MS, Harvard College Library).

42. November, 1849, MS, Craigie House.

43. November, 1849, MS, Craigie House.

44. Griswold, *Correspondence*, p. 293.

45. August 24, 1855, MS, Huntington Library.

46. March 11, 1856, MS, Huntington Library.

47. September 13, 1856, MS, Huntington Library.

48. January 10, 1863, MS, Huntington Library.

49. August 25, 1858, MS, Huntington Library.

50. Andrews and Punchard to Griswold, May 24, 1852, MS, Boston Public Library.

51. March 28, 1856, MS, Massachusetts Historical Society.

52. December 22, 1855, MS, Huntington Library.

53. December 13, 1855, MS, Huntington Library.

54. That Fields, during the later years of the firm's history, had a fund for "entertainment" purposes is suggested by the articles of agreement governing the company (beginning in 1864), in which he is allowed "the sum of *One Thousand Dollars* per annum as consideration for his personal services . . . to be charged to the expense account of the firm." Information from Professor W. S. Tryon, who is writing a history of the firm of Ticknor and Fields (*Parnassus Corner* [Boston, 1963]—ED.).

CHAPTER ELEVEN

Melville's Income

WHEN Herman Melville died on September 28, 1891, he left an estate worth $13,261.31. When his wife died on July 31, 1906, her property was appraised at $170,369.62. This information may be a surprise to those who have imagined that the Melvilles subsisted on air after the death of Elizabeth Melville's father in 1861 (by which time Melville had almost ceased to write for the general book market), and on his custom-house salary after 1866. The fact is, however, that his situation was neither so bad as tradition suggests, nor so prosperous as these bare figures might lead one to think. At any rate, an investigation of the two wills and of Melville's financial condition after 1851 throws much light on his later years.[1]

I

Melville's holograph will, which is preserved in the Hall of Records in New York City, is as follows:

New York City

I, Herman Melville, declare this to be my will. Any property, of whatever kind, I may die possessed of, including money in banks, and my share in the as yet undivided real estate at Gansevoort, I bequeathe to my wife. I do this because I have confidence that through her our children and grand-children will get their proportion of any benefit that may accrue.—I appoint my wife executrix of this will.—In witness whereof I have hereunto set my hand and seal this 11th day of June 1888.

HERMAN MELVILLE

Signed and sealed by the above-named Herman
Melville as his last will, in prescence of us who at
his request and in his prescence and in the pres-
cense of each other have hereunto subscribed our
names as witnesses.

H. Minturn Smith

S. N. Robinson

H. B. Thomas[2]

The will itself is less interesting than the appraisal of the estate,
which was made on March 28, 1892, and filed on May 3, 1892:

Cash	$4,532.56
7 $1,000. U. S. 4% Registered Bonds (of the market value of $1.16 1/8 at the time of decedent's death)	8,128.75
Personal books numbering about 1,000 volumes	600.
Copyright of two works expiring in 1892 and 1893, which give no income and have no market value	
	13,261.31

Expenses		
Last illness	$413.	
Funeral	474.35	
Legal fees	170.	
Commissions allowed by statute	307.	
	1,364.35	
Net value		11,896.96
Transfer tax		118.97

One asks at once how and when Melville managed to accumu-
late almost $13,000 in cash and bonds, but some minor points
about these documents should be settled first.

1. *The library.*—It is well known that Melville was an assiduous book-buyer even in his leanest days, but the $600 valuation on his library turned out to be wildly optimistic. According to Oscar Wegelin, who, in his youth, worked in a bookstore which Melville patronized, Elizabeth learned the bitter truth about secondhand bookdealers when she failed to realize more than $110 from the sale of the whole collection.[3]

2. *Copyrights.*—By the laws in effect in 1892, an author had control of his work for twenty-eight years, plus fourteen years if he or his widow or children were living, making a total of forty-two years. Thus the copyrights expiring in 1892 and 1893 must have been *White-Jacket* and *Moby-Dick,* published in 1850 and 1851. That these copyrights had "no value" would seem to be a pathetic comment on Melville's reputation at the time of his death. But Elizabeth Melville was in error, for in 1892 the United States Book Company brought out new editions, under her copyright, of four of Melville's works: *Typee, Omoo, White-Jacket,* and *Moby-Dick.*[4] Moreover, in 1897 she wrote that the paper edition of these four works published in 1896 had had "a very good sale."[5] One wonders, however, why the appraisal contains no reference to the six works (other than the privately printed poems) published after *Moby-Dick.* Obviously they would not have been omitted from the inventory merely because they had "no value." It seems probable, therefore, either that Melville sold the six copyrights on publication or at some time when he was badly in need of the money, or that he neglected to renew them at the end of the twenty-eight-year period.

3. *Real estate.*—It will be noted that the Gansevoort property (near Saratoga Springs, New York) mentioned in the will is not listed in the inventory. This property was deeded to Melville and his brother Allan by their uncle, Peter Gansevoort, in December, 1848; was held in trust by them for a time; and finally was conveyed to Melville's sister, Frances Priscilla. When the latter died in 1885, she seems to have left the property to Melville and other members of the family. But on September 1, 1888, about three

months after Melville made his will, the property was sold at auction.[6] Inasmuch as Melville gave receipt on March 16, 1889, for $1,123.79, "being my portion under [the] will of the remainder of the estate of said Priscilla F. Melville,"[7] it would seem that the clause referring to the Gansevoort property became irrelevant before Melville died but that he neglected to change the will accordingly.

It should be noted also that in neither the will nor the appraisal is there any reference to the Melville house at 104 East 26th Street, New York City, although Melville's biographers say that he bought and paid for it with his wife's legacies. The Records of Conveyances at the Hall of Records show that the house was the property of Elizabeth; that she bought it from Allan Melville on April 25, 1863, for $7,750 and the Arrowhead place in Pittsfield (which also belonged to her, not to him, as is usually stated);[8] and sold it on April 15, 1892, after Melville's death, for $16,250.

2

The major question, of course, is Melville's sources of income. During the first five years of his literary life (1846–51) Melville seems to have made a good living from his writings. A document[9] in Allan Melville's hand shows that by April 29, 1851, Melville had realized from the English and American sales of his first five books and the English sale of his sixth—*Moby-Dick*—a total of $8,069.34—an average of over $1,600 a year for five years. Few American authors in the first half of the nineteenth century made as good a financial showing. But income seems to have been exceeded by outgo, for in spite of his success Melville owed, in 1851, $695.65 to the Harpers and at least $5,000 to Judge Shaw.[10]

For the next few years the American sales of his works held up fairly well. The Harpers advanced him $500 in February, 1852, and $300 in December, 1853, but from then until 1864 he was in debt to his publishers and drew nothing. Such royalties as accrued were applied to his debt until February 9, 1864, when Melville paid the Harpers $200. From then until 1887, when the records stop, his income from this source was negligible.

I have no information about Melville's income from books brought out by other publishers, but it appears that no one of them had a large sale. Moreover, Putnam was forced to sell the plates of *Israel Potter* during the panic of 1857, and Dix and Edwards, publishers of *The Piazza Tales* and *The Confidence-Man,* went bankrupt in the same year.[11] Melville's dealings with English publishers after he sold *Moby-Dick* to Bentley for £150 have not yet been investigated, but Arthur Stedman stated that about 1851 the "English rights in *Typee* and *Omoo* had been bought outright by a London publisher for small sums and were held by him until Melville's death, so that soon all income from 'oversea' was ended."[12]

When his income from books began to fail, Melville turned to other outlets. Between 1853 and 1856 he contributed *Israel Potter,* fourteen essays and stories, and a few poems to *Putnam's Monthly Magazine* and *Harper's New Monthly Magazine,* for which he probably received a little over $725—an average of about $240 a year.[13] From 1857 to 1860, lecturing brought him gross receipts of $1,273.50—an average of $423 a year.[14]

After 1853, then, Melville's income from literary work seems to have been meager. It should be remembered, however, that during this period he had no rent to pay, and that he was probably able to support himself to some extent by farming at Arrowhead.

3

But what of the years from 1860 to 1866 when he had almost no income from magazines, lectures, or books, and during the latter half of which he did not even have a farm? It is true that in 1862 he received a small legacy—$900—from his Aunt Priscilla,[15] but that could not have lasted long. The solution of the problem is obvious when we remember that it was Elizabeth Melville who paid for the New York house two years after her father died. Though everyone is aware that Judge Shaw was generous to the Melvilles while he lived, no one has considered what his death must have meant to them in terms of financial relief.

Lemuel Shaw died on March 30, 1861. In his will,[16] dated October 4, 1860, he directed that the bulk of his estate be divided equally among his wife, his three sons, and his daughter Elizabeth. The inventory of the estate, filed July 26, 1861, showed a gross valuation of $114,320. After debts, expenses, and special bequests had been paid, Elizabeth's fifth share amounted to $15,114.27. This sum was, apparently (the records are not quite clear), paid out to her in three separate instalments during the years 1861–62.

There was no bequest for Melville, though he signed one of the probate documents as an interested party. But the will itself contains some interesting references to him. One clause runs as follows:

> And whereas since the marriage of my said daughter, I have loaned and advanced to her said husband, certain sums of money, I do hereby release, exonerate and discharge the said Herman Melville from all debts, dues and demands for any such loan made to him or on his account.

Inasmuch as Shaw had canceled all of Melville's debts to him five months before he drew his will, in return for title to Arrowhead which he then transferred to his daughter,[17] it is likely that this provision was mere legal formality.

Still another clause refers to a hitherto unknown marriage contract:

> Item.   Whereas at the marriage of my daughter with her present husband Herman Melville, a certain fund of three thousand

dollars was placed in trust under a certain contract or marriage contract and settlement between the said Herman Melville of the first part, the said Elizabeth V. [error for "K."] Shaw of the second part, and the said Curtis and myself of the third part, to which reference is to be had for the more particular provisions and trusts thereof; and whereas the principal of said fund of three thousand dollars has ever since remained in my hands and has not been specially invested,—I do order and direct my executors, unless the same shall be invested in my life-time,—to pay over to said Benjamin R. Curtis, surviving trustee, the said sum of three thousand dollars to be held and invested, and the income and principal thereof to be appropriated and disposed of according to the trusts and terms of said contract and marriage settlement.[18]

It would seem, therefore, that during the difficult years after 1853 the Melvilles had a backlog in this small trust fund, and that from 1861 to 1866 they must have been almost completely dependent upon it and the bequest, a sum totaling about $18,114. At 6 per cent this would have brought in an income of over $1,000 a year: but if, as is likely, the New York house was paid for out of the bequest, the principal must have been cut by $7,750 in 1863.

4

Secure as this income may have been, it was too small for the father of four children (whose ages, in 1866, ranged from eleven to seventeen), and especially for a man whose house seems frequently to have been full of relatives. It was, therefore, a financial as well as a moral necessity for Melville to obtain employment. On December 6, 1866, he was appointed Inspector of Customs in the District of New York at a salary of four dollars a day[19]— approximately $1,250 a year, though this was probably reduced by annual party assessments.[20] Together with income from the funds, this should have provided an adequate living, particularly since the Melvilles owned their New York house. Money for "extras" was occasionally provided by more well-to-do relatives. It appears from a letter of Elizabeth's in 1872 that Melville's uncle, Peter Gansevoort, made a gift of money when misfortune, the nature of which is not entirely clear, was suffered by the family:

> The fire is the all absorbing topic, and friends on every side have met with losses greater or less—I have plenty to keep me company—but I feel so much relieved by your father's kind and generous gift to Herman (removing the necessity of renting our house or part of it, which I feared) that I can bear my loss with equanimity.[21]

It is well known that the same uncle gave $1,200 for the printing of *Clarel* (1876), and Melville must have benefited by any sales of a book on which the publisher took no risk. It is not generally known, however, that in 1877 Melville received a bequest of $500 from Peter Gansevoort.[22] In 1876 Elizabeth's brother Lemuel paid for the Melvilles' vacation trip to the White Mountains, and in the following year a bequest of $100 from a relative enabled her to make badly needed improvements in her back parlor.[23]

Unfortunately, Melville's government job was not entirely secure, for, like Hawthorne, he was of little practical use to the party in power, and at least twice he was threatened with removal. One of the worst nests of corruption in Roscoe Conkling's machine, the New York Customhouse was under the constant surveillance of civil service reformers.[24] In 1877, early in Hayes's administration, the Jay Commission investigated irregularities at the customhouse, then ruled by Collector Chester A. Arthur. As might be expected, the commission found a heavily overloaded staff and evidence of bribery. No scandal seems to have touched Melville's name,[25] though his salary and the date of his accession to office appeared in lists of officeholders which were sent to Congress.[26] Nevertheless, his job was in jeopardy.

As a result of the investigation, Secretary of the Treasury Sherman ordered that the staff be reduced 20 per cent by June 30, 1877, and two hundred employees were dropped. It is barely possible that a literary man saved Melville, for one of the committee of three employees whom Arthur selected to draw up the list for decapitation was Richard Grant White, the Shakespearian scholar.[27] As it turned out, Melville was affected only by a general increase in working hours, from ten-to-three to nine-to-four daily. His reaction to all this was apparently stoical. On May 7, 1877, he wrote to a relative, "Now about President Hayes? I chanced to turn over a file of your Albany Argus yesterday, and was all but blown off the stool by the tremendous fulmination of that indignant sheet.—But what's the use? life is short and Hayes' term is four years, each of 365 days." [28] On the other hand, there is a possible reference to quite a different mood in a letter which his wife wrote on June 5, 1877: "—poor fellow he has so much mental suffering to undergo (and oh how *all* unnecessary) I am rejoiced when anything comes into his life to give him even a moment's relief. . . ." [29]

A second threat came in 1885, when Elizabeth wrote Catherine Lansing, "Of course there have been removals, and he may be removed any day," and suggested that she ask her husband, Abraham Lansing, who was politically influential in New York State, to intercede for Melville.[30] Within six months, however, she wrote the Lansings again, thanking them for their efforts but informing them that Melville had resigned on December 31, 1885.[31]

5

The reasons she gave the Lansings for Melville's resignation were age and ill health, but financial considerations must have entered into it. In August, 1885, Melville's sister Frances had

died, and he was undoubtedly looking forward to the liquidation
of the Gansevoort property on which she had lived but in which
he had an interest. By the will of his sister he received, on August
19, 1886, $3,019.50; on October 15, $96.49, which was intended
for his son Stanwix, then dead; and on March 16, 1889, $1,123.79
—a total of $4,239.78. By the same will his wife and his daughter
Elizabeth received unknown, but probably smaller, amounts.[32]
These facts have been generally overlooked in discussions of
Melville's decision to retire. Quite rightly, emphasis has been
put on the legacy which Elizabeth Melville received from her
brother at about that time, but hitherto details have been lacking.

The will of Lemuel Shaw, Jr., was signed June 27, 1882, and
the executors' inventory, filed December 3, 1884, evaluated the
estate at $323,450.70.[33] According to the will, the residue of the
estate was to be divided equally between Elizabeth and her two
brothers, John and Samuel. Elizabeth's share was $37,949.20, but
inasmuch as we are interested only in the amount received before
Melville's death, it should be noted that $33,516.67 was paid to
her before that time. In addition, the three Melville children
(Stanwix, Elizabeth, and Frances) received $2,000 each.

For the rest of the financial facts, we must turn to Elizabeth
Melville's will, which was signed on October 11, 1905.[34] It is a
comforting thought that the writer's widow and children were
well provided for; but, except for a few matters which bear upon
his interests, the details of the will and its administration are
irrelevant. The two daughters shared equally the residue of the
estate, Elizabeth receiving in addition $16,250, "being the sum
realized from the sale of my house and lot at 104 East 26th
Street, New York, which property was given to her by me
in a former will." Another clause shows that Melville's wish that
his children should benefit by his estate was scrupulously carried
out by his wife, who bequeathed to Elizabeth a special sum of
$5,000, representing "a portion of her father's estate devised
to me," a like sum having already been paid to Frances.

Of special interest among the probate documents is a deposition, made on June 12, 1907, by H. B. Thomas, her son-in-law and executor, that "at the time of her death she had no copyrights, nor any interest therein; that for several years before her death he had collected her income and during that time she had received nothing from copyrights."

6

Obviously more facts are needed to complete this picture, for the legacies and earnings listed are not sufficient to account for the size of Melville's estate—particularly when one considers that his funds must have been reduced by his private publication of *John Marr* and *Timoleon* in 1888 and 1891. Furthermore, his records of accounts with the Harpers have not been thoroughly studied, and little or nothing is known of his business relations with his other publishers—Putnam, and Dix and Edwards, or with his English publishers after 1851. Nevertheless, the major sources of his income are known, and tentative conclusions may be drawn.

From 1846 to 1851 Melville was a financially successful author, able to support his family by his writings. From 1851 to 1866, during which time his literary work tapered off, his income from magazine contributions, lectures, and from books published by Harpers, was about $3,430, an average of $228 a year; but inasmuch as the bulk of this income was earned by 1861, it is more useful to know that for this period of ten years he averaged at least $320. This was insufficient, of course, and only the trust fund and the legacies of 1861-1862 made it possible for him to do without a job until 1866. His luck in respect to legacies was phenomenal, for he and his family received a total (including the trust fund) of at least $63,370 during his life, and, through the generosity of his father-in-law, they lived rent-free from 1851 on.

"[Household] economy is a science, and must be devoutly studied," wrote Emerson.[35] Of such science, Melville seems to have been innocent. This, of course, is no reflection on either his personal or his artistic integrity; yet it and such information as I have here given must be considered in any discussion of that important but neglected problem—the relation between Melville's (or any author's) works and the financial and domestic strains which he endured. The conclusion that Melville was a poor manager seems inescapable, for even at the height of his literary fortunes he was heavily in debt. His wife wrote to a friend in 1872: ". . . Herman from his studious habits and tastes being unfitted for practical matters, all the *financial* management falls upon me—and one cannot make bricks without straw—you know." [36] When one remembers that in spite of connections with such powerful political figures as Judge Shaw, R. H. Dana, Jr., Abraham Lansing, Peter Gansevoort, and Marcus Morton, Melville was unable to get a political appointment better than an inspectorship, it is possible to infer that this estimate of his practical ability was shared by his relatives and acquaintances.

1. Willard Thorp has collected some of the details of Melville's later life in "Herman Melville's Silent Years," *University Review*, III (Summer, 1937), 254–62.

2. In other documents Robinson deposed that he had known Melville for more than three years before his death; Thomas (Melville's son-in-law), that he had known him for fourteen years; and both, that Melville was of sound mind when he made his will.

3. "Herman Melville as I Recall Him," *Colophon*, N.S. I (Summer, 1935), 21–24.

4. See the *American Catalogue* for 1890–95 and 1895–1900; and Meade Minnigerode, *Some Personal Letters of Herman Melville and a Bibliography* (New York, 1922). The bibliographical facts about these editions (supposedly edited by Arthur Stedman) are by no means clear. The latter explains in his Introduction to the 1892 edition of *Typee* that he made minor changes in the text, which, together with the Introduction, explains the occasion for a new copyright.

5. V. H. Paltsits (ed.), *Family Correspondence of Herman Melville* (New York, 1929), p. 66.

6. *Ibid.*, pp. 12–13.

202 THE PROFESSION OF AUTHORSHIP

7. *Ibid.*, p. 64.

8. The transfer of Arrowhead to Allan does not appear in these records, but that title passed from Melville to his wife in 1860 is made clear in a letter from her father to Melville, May 15, 1860 (Raymond Weaver, *Herman Melville, Mariner and Mystic* [New York, 1921], pp. 366–69).

9. For this information and the details on Melville's business with Harper and Brothers, I am indebted to Professor Raymond Weaver, who has generously allowed me to use his copies of Melville's manuscript accounts, which are now a part of the Herman Melville Collection in the Houghton Library at Harvard University. Subsequently, the Committee on Higher Degrees in the History of American Civilization at Harvard University permitted me to examine the original manuscripts for the purpose of checking some of the details and general conclusions.

10. Weaver. *op. cit.*, p. 367.

11. Information from Dr. John H. Birss, who has a copy of a letter by Melville on the subject which will be published in his forthcoming edition of Melville's correspondence. (See Melville to George William Curtis, September 15 and 26, 1857, *The Letters of Herman Melville*, ed. Merrell R. Davis and William H. Gilman [New Haven, 1960]—ED.).

12. *Review of Reviews*, IV (November, 1891), 430.

13. This estimate is based on a count of the pages of Melville's contributions at the rate of $3.00 a page, which, according to F. L. Mott (*A History of American Magazines, 1850–1865* [Cambridge, Mass., 1938], pp. 20, 21) was "normal" for *Putnam's* and probably for *Harper's*.

14. See Weaver, *op. cit.*, pp. 369–70.

15. *Ibid.*, p. 258.

16. Case No. 43419, Probate records, Suffolk County Probate Court, Boston.

17. Weaver, *op. cit.*, pp. 366–69.

18. I have not found the marriage contract. It should be noted that such arrangements were very common in the nineteenth century. Another document, dated June 3, 1861, indicates that the contract was made on August 2, 1847 (two days before the marriage) and that Curtis resigned the trusteeship to Elizabeth's brothers, Lemuel and Samuel.

19. Information from the Treasury Department.

20. G. F. Howe, *Chester A. Arthur: A Quarter Century of Machine Politics* (New York, 1934), p. 53.

21. *Family Correspondence*, pp. 28–29.

22. Records of the Surrogate's Court of Albany County, Albany, New York. The will was proved December 6, 1876. This is probably the matter referred to in Elizabeth's letter to Gansevoort's daughter on June 5, 1877 (*Family Correspondence*, p. 50). It probably also explains the painting, renovation, and new furniture described in her letter of October 9, 1877 (*ibid.*, pp. 52–53).

23. *Family Correspondence*, p. 56.

24. Howe, *op. cit.*, pp. 49–83, and Lee Newcomer, "Chester A. Arthur, The Factors Involved in His Removal from the New York Custom House," *New York History*, XVIII (October, 1937), 401–10.

25. Elizabeth Melville, January 10, 1886: "This month was a good turning point, completing 19 years of faithful service, during which there has not been a single complaint against him—So he retires honorably of his own accord."— *Family Correspondence*, p. 62.

26. *U.S. House Executive Documents*, 45th Cong., 1st Sess., Vol. I, No. 8, p. 28.

27. *New York Tribune*, June 7, 1877.

28. *Family Correspondence*, p. 47.

29. *Ibid.*, p. 50.

30. *Ibid.*, p. 61.

31. *Ibid.*, p. 62.

32. *Ibid.*, pp. 62–64.

33. Case No. 71419, Probate records, Suffolk County Probate Court, Boston.

34. Probate records, Hall of Records, New York City. She died July 31, 1906.

35. R. L. Rusk (ed.), *The Letters of Ralph Waldo Emerson* (New York, 1939), II, 64.

36. *Family Correspondence*, pp. 28–29.

CHAPTER TWELVE

Melville

HERMAN MELVILLE'S conflict with his readers, which lasted the whole ten years of his professional writing life and ended in a defeat which even in our time has not been completely reversed, began in the first paragraph of his first book— *Typee*. The conventional, cozy, reader-writer relationship in the second sentence is promptly undermined by the apostrophe to "state-room sailors":

> Six months at sea! Yes, reader, as I live, six months out of sight of land; cruising after the sperm-whale beneath the scorching sun of the Line, and tossed on the billows of the wide-rolling Pacific. . . . Weeks and weeks ago our fresh provisions were all exhausted. . . . Those glorious bunches of bananas . . . have, alas, disappeared! . . . There is nothing left us but salt-horse and sea-biscuit. Oh! ye state-room sailors, who make so much ado about a fourteen-days' passage across the Atlantic; who so pathetically relate the privations and hardships of the sea, where, after a day of breakfasting, lunching, dining off five courses . . . and drinking champaign-punch, it was your hard lot to be shut up in little cabinets of mahogany and maple, and sleep for ten hours, with nothing to disturb you but "those good-for-nothing tars, shouting and tramping over head. . . ."

The author, of course, is a "good-for-nothing tar," and although he does not say that his readers are self-pitying state-room sailors, he invites such identification, as well as a hostile comparison of the self-pity imputed to them with his own. What he probably intended as playfulness he apparently later recognized as tactlessness (ever a weakness of Melville's), for he deleted the apostrophe in the second edition. But the basis of the conflict remained. A former member of that dispossessed class—the common sailor—with which he remained in permanent sympathy, he was now, as journalist, trying to sell prose to the world which dispossessed him. Within a page or two he resumed the sales talk with which he had begun: "The Marquesas! What strange visions of outlandish things does the very name spirit up! Naked houris —cannibal banquets . . . —and bamboo temples . . . carved canoes . . . savage woodlands guarded by horrible idols—*heathenish rites and human sacrifices.*"

Some of his professional problems (in his later and better, as well as in his apprentice, works) were the result of poor craftsmanship. The promise of "naked houris" in the passage above was to cause him trouble, but not for the reason one would expect. In the early Victorian age few objected to the nude females with which *Typee* is richly equipped, for the times granted general immunity to the representation in art of unclothed pagans. In literature, as in painting and sculpture, ladies could be naked from the waist up if they were Indians, ancient Greeks, or other heathen. Melville's real mistake here was technical—a matter of point of view.

As his ship "approached within a mile and half" of Nukuheva Bay, he observed what seemed to be a shoal of fish sporting on the surface but which was in reality a "shoal of 'whihenies' (young girls) who in this manner were coming off from the shore to welcome us," resembling, as they came closer, "so many mermaids." The "swimming nymphs . . . boarded us, . . . seizing hold of the chain-plates" and "bob-stays," where they "hung dripping with the brine and glowing from the bath, . . . sparkling with savage vivacity, laughing gaily . . . , and chattering away with infinite glee. . . . " Each one "performed the simple offices of the toilette for the other. Their luxuriant locks . . . were freed from the briny element; the whole person carefully dried . . . anointed with a fragrant oil. . . . " Clad only in a few folds of white tappa "in a modest cincture, around the waist," they were "quickly frolicking about the decks" or "reclined at full length. . . . " Extremely youthful, with "delicate features and inexpressibly graceful figures, their softly moulded limbs, and free unstudied action, seemed as strange as beautiful."

Thus far the writing is at least journalistically skilful. The native word "whihenies" establishes the necessary distance between the civilized reader and the naked savage; the metaphors "nymph" and "mermaid" are a demure transition to the more respectable classical heathen world; and in a whole series of phrases the nymphs are endowed with the charms attributed to females in parlor novels—"delicate features," "graceful figures," the ceremony of the "toilette," vivacious chatter. There is much evidence that this kind of thing in *Typee* beguiled even the feminine reader. But the distance between the author and his idyll is closed up by an arch and clumsy comment (also deleted in the revised edition): "What a sight for us bachelor sailors! how avoid so dire a temptation? For who could think of tumbling these artless creatures overboard, when they had swam miles to welcome us?" And the idyll becomes a brawl as the nymph-sylph metaphor, with its implication of innocence subjected to gross mortal aggression, becomes confused with images of piracy. The girls are a "party of boarders," the "bachelor sailors" are "prisoners . . . completely in the hands of the mermaids." The "sylphs" get up a "ball in great style," but it is not a parlor affair: "there is an abandoned voluptuousness in their character which I dare not attempt to describe." The figure shifts again and the voluptuous pirates become victims:

> Our ship was now wholly given up to every species of riot and debauchery. *Not the feeblest barrier was interposed between the unholy passions of the crew and their unlimited gratification.* [Deleted in the revised edition.] The grossest licentiousness and the most shameful inebriety prevailed. . . . Alas for the poor savages when exposed to the influence of these polluting examples! Un-

sophisticated and confiding, they are easily led into every vice, and
humanity weeps over the ruin thus remorselessly inflicted upon
them by their European civilizers. Thrice happy are they who . . .
have never been brought into contaminating contact with the
white man.

We are not concerned here with the false note in this last
passage except to the extent that he exposes the sentimentality
of his early liberalism by slipping into the language of the conventional morality which even this early he had rejected—
"licentiousness," "polluting," "temptation," "ruin." More ger-
mane to our point is that he has confused the point of view of
his old self with that of a new self which emerged only when
he began to write. Up to the didactic passage he talks with
journalistic casualness of the life of the common-sailor Melville
of 1841; then suddenly, he shifts to the point of view of the
socially conscious Melville writing in 1845. In the first part he
reports sympathetically from the point of view of sex-starved
bachelor sailors subjected to dire temptation; in the second,
the crew becomes an abstraction of the polluting "white man."
He sees himself in both cases as an anonymous member of a
group whose group behavior can be explained; thus he, as an
individual, is exculpated. But his own name was on the title
page, and his guarantee that this personal narrative was the
"unvarnished truth" was in his Preface. He was therefore anything but anonymous, and hostile critics reminded him of his
scandalous past for years. Thus did Melville learn the first of
many stumbling lessons in the necessity of putting some kind
of distance between himself and his materials. Never thereafter
in his work was the author a bona fide "common" sailor.

In his next book, *Omoo*, he separated himself from his mates
by describing them as the licentious "reckless seamen of all
nations," and himself as a man of education and therefore, inferentially, as one qualified to pass judgments on institutions. Early
in *Mardi*, the anonymous narrator is spotted as a gentleman by
his mates because of his language, his table manners, and his

"unguarded allusions to *Belles Lettres* affairs." And in *Redburn* and *Moby-Dick* distance is effected through an imagined spokesman who is not Herman Melville.

In this matter Melville might have learned something from Dana's *Two Years before the Mast* (1840). On Dana's first page we find the Cambridge gentleman discarding the "tight dress coat, silk cap and kid gloves of an undergraduate at Cambridge," for the loose duck trousers of a sailor. In his Preface we learn that he is intent on calling "attention to the welfare of seamen," and "promoting their religious and moral improvement." It is probable that Dana's book has always been a more popular classic than *Typee* because the common reader feels secure in Dana's clearly defined point of view—that he knows its "facts" can be trusted because the writer stands outside his material where the reader is, and never becomes imaginatively involved in the life he describes.

2

All the evidence shows that Melville, when he entered the literary life, thought of himself not as an artist but as the kind of practical writer who can be called, without prejudice, a journalist. That is, his intention was to communicate, in familiar language and literary forms, materials which readers could absorb and understand without special antecedent knowledge and without any great concentration or effort. His material—travel—was of established appeal, but he was aware that traditional travel-writing, shaped by eighteenth-century rationalism, and pretending to be both objective and "philosophical," was dull and pretentious, and that the new reading audiences found it tiresome. Irving and Longfellow had popularized European travel by romanticizing and sentimentalizing it, and Melville profited by the styles they developed without imitating them much. But Pacific travel-writing, still dominated by the ponderous British scholarly tradition, had as yet been unaffected by the tastes of the journalist's audience.

Melville's first book title reveals his intention to get away from tradition. In *Typee: a Peep at Polynesian Life. During a Four Months' Residence in a Valley of the Marquesas,** "Typee," "Polynesian," and "Valley of the Marquesas" are texture words suggesting the exotic; "Four Months' Residence" promises that the exotic will be nevertheless based on "real"; and "Peep" (like "glance," a word much exploited in contemporary journalism) is an assurance that reality will not get the heavy "philosophical" treatment. When the word "Typee" failed to appear on the title page of the first British edition, Melville assured the publisher that to restore that "magic, cabalistic, tabooistic" word would have a gratifying effect on sales.

<The title of the London edition of his second book rode on the tail of the first: "Omoo: a Narrative of Adventures in the South Seas; being a sequel to The 'Residence in the Marquesas Islands.' By Herman Melville, author of 'Typee.' " Melville's sales letter to John Murray said that *Omoo* "embraces adventures in the South Seas (of a totally different character from 'Typee') and includes an eventful cruise in an English Colonial Whaleman . . . and a comical residence on the island of Tahiti."

Melville's close interest in public taste is also reflected in his prefaces. Prefaces have historically had the function of setting the writer in relation with his reader. In general the pattern has been that prefaces are longer at the beginning of a writer's career, or at crucial points in his development when he is uncertain about his work; and that when his status, whether high or low, has become established, he stops writing prefaces altogether. Melville's practice fits the pattern. The Preface to *Typee* is a piece of salesmanship.> The reiterated words are "adventure," "occurrence," "incident," "yarn," "singular," "strange," "fact," these serving at once as guarantee and apology that he is diverg-

---

* This was the title of the New York edition.—ED.

ing from the traditional mode of travel-writing. He will refrain from "entering into explanations concerning [the] origins and purposes" of native customs, because such material is usually "diffuse," i.e., non-journalistic. He will omit the customary dates, i.e., the kind of facts that do not serve to maintain interest. He will ignore formal chronological order whenever he wishes to serve the readers' interest in recent events in the South Seas. He will not be scholarly about Polynesian pronunciation, knowing that the reader is less interested in philology than in "beautiful combinations of vocal sounds."

In the narrative itself, Melville's defense of journalistic method becomes an offensive against the "scientific voyagers"—the learned tourists who get their "facts" about primitive religions from "retired South-Sea rovers." The beachcomber is flattered when interviewed by the scholar, and "his powers of invention increase with the credulity of his auditors. He knows just the sort of information wanted [exaggeration of the "evils of Paganism"] and furnishes it to any extent." When the scientist gets home he writes a "learned" account of superstitions and practices, about which he knows as little as the islanders do themselves, for "they are either too lazy or too sensible to worry themselves about abstract points of religious belief."

Although, apparently, Melville did not know it, such skepticism was in harmony with the mid-nineteenth century attack on inherited rationalistic methods of speculating about primitive cultures—on all the glorified guesswork and a priori thinking that went under the name of "philosophic research." The *London Spectator* missed the point when it said that Melville was not "trained in those studies which enable men to observe with profit." To the journalist such "profit" was spurious; his road to truth was through "what he had seen." Twenty-five years later, American journalists were still on the offensive against the tradition, on behalf of the common reader. Mark Twain's Preface to *Roughing It* asserts that his book is "merely a personal narrative"; that his material is "interesting," "curious," "peculiar";

that his book is not a "pretentious history or a philosophical dissertation"; and that he will not "afflict [the reader] with metaphysics or goad him with science."

3

These two books, to Melville's eventual chagrin, were accepted largely on his own terms: they were instantly labeled, on both sides of the Atlantic, as "popular" writing "for the million." In dozens of reviews the same adjectives appeared: fresh, lively, light, animated, vigorous, racy, readable, easy, interesting.

But there was a powerful, if small, dissenting minority who were to become more influential once Melville's novelty had worn off and his later books spelled out the implications of the first two. It was to be expected that the missionary and denominational groups should resent his criticisms, attack him in their periodicals, and attempt to coerce his publisher. When the American Board of Foreign Missions appended to a large order of Wiley and Putnam books a statement of its "regret that [*Typee*] bears the respectable name of your house," Wiley promptly got Melville to prepare an expurgated edition, and was reported to be "agitated" in his "conscience" when he was offered *Omoo*.

The fact that *Omoo* was actually published by the Harpers, a firm which had religious connections with Methodism, suggests the problem faced by many American writers of that time—a reading audience so mixed that it was difficult to predict public reactions to deviations from common beliefs and accepted standards of decorum. Audiences have always been more or less mixed, of course, but in various times and cultures it has been possible for writers to address themselves to reader groups of definable degrees of tolerance and sophistication. The stratification which gives writers a degree of freedom in our time did not begin in America until well after 1850. In 1846, when *Typee* appeared, books were offered to an undifferentiated audience of men, women, and adolescents, and were therefore subject to fantastically wide ranges of response. Melville's book, with its criticism of religious institutional activities, its naked "houris," voluptuous dances, and sailor orgies, was recommended for its "pretty and spirited pictures" by Margaret Fuller in the *New York Tribune,* who predicted that it would be read aloud in the "sewing societies of the country"; the columnist "Grace Greenwood" called it "charming"; and there is abundant evidence that it and *Omoo* were read aloud in families (including Longfellow's) and were popular with the young. At the other extreme, a representative New York magazine said that *Typee* catered to the "vicious appetites of [the] sailor"; and that *Omoo* was "vendible," "venemous," and "venerous." The London *Times* predicted that *Typee* would "exhilarate the most enervated and blasé of the circulating library loungers"; and Sir Walter Farquhar urged Lord Ashley to tell John Murray that Melville's works were not such as "any mother would like to see in the hands of her daughters," and that he was not living up to his pledge that the "Home and Colonial Library" (in which the two books were issued) would contain "nothing offensive to moral and good taste."

Between these extremes there was wide recognition that the books were "racy." Some, like Hawthorne in the *Salem Advertiser,* reminded the reader that the life of a young sailor "renders him tolerant of codes of morals . . . little in accordance with our own." But it was Horace Greeley, Miss Fuller's employer on the *Tribune,* who saw the problem of reader levels: Melville was a "born genius"; but his books are "dangerous reading for those of immature intellects and unsettled principles. Not that you can put your finger on a passage positively offensive; but the *tone* is bad . . . if not morally diseased."

Greeley's last sentence focuses for us the matter of the sophistication of Melville's readers. The editor did not put his finger on that passage in Chapter XX of *Typee* where the half-naked, beflowered girls dance in the moonlight, "all-over, as it were," in a way that was "almost too much for a quiet, sober-minded, modest young man like myself." In the revised edition Melville wisely corrected this defect in "distance" by removing the last-quoted phrase. Apparently at this point, also, he removed from the manuscript a detailed description of the dance which he "thought best to exclude from *Typee*," but used it, "modified and adapted," in Chapter LXIII of *Omoo*.

To the modern reader that dance is plainly phallic, its patterns representing coition and orgasm. Two taller girls, their hands joined overhead, stand in the middle of a ring of dancers. Taking their cues from the pair within, the ring expands and contracts, its movements varying from wild abandon to languorous stillness. At the climax the ring-dancers reel forward, "their eyes swimming in their heads," and joining in "one wild chorus," they sink into each other's arms. Greeley did not put his finger on this passage either, but note its new context: the observer is no longer a "modest young man" but, instead, two men with a touristic and anthropological interest in the "heathenish games and dances" which "still secretly lingered in the valley" after the advent of the missionaries. Far from being a part of the life openly observed and shared by the author in *Typee,* the dance is surreptitious, the girls being guarded by "hideous old crones, who might have been duennas," and the two spectators are hidden at a distance. Personal response comes not from the young writer but from his disreputable companion, the "ruined gentleman," Dr. Long Ghost, whom the narrator with difficulty restrains from "rushing forward and seizing a partner." When, the next day, the doctor recognizes a girl who took part in the dance and makes overtures, he gets his ears boxed.

If Greeley and other commentators understood either the dance or the doctor's reaction to it, they did not say so. It may have been at this time that Melville began to develop his conviction that the unpalatable may, through disguise, be concealed from "superficial skimmers," as he called the common readers. At any rate, he seems to have got away with certain crude passages, and with the chapter on the whale's penis in *Moby-Dick*, and with allegory of gestation and childbirth in the "Tartarus of Maids," which he published in *Harper's New Monthly* in 1854.

Yet Greeley did say that Melville's tone was bad, if not morally diseased, and there is other evidence that even at the height of his early popularity, he was beginning to be recognized as an enemy of society as well as of common standards of taste. Seen in strictly historical perspective, the most perceptive reader of his books was George Washington Peck, a self-described "conservative" whose allegiance to certain aspects of Coleridge's thought entitle him to be considered a "new conservative" of that day. He declared himself impatient with writers like Melville who were producing "literature for the million" instead of for the "judicious few"; and as a spokesman for that class of readers (rather than for the mass or for the artist), Peck rightly condemned the "tone and spirit" of *Omoo* as effects of the author's bad intellectual and moral character. As a believer of the culture of which he was a part, he understandably interpreted Melville's hostility to civilized institutions as "cool, sneering wit, and . . . perfect want of *heart*." "If these writers would only leave us alone in our simple religious faith, in our common views of God, ourselves, and the world. . . . But they muddle the mind, and make the voice of reason and conscience 'an uncertain sound.'" Such candid recognition that literature is inimical to common beliefs was as rare in criticism then as now, but the implications of many less honest reviews of Melville were the same. Peck would probably have agreed with the writer of a rejoinder who said that the "vast majority of readers" accept *Omoo* "with unmixed delight," for only his "judicious few" would let Melville's social criticism spoil their pleasure in his narrative. And Peck did not, like most of the rest, mistake Melville's developing subversiveness for the sentimental primitivism of that day.

4

In England, where it was assumed that if a gentleman went to sea it was as an officer, never as a common sailor, some critics objected that *Typee* must be a faked narrative, for no common sailor, if he could write at all, could command such a style. These, then, must be the fabricated adventures of a gentleman-author. More perceptive British reviewers pointed out that things were different in America—where "popular education bestows upon the American a greater familiarity with popular attitudes and a readier use of the pen than is usual with classes of the same apparent grade in England," and that therefore Melville could be a social nobody. Yet the suspicion persisted that Melville was a gifted Munchausen, or that, at the very least, if his story was true, it had been "touched up" by some "literary artist." The controversy spread to America where commentators took sides— not one of two sides, but as many sides as there were attitudes toward fact and fiction.

In the forties, fiction, though increasingly popular, still had in general a low status as an art. One common opinion posited an absolute dichotomy between "fact," which was "truth," and "fiction," which was "falsehood." It was reported that when John Murray (a connoisseur of travel books whose contempt for fiction was well known) read the manuscript of *Typee,* he "scented the forbidden thing—the taint of fiction"; and that the house of Harper, after some disagreement, rejected it because "it was impossible that it could be true and therefore was without real value."

Melville himself contributed to the confusion (and shared it) by insisting that he had told the "unvarnished truth." It is hard to tell what he meant by "varnish," but his style is proof, if we need it, that his eye had its own way of seeing: a Marquesan girl seen as a "nymph" is certainly "touched up." He tells us that natives eat live fish, which is truth; he also tells us that when the beautiful Fayaway eats one it is "as delicately as a lady eats a biscuit"—which is not untruth but probably varnish. Even his ordering of the events in such a way as to create suspense by balancing his idyllic existence against the fear of being cooked by cannibals was a kind of varnish, if not a kind of fiction. But some readers associated this suspense with the artificial manipulations of "plotted" fiction, and therefore questioned the truth of the events. Hostile readers called him Munchausen, but the great majority called him the American Defoe, his book *Robinson Crusoe*, and his skill verisimilitude. Whatever genre *Typee* and *Omoo* may belong to, Melville had not yet explored the problem of the relation of fact to the imagination, for in his Preface to *Omoo* he was still talking in terms of "correct observation." But only a year or two later, he says, through one of his mouthpieces in *Mardi*, "Things visible are but the conceits of the eye: things imaginative, conceits of fancy. If duped by one, we are equally duped by the other." Sometime during the years 1847-48, Melville began to think like an artist.

Up to that point there is as little evidence in his books as outside of them that he was, or regarded himself as, any more than a gifted journalist and yarn-spinner whose major motive was to divert readers. He was untouched then (but not later) by that tradition of authorship which put a value on the writer's privacy and shunned vulgar promotion and publicity. He co-operated gladly in getting editors to publicize his books, and even wrote an anonymous defense of *Typee*. In a review of another man's nautical work he celebrated the triumph of "plain, matter-of-fact" sea narratives over "spiritual" addresses to the ocean, like Byron's.

Nor had he at this time the serious writer's feeling about the inviolability of his text. When he expurgated *Typee* at the request

of his timid American publisher, he remarked complacently that
"I trust as it now stands the book will retain all those essential
features which most commended it to the public favor"; and he
was not quite honest, in the Preface to the revised edition, in saying that "several passages, wholly unconnected with that adventure, have been rejected as irrelevant," for the passages were not
several but many, and some were anything but irrelevant.

Seen in relation to his later works, *Typee* and *Omoo* are something more than good diversion. The social criticism in them is
more conspicuous to us than to contemporary readers because
we have been taught to look for it. Moreover, we know now that
in the process of recalling his adventures Melville was beginning
to discover the self which was to produce *Moby-Dick*. But more
serious and socially responsible readers like Greeley and Peck
looked past his pretty nymph Fayaway and found the heathen
mistress of a man who respected heathens as if they were people;
looked past his idyllic valley to find an indictment of the valleys
of the Thames and the Hudson; past his criticism of missionaries
to find fundamental doubts about Christian culture. These few
were in the vanguard of what was to become majority opinion
about Melville.

5

Sometime between January 1 and March 25, 1848, Melville
was transformed from a journalist into a writer who identified
himself with the great tradition of Western art which grew out
of the Renaissance. Before that time he had conceived of his
third book, *Mardi*, which he began before *Omoo* was published in
March, 1847, as "another book of South Sea Adventure (continued from, tho' wholly independent of, 'Omoo')." He was still
thinking in terms of commercial originality: the scenes will be
"altogether new," and the new work will "possess more interest

than the former, which treated of subjects comparatively trite"; the field is "troubled with few & inconsiderable intruders." Fearing that he had worked out the vein of factual, personal adventure in his first two books, he worked out a plan which "clothes the whole subject in new attractions & combines in one cluster all that is romantic, whimsical & poetic in Polynusia. It is yet a continuous narrative." Certain that it would make a "hit," he asked of Murray double the advance he had received for *Omoo*.

On March 25 Melville wrote John Murray the letter which announced the crucial change in his creative life. He now, a year before *Mardi* was actually published, informed the publisher who was to refuse his book that it would not be the continuation of South Sea adventures that he had promised. "To be blunt: the work I shall next publish will in downright earnest a 'Romance of Polynisian Adventure.' But why this? The truth is, Sir, that the reiterated imputation of being a romancer in disguise has at last pricked me into a resolution to show . . . that a *real* romance of mine is no Typee or Omoo. . . . " This was his "main inducement" in altering his plans, and he was to repeat it in the published Preface of the book. But he qualifies the motive at once: he had apparently conceived such a work much earlier. "I have long thought that Polynisia furnished a great deal of rich poetical material that has never been employed hitherto in works of fancy," and he had thrown off "occasional sketches" for such a work, but postponed the project. But as he wrote the first *Mardi*, which was a "narrative of *facts* I began to feel an incurable distaste for the same; & a longing to plume my pinions for a flight & felt irked, cramped & fettered by plodding along with dull common places,—So suddenly standing the thing alltogether, I went to work heart & soul at a romance which is now in fair progress. . . . "

<At this point he announced his departure from those current traditions of fiction which few but Poe and Hawthorne and Brown had thus far managed to escape from, and they only at

the cost of popularity. At a time when almost all vendible
American fiction was based on either history or "real" contemporary life, Melville conceived an imagined narrative which,
though it derived from Rabelais and Swift (and the tradition of
allegory), was not classifiable with anything that readers were
currently consuming.> Aware that the fiction-hating Murray
would misunderstand his use of the word "romance" (which
indeed had no fixed meaning), he begged him not to "exclaim
'Pshaw! Puh!'—My romance I assure you is no dish water nor
its model borrowed from the Circulating Library [where Murray
found most of his customers]. It is something new I assure you,
& original if nothing more. . . . It opens like a true narrative—
like Omoo for example, on ship board—& the romance & poetry
of the thing thence grow continually, till it becomes a story
wild enough I assure you & with a meaning too." He saw the
commercial risk in "putting forth an acknowledged *romance*
upon the heel of two books of travel," but "My *instinct* is to out
with the Romance, & let me say that instincts are prophetic, &
better than acquired wisdom. . . . "

In the light of the statement that "it opens like a true narrative," one wonders whether he really "abandoned" his original
project altogether. Certainly, in the finished work, the first forty
chapters might have served as the beginning of the work Melville
first proposed to Murray. The narrator and a shipmate, Jarl,
desert a whaler in a small boat; encounter another ship, unman-
ned except for a Polynesian couple; hear the antecedent story
of the couple and their ship; are forced to abandon the ship in a
storm; and continue on in the small boat with the couple in
search of certain islands. They meet an island craft full of
natives who hold captive a beautiful maiden doomed to be sacrificed. The group rescues her, and the narrator kills the head priest.

Up to this point the story is a "narrative," in Melville's sense—
imagined rather than autobiographical, it is true, but derived
from physical rather than spiritual experience. Melville fans

might well have expected the maiden to be another Fayaway, and subsequent adventures to be itinerant as in *Omoo*. But at the point where the maiden is revealed to have been transformed by supernatural means from an olive-skinned brunette to a golden-haired, blue-eyed blonde, with whom the hero, in quite un-Tommo fashion, experiences transcendental love-at-first-sight, a new book begins. Though the hero and the girl are said to have "lived and loved," admirers of Fayaway found this romance antiseptic—and somewhat spoiled by the hero's growing doubts of his own motives in rescuing her and killing the priest. After the Mardi islanders, unlike the matter-of-fact Typees, mistake this jump-ship tar for a demigod (a "Taji"), the physique becomes insubstantial and translucent, and the continuing solidity of Jarl and Samoa are embarrassing to the story. When Yillah mysteriously disappears, and Taji begins his search—as abstract as Thoreau's quest after the hound, the bay horse, and the turtle dove—Jarl and Samoa are out of a job. Melville does not exactly drop them down a well, as Mark Twain said he did with his stranded characters in the first version of *Those Extraordinary Twins*, but he has to do some shifty footwork to get them off the scene. He may have guessed that many of his Circulating Library customers would exit with them, for among his alternative explanations of Samoa's refusal to continue the search (he was "not the first man, who had turned back, after beginning a voyage like our own") was his distaste for Babbalanja's "disquisitions" (which were indeed distasteful to most reviewers), and for a Mardi which had not met his expectations. A year after the London publication of *Mardi* in three volumes, Bentley, the publisher, wrote the author that the "first volume [which included all the first forty chapters] was eagerly devoured, the second was read," but the third was so ill adapted "to the class of readers whom . . . the First Volume . . . gratified" that it virtually "stop[ped] the sale of the book." The reviewers agreed that there was a general exodus of readers along with Samoa.

The exodus is understandable if one approaches *Mardi* as a book rather than as a revelation of Melville's intellectual development. Though every paragraph of the world-allegory that follows Chapter XL may be interesting for its speculative commentary on man's problems, it is allegory rather than narrative—and as tiresome and confusing as nineteenth-century allegory had to be, deprived as it was of a basis in common belief such as Spenser and Bunyan had been able to build on. Taji's quest for Yillah quite properly ended in suicide, not in a new version of the meaning of life which traditional allegory had offered.

The design of the allegorical part of *Mardi* can be explained largely in terms of Melville's need for scope and for protection from readers who insisted on typing him as an uneducated sailor with a gift for "popular" writing. The new Melville was overflowing with speculations on the nature of the individual, on the relation of genius to society, and on all the major problems of contemporary civilization. He needed a form in which his unordered, unfocused, many-sided, often contradictory speculations could be given free play—in which, indeed, he could *play* with ideas without committing himself to a position.

The form he found was that of the expanding "self." The first-person narrator, who on the title page and in the Preface is the well-known traveler-Melville, becomes in the first few chapters a learned, philosophic, poetic tar who is to record fictional adventures loaded with commentary. But after he loses Yillah, and is joined in his search for her by three mortals—Yoomy, the Poet; Mohi or Braidbeard, the Chronicler; and Babbalanja, the Philosopher—and by a real demigod, King Media (the Mediator), his status changes, his function as commentator being wholly taken over by his companions, especially Babbalanja. Even his role as narrator becomes obscure and confused. The "I" of the first chapters becomes "we" in the allegory, and even the "we" often becomes the voice of authorial omniscience released from the control of the grammatical first person. Sometimes, within the space of a page or two, Taji speaks as "we," is addressed *by the author* as "you," and is referred to by his companions in the third person as if he were not there. In one spot, Melville even shoulders him aside and speaks directly *as* author: "My cheek blanches while I write . . . while I slave and faint in this cell." (In context, "cell" can mean only Melville's study.)

Taji's disintegration as narrator is at the center of the structural weakness of the book. Nothing but his restlessness in the narrative portion motivates his quest for the bloodless lost blonde, or justifies his suicidal pursuit of her after his companions have deserted him. Both he and his quest are lost sight of entirely in long stretches of the allegory. The convincing quest in this book resides not in his search but in the speculative discourse of his mouthpiece, Babbalanja.

When Melville becomes Taji, his commentary becomes speculative discourse distributed among the three other mortals, with Media acting as a kind of chairman. Although Mohi, the chronicler, sometimes contributes stories, and sounds like Melville when he does, he functions mainly as the scorner of fanciful and imaginative elements in the discourse of Yoomy and Babbalanja. He is a compound of Melville's former self and of those critics who had doubted his "authenticity." Yoomy is the poet in the new Melville, a tender-minded believer, sympathetic with fancy and impatient of raw fact, but "capricious . . . swayed by contrary moods . . . made up of a thousand contradictions . . . [and] no one in Mardi comprehended him." In these respects he is counterpart to Babbalanja, though, unlike him, he is strongly affirmative: he is that in Melville which believed that the principle represented by Yillah (enduring truth and beauty) *might* be discovered in the United States.

The dominant character and chief talker is Babbalanja, who, from the beginning, is "not so buoyant of hope concerning lost Yillah" as Yoomy, but who nevertheless joins the party "in quest of some object, mysteriously hinted." He is the seeker after meaning, and the believer in "polysensuum," or many meanings. He is the "everlasting foe" of all Mohis. He is the man who fights "the armed and crested Lies of Mardi." He is also a poet, though he "dives," unlike Yoomy, who "soars." Through his explanations and defenses of the great mythical authors, Bardianna, Vavona, and Lombardo, he becomes the spokesman for art and the enemy of Philistinism. <In this role he is the outlet for Melville's insatiable reading (at least one of his "quotations" is taken verbatim from _____) and his new commitment to the world of art and thought.>

But even this expansion of self through the great thought of the past is insufficient. He is in search of the very principle of "self," and finds his own self multiple. He declares himself inhabited by a "stranger" whom his friends know but who is "independent of me." When, in the pursuit of truth, he reaches the limits of the communicable, he is possessed by his demon, Azzageddi, and lapses into gibberish, muttering "fugle-fi, fugle-fo, fugle-fogle-orum." And at times he puts both the "stranger" and Azzegeddi aside and regards himself as a "lunatic," but this is only in moments when "I most resemble all other Mardians."

Through these many personae, then, but mainly through the line of Taji, Babbalanja, Bardianna, and Azzageddi, Melville found his needed scope, and, he futilely hoped, the protective barrier behind which he could make many bold explorations with few commitments.

From first to last Melville was a trial-and-error experimental writer who never quite knew what he wanted to do—or did not want to do—until he had done it. And the allegory of Mardi was one of his errors. (A year after publication his "mood" about the book had changed: he has never looked at it "since I thanked God it was off my hands.") But the first forty chapters were a trial in which he found his proper form—a form which became the base (but not the superstructure in all cases) of his subsequent books. And it was a form through which he might have acquired a sophisticated as well as a popular audience, as Shakespeare did with his plays.

That form consisted of a loose, episodic narrative—not at all dramatic (that is, it is not a *story* which delivers its chief weight through action and character), but dependent for its effect on vivid description and the graphic presentation of isolated incident. To his skill in this kind of narrative, as first displayed in the travel books and perfected in *Mardi*, his generation paid full tribute. But this to Melville was mere craft, and he felt cramped within its restrictions. To the narrative part of *Mardi* he added a new dimension which raised narrative to the realm of poetry. The episodic narrative becomes a vehicle for reflection and commentary—humorous, satirical, learned, allusive, philosophical, speculative, image-laden. If he learned this art of rich and varied commentary from Rabelais and Sir Thomas Browne, he made it an art of his own more completely than he was able to do with the dramatic art that he was shortly to learn from Shakespeare but never to master.

In a sense it is an art of digression: digression becomes art in that, though it is structurally separable, like a parenthesis in a sentence, it is still relevant to the embracing purpose. Thus, in Chapter II ("Calm") the narrator's wish to desert the whaler is intensified by the harrowing experience of a prolonged and absolute sea-calm. He is reminded of his first experience as a landsman with such a calm: "These impressions may merit a page." He then by intense imaginative exploration of the experience evokes what he elsewhere calls the "metaphysics of the thing." "It not only revolutionizes his abdomen, but unsettles his mind," undermines his conceptions of time and space, renders the "parallels and meridians" of the globe truly imaginary, shakes "his belief in the eternal fitness of things; in short, almost makes an infidel of him," and he grows "madly skeptical."

Some of Melville's finest writing is in his digressions on "wonders of the sea." It is in *Mardi* that Melville first emerges as one of the greatest of all American popularizers of natural history and the technology of seamanship. When, for example, he sees a devilfish, he makes it the occasion of an informal but learned essay on sharks. All of his book-learning on the subject comes to life through his actual observation of sharks in their element. Reflections on natural violence develop into a dissertation on love, hate, and Timonism.

Though no one can, with certainty, say exactly what numerous reviewers meant when they said *Mardi, White-Jacket,* and *Moby-Dick* were "poetic," it is evident that they were pleased with his combination of "fact and fancy" even when they disapproved of his books as totalities and distrusted the tone of his mind. It is possible that his new episodic-digressive method might have enabled the newborn poet to continue as self-supporting professional writer. But it did not. The new Melville needed even greater scope for self-expression than this method afforded, and in shifting to allegory after Chapter XL, he was only beginning his ceaseless and, on the whole, fruitless, search for an art structure (as opposed to method) adequate to his aspirations. And the further he searched, the more he alienated readers who were willing to meet him halfway on the road he had taken from journalism to poetry.

The search and the alienation began while he was writing *Mardi,* and both were products of two new developments in his vocational character. The search grew out of a new and exalted conception of the function and nature of the artist, a conception which was the product of the insatiable reading which began after his return from the Pacific. As he absorbed the masters—Dante and Rabelais and Browne and Milton and the King James Bible, to name only a few—he became aware of, almost obsessed with, a sense of his affinity with the creative spirit in Western art from Homer to Hawthorne, and with the need to do something "big." It was in a spirit of malice that some critics of *Mardi* said he had discovered he was a genius, but it would be fair to say that he had acquired a consciousness of what it means to be a genius. And part of that meaning he defined as doom: it had always been the fate of the creative artist to endure suffering, frustration, and misunderstanding in his time. Only after it had broken and buried him had society ever been willing to celebrate (without comprehending) his art.

His own developing sense of doom, however, it must be emphatically said, was not the result of being rejected but of being accepted and admired for the wrong reasons. He had expected *Typee* and *Omoo* to be read as entertaining but truthful autobiography, and as accurate observation of the impact of civilization on primitive cultures. But in the critical debate over their authenticity, he was probably less amazed that the hostile minority called him Munchausen than that the friendly majority called him Defoe, for who believed that Robinson Crusoe's adventures were Defoe's own? Moreover, those who most admired him as a Defoe seemed to ignore his social criticism. Hence the belligerence of the *Mardi* Preface in the face of the "success" of *Typee* and *Omoo*: inasmuch as these had been received with incredulity, he would see whether this "fiction" would be "received for a verity." In the book itself he reiterates his resentment. When Samoa told his "incredible tale . . . he told it as a traveller. But stay-at-homes say travellers lie." Yet "few skeptics are travellers; fewer travellers liars." In the chapter on "Faith and Knowledge" (XCVII) he says, "And many infidels but disbelieve the least incredible things; and many bigots reject the most obvious. . . . The higher the intelligence, the more faith, and the less credulity. . . . " Then, almost perversely, he challenges the reader's capacity for imaginative truth: "In some universe-old truths, all mankind are disbelievers. Do you believe that you lived three thousand years ago? . . . No. But for me, I was at the subsiding of the Deluge, and helped swab the ground. . . . " In the opposition of *I* to "all mankind," the alienation of the romantic artist is revealed.

The quarrel with the reader continues in Babbalanja's discussion of the problem of contemporary reputation in relation to posthumous fame—commentary we can be sure is authorial because it is echoed in Melville's correspondence. He, like all American professional writers after 1800 from Irving to Faulkner, was a victim of the circumstance that literature was a potential commodity and the writer's personality a sales factor. He had already felt the humiliation of being typed as "Herman Typee Melville," "Mr. Omoo," and Fayaway's lover, and he was often to refer to himself bitterly as "Author of 'Peedee,' 'Hullabaloo' and 'Pog-Dog.'" It was the public's relentless determination to identify a book with their limited conception of the person who wrote it that impelled Melville to cry, through Babbalanja, when Yoomy sings an immortal but anonymous song, "This were to be truly immortal; to be perpetuated in our works, and not in our name. Let me, oh Oro! be anonymously known." The Melville who asked Murray to omit "by the author of *Typee* and *Omoo*" from the title page of *Mardi* is the Babbalanja who asks, "Does not all Mardi by its actions declare it is far better to be notorious now than famous hereafter?" Yoomy suggests that the "unappreciated poet" may "console himself for the neglect of his contemporaries" by the hope of fame in the future. But Babbalanja asserts that there is "more likelihood of being over-rated while living than of being under-rated when dead." Writers have a "feverish, typhoid" wish to believe that "now, while living they are recognized as those who will be as famous in their shrouds as in their girdles." But this is illusion. The "ravening for fame," even if appeased, "yields no felicity. . . . To insure your fame, you must die."

Later in the book Melville joins the long procession of American writers who, in their insecurity and their wish to be understood *as writers,* write literature about literature. One chapter, "Dreams" (XV), a direct utterance of Taji-Melville, constitutes a testament of romantic art to which most of his great contemporaries could have subscribed. In part it is a Whitmanian catalogue identifying self with everything outside of self—a breaking down of all barriers of time and space, of all barriers between souls. In a catalogue of great writers of all times, it affirms the great "community of genius" in which a Melville is one with Montaigne, "blind Milton sings bass to my Petrarchs and Priors, and laureats crown me with bays." All geniuses being but mouthpieces of the eternal, the flow of wisdom and light runs both ways in time, so that as Babbalanja says later, "I do not so much quote Bardianna as Bardianna quoted me, though he flourished before me."

The exaltation of this feeling of community is not unmixed with terror, for as the vehicle of a "memory [of] a life beyond birth," the poet is ridden by a Dionysus, and devoured by his "mad brood of eagles." Nor is it unmixed with the romantic writer's self-pity—the wish to let the world know that writing is agony, that the masterpieces it reads are the products of killing labor and exhausting involvement. "Oh!" says Lombardo, through Babbalanja, "could Mardi but see how we work, it would marvel more at our primal chaos, than at the round world thence emerging."

Most of the commentary on writing, however, is conceived in defensiveness against the reader. A better part of twelve pages of Chapter CLXXX is devoted to corrections of the public's vulgar conceptions of the creative process.

Though the discussion centers on Lombardo, author of "Koztanza," who stands for any great artist of the past who received "coppers then, and immortal glory now," the applicability of the passage to Melville himself is obvious. Lombardo's motive for writing his great work was double: first, a "full heart," and second, the need to "procure his yams." Without the second —that is, lacking poverty, "fierce want," or adversity—the genius has no lever to make him communicate. (Here speaks the Melville who, during the course of writing *Mardi*, married, borrowed to buy a house and got into permanent debt with his publisher and his father-in-law.)

In the conversation King Abrazza, the arch-Philistine of the group, utters platitudes about writers and writing (which are still current), and is refuted by Babbalanja. Says Abrazza, Lombardo deserves small credit because it must have been easy work to set down full-fledged inspirations. (No, says Babbalanja, his thoughts were at first callow, though eventually they soared.) To get into the writing mood, he probably fasted and invoked the muses. (No, he bought vellum and quills, and had a good meal. "What fasting soldier can fight? . . . the fight of all fights is to write.") Then he "dashed off. . . . " (He dashed off nothing. In ten days he wrote fifty pages—and then burned them.) Oh, so this genius wrote trash! (Genius is full of trash, but tries to get rid of it: "giving away its ore, [it] retains the earth.") Then genius is inspired after all. (All men are inspired, even fools; but Lombardo wrote deeper and deeper into himself until he knew what he sought.) Did he not keep himself inspired by drinking? (No; "though he loved it, no wine for Lombardo while actually at work.") Why did he "choose a vehicle so crazy?" "The unities . . . are wholly wanting in the Koztanza." It "lacks cohesion; it is wild, unconnected, all episode." (He chose that vehicle because "it was his nature." Mardi itself is "nothing but episodes; . . . rivers, digressing from plains; vines, roving all over; boulders and diamonds; . . . And so, the world in the Koztanza.") I suppose he admired his own work? (Hard to say. Sometimes when alone he thought well of it; but when among men, he despised it, and asked, Who will ever read it? At last, he had to send it off to be published before it was really finished, to get bread for himself.) Abrazza, finally: "I never read it."

"Who is this Abrazza?" Babbalanja asks again and again, and discovers that he can be identified only in terms of his ancestry, his wealth and status, his sensuality, and his refusal to be disturbed by unpleasant realities—among which are literature and writers, concerning whom he is by turns condescendingly ignorant, unsympathetic, and spiteful.

Against the Abrazzas of the world the writer must put up defenses. It is King Media who, in shutting off Babbalanja's discussion of an allegorical adventure in religion, lays down a principle which is operative in *Mardi* and all Melville's subsequent writings. Serious discussion of religion is something which "all gay, sensible Mardians, who desired to live and be merry, invariably banished from social discourse." Says Media:

> Meditate as much as you will, . . . but say little aloud, unless in a merry and mythical way. Lay down the great maxims of things, but let inferences take care of themselves. Never be special; never, partisan. In safety, afar off, you may batter down a fortress; but at your peril you essay to carry a single turret by escalade. And if doubts distract you, in vain will you seek sympathy from your fellow men. For upon this one theme, . . . even the otherwise honest and intelligent, are the least frank and friendly. Discourse with them, and it is mostly formulas, or prevarications, or hollow assumption of philosophical indifference, or urbane hypocrisies, or a cool, civil deference to the dominant belief; or still worse, but less common, a brutality of indiscriminate skepticism.

Melville revealed this position as his own often in the years between *Mardi* and *Pierre*. "Even Shakespeare," he wrote Duyckinck, "was not a frank man to the uttermost. And, indeed, who in this intolerant universe is, or can be?" And he believed that Hawthorne took delight in "hoodwinking the world"—in "egregiously deceiving the superficial skimmer of pages." Though no one can say that he intended his rapidly developing techniques of symbolism, microcosm, irony, and ambiguity to serve the purpose of oblique and disguised statement of the unpalatable, they often had that effect. And it is demonstrable that his shift from straight narrative to various forms of dramatized narrative was partly motivated by his need to put a protective distance between his speculations and the readers' prejudices. For within the dramatic frame he could avoid direct statement by manipulating point of view. "Through the mouths of the dark characters of Hamlet, Timon, Lear, and Iago," he wrote in his review of Hawthorne, "[Shakespeare] craftily says, or . . .

insinuates the things which we feel to be so terrifically true, that it were all but madness for any good man, in his own proper character, to utter, or even hint of them." In *Typee* and *Omoo* he had been "special" and "partisan"—had uttered unpopular opinions "in his own proper character." In *Mardi* opinion is so refracted, so broken up and distributed among invented characters, so often deceptively labeled as crazy and irresponsible by other characters, that readers could only complain that Melville was capable of imagining the kind of people who could hold such opinions. His confidence in his methods of deception achieves the status of impudence when, a scroll having been read which constitutes a warning to the American democracy and a mob is so infuriated that it looks for a victim, Babbalanja and Media accuse each other of having written it. The document resembles in some ways the thinking of both, different though they are, yet is not wholly characteristic of either. "The settlement of this question," says Taji-Melville coyly, "must be left to the commentators on *Mardi* [the world or the book?], some four or five hundred centuries hence."

6

Nevertheless, the critics who guarded the fortress of congealed prejudice and indifference caught Melville on a turret and knocked him off, for even if he was not Babbalanja, they did not like Babbalanja. The attack on *Mardi* was lethal. In its whole nineteenth century only 3,510 copies were printed (it took seven years to sell the first edition of 3,000), and many of these were bought by mistake, as it were.

It was a book which, from the professional point of view, should never have been published in its present form—or perhaps at all, not because it turned out to be a failure, but because it was a laboratory job—an intensely personal purgation and reconstruction of himself. He learned much about art and thought and himself in the course of writing it—learned, indeed, almost everything that was to make him the great writer of *Moby-Dick*. But what the book offers, even to the modern reader, is the *process* by which Melville explored his own mind. The general reader, then as now, is interested in results, not process, and he must look to Melville's later books for the results of the writing of *Mardi*.

A part of the process was Melville's reading, during the time he was composing *Mardi*, of certain authors who helped him find himself—Rabelais, Burton, Browne, and Dante—writers who could not be digested as rapidly as Melville tried to do. Melville apparently recognized this fact a few years later. A passage in *Pierre* that almost certainly refers to *Mardi* describes the young Pierre's reading, which "poured one considerable tributary stream into that bottomless spring of original thought which the occasion and time had caused to burst out in himself," not realizing then that "to a mind bent on producing some thoughtful thing of absolute Truth, all mere reading is apt to prove but an obstacle. . . . Mere book-knowledge would not congenially weld with . . . spontaneous creative thought." One can hardly dissent from Hawthorne's judgment that it was a book Melville had "not brooded over long enough."

7

A simple count of favorable and unfavorable American reviews shows that they were about equally divided, but Melville knew better than to be comforted by this fact. He must have known, for one thing, that the powerful Harper Brothers sent out "canned" reviews of their books for the benefit of lazy or overworked critics, some of whom knew how to keep on getting review copies of expensive books from Harper's tremendous list. Many of the most favorable comments were superficial, uncomprehending, and even stupid, and must have exasperated Melville more than some of the attacks. Some reviewers, like the one who wrote in the *Literary American* that there was little difference between *Mardi* and the earlier works, could not have read more than the first third of the new one.

On the whole, the most influential journals were hostile, and many of these seem to have taken their cue from reviewers in England, where the book had appeared a month earlier. The British were almost unanimously hostile. To a certain extent they had been misled by the format and the title page of the London edition. As Melville protested to the disgusted Bentley (who had paid Melville £210 and three years later was still £68 out of pocket), the book had been printed in the three-volume format of "dish-water" novels intended only to entertain the circulating library devotees. Moreover, against Melville's express wishes, the London title page (unlike the New York) carried his authorship of *Typee* and *Omoo,* thereby encouraging his former fans to expect the same kind of thing. For all the latter knew, Mardi was another real place, like Typee.

As usual, reviewers tried to "place" *Mardi* by associating it with works of similar genre that they knew, and Melville was universally charged with being an unsuccessful imitator of Swift, Rabelais, More, Browne, and Carlyle. This charge to a certain extent derived from the reader's immemorial defense against whatever is at once puzzlingly new, strange, unintelligible, and therefore offensive: there is "nothing new in it"; it has been done before and done better. Indeed, the reception of *Mardi* is a striking example of the way in which the general reader's latent, deep-rooted hatred of the seriously experimental is flushed to the surface by a work that takes him off base when he is seeking amusement.

The recurrent and revealing words in the reviews are "crazy," "affected," and "unintelligible"; all three represent protest against Melville's departure from the publicly accepted norms of fiction. Sanity had been an issue in the warfare between writers and readers since the beginning of Romanticism. Readers were willing to be diverted by "mad" fictional characters if they were clearly labeled thus, as in popular Gothic fiction. But when writers from Byron and Shelley to Poe and Hawthorne, Emily Brontë and Emerson, began to break down the artificial distinctions of the previous age between sanity and insanity, to find infinite variations between the two theoretical extremes, to see positive values in types of irrationality, and even to identify art and thought with the abnormal, the common reader was made to feel uncomfortably uncertain of his standards of normality. It is therefore not surprising that nineteenth-century reviewing tends to identify the serious treatment of irrationality in a work of literature with irrationality in the author, much as it used Poe's alcoholics and narcotic addicts as evidence about the author's private life. Melville himself confirmed the implicit charge that he found positive values in mental abnormality. During the British onslaught on *Mardi* he wrote Duyckinck concerning the sickness of the writer Charles Fenno Hoffman, "This going mad of a friend . . . comes straight home to every man who feels his soul in him,—which but few men do. For in all of us lodges the same fuel to light the same fire. And he who has never felt momentarily what madness is has but a mouthful of brains." From incoherent Azzageddi and suicidal Taji through Ahab and Pip to Claggart, Melville was to tempt the reader to make assumptions about him.

For lack of examples in the reviews, one cannot be sure what was meant by the charge of "affectation," but apparently it referred, in part at least, to his style, and was used as a contrast to the terms "natural" and "easy" which had been so widely applied to the style of his earlier books. Certainly he was open to the charge that since his style had been simple when he was

MELVILLE   235

writing of his personal adventures, his mixed, sometimes elevated, often hectic style in this work of fancy was strained and artificial—an attempt at "fine" writing. Other reiterated words in the reviews, especially "conceits" and "pedantry," seem to refer not only to style but to substance—to his elaborate metaphors, his speculations, and his allusiveness. "Every page fairly reeks with the smoke of the lamp," said Park Benjamin. In all such criticisms there was an implication of an underlying resentment that the journalist who had hitherto pretended to be no more profound or learned than his readers had suddenly become pretentious about his own culture and intellect. Though there is evidence enough that Melville at this time was taking himself too seriously (he was capable in 1849 of speaking of "building up [a] permanent reputation"), the reviewers seemed to be objecting to his taking his *subject* too seriously as well.

He seems to have been particularly exasperated by the accusation of unintelligibility—a charge which few major writers after 1800 escaped. The oft-repeated words in the reviews were "fog," "obscure," "indistinct," "dark," "dim," and "nonsense." A few recognized the book as an allegory—a "three-volume metaphor," one of them called it—but confessed to being baffled by its meaning. Even George Ripley, trained in the abstractions of Transcendentalism, felt defeated—and angry. Melville thought the allegory was crystal clear, and the denial that it was led him to exclaim to his father-in-law, " 'There's nothing in it!' cried the dunce, when he threw down the 47th problem of the 1st Book of Euclid—'There's nothing in it—' " He must have felt that if his clues and keys were less obvious than those in *Pilgrim's Progress*, they were at least as clear as those of Rabelais and Swift, whom everybody pretended to understand.

The allegory was not as transparent as he thought, even to the modern reader, equipped though he is with accumulated explications, but it was clearer than many critics found it. Only one of them made the necessary point about the general reader's

immemorial habits: a book like this, not meant for mere entertainment, will escape the "careless reader" who "dozes" through
it on "a summer afternoon." Parts of it "require a wide-awake
application," or, as with *Gulliver's Travels*, "one half the aroma
will be lost. . . . The book invites study, and deserves . . .
close investigation." Melville's *Mardi* does not deserve to be read
as closely as Swift, but a public that read *Gulliver's Travels* as a
child's book was not going to take much trouble with an author
whose hostility to them was clear even if his book was not.

8

Melville appears never to have defended *Mardi* as a book, and
apparently he had his doubts about it if we may judge by the
quotation from *Pierre*, and by a letter he wrote a year after
publication: " . . . My mood has so changed, that I dread to
look into it, & have purposely abstained from so doing since I
thanked God it was off my hands." Yet he was deeply hurt by
the attack, because whatever the book's merits, the book was
himself. "Hereafter I shall no more stab at a book . . . than I
would stab at a man. . . . For [*Mardi*] was stabbed at— . . .
therefore, I am the wiser for it."

For a while he gave up the struggle to write above the level
of diversion. His next two books were conceived in a mood of
contempt for his readers, who promptly made them his third
and fourth most popular works. We are bound to accept his
reiterated statements that *Redburn* and *White-Jacket* were, to
him, pot-boilers. The pair were written within the space of nine
months, under dire pressure of debt. "But no reputation that
is gratifying to me, can possibly be achieved by either of these
books. They are two *jobs*, which I have done for money—being
forced to it as other men are to sawing wood. . . . My only
desire for their 'success' (as it is called) springs from my pocket,
& not from my heart." Forgetting Babbalanja's words about

necessity as being the mother of art, he lamented that when a man is surrounded by duns, nothing better can be expected of him than "a beggarly 'Redburn.' " (The duns were real. Melville was living off advances on his books, and spending the advances before the books appeared. By the time *Redburn* was published, he owed the Harpers $832.) Melvillites deny that *Redburn* is beggarly, and can rightly argue that a writer's judgments about his own works are notoriously unreliable. But there is no denying the contemptuous tone of his sales letter to Bentley. Having expressed his bitterness about readers who wish only to be amused, Melville offered *Redburn* as "a thing of a widely different cast from 'Mardi':—a plain, straightforward, amusing narrative of personal experience . . . no metaphysics, no conic-sections, nothing but cakes & ale." When it was praised, he wrote, "I hope I shall never write such a book again." "I know it to be trash"—a "nursery tale."

It was not much of a book, at that. Following predecessors like Captain Marryat, he was exploiting a popular formula: the adolescent middle- or upper-class greenhorn provides comedy and/or pathos as he flounders in the alien environment of the forecastle. There are some passages of pure Melvillian power, but on the whole he was not possessed by his subject: the whole episode of adventure in London sounds like a job of bored padding; and with his usual carelessness in the management of point of view, he lets his child hero slip into knowing adult commentary. The Melvillian theme of the initiation of innocence into evil is in the background, but if the trip to England which Melville made when he was twenty had any deep effect upon him, it is better, if more indirectly, reflected in his other books. On the whole he seemed here to be using up another segment of his experiences for quick returns.

The public response to the book is a good example of the audience's compulsion to "type" an artist and coerce him into doing—over and over—what it wants him to do. A few reviewers saw its faults, and most British critics recognized the Marryat formula. But in general, they sang its praises as a piece of "realism," scolded him for having deserted them in *Mardi*, and welcomed his return to sanity and intelligibility. The reigning note was one of condescension: again and again he was "advised" to stick to straight sea stories, to develop himself as an "agreeable writer" of "nautical yarns." What they meant by "stories" and "yarns" reveals something about the contemporary attitudes toward narrative. They showed little concern over "authenticity." It "reads like a true story"; "everything in it might have happened"; and Melville is "the Defoe of the ocean." In other words, what matters is that these things could have happened to someone within the limited range of the reader's understanding and sympathy. The boy Redburn was within this range (as Taji, or, to anticipate, Ahab, was not).

Melville himself, though he had described it to Bentley as a "narrative of personal experience" made up of materials "picked up by my own observations," was surprised that *Blackwood's* treated "the thing as real." Obviously there was a widening gulf between the public's conception of reality and Melville's. To him the actual event was real only to the extent that it was transformed and ordered by the imagination. He had shaped *Redburn*, as his sales letter indicates, not from the imagination but from stock formulas of the "amusing" and "the comic," such as are appropriate to minds still in "the nursery." When he had something serious to say in the book, he simply stepped out of the skin of his stock character and talked like Melville.

9

It is puzzling that Melville classed *White-Jacket; or The World In a Man-Of-War*, with *Redburn* as a potboiler, but it is significant that he made no further contemptuous references to this, one of the richest of his books. It is a more serious book, even on the surface, than *Redburn* in so far as it is focused on a serious abuse that needed reform—the treatment of sailors in the navy. But this subject is only his vestibule to a world of ideas about authority, religion, and the sources of evil and corruption. He put no puppet like Wellingborough Redburn between himself and his reflections, but spoke in his own person, even asserting his status by referring to "my friend Dana" and my "fine countryman, Nathaniel Hawthorne." Resuming the latitude he had given himself in *Mardi*, he made copious allusion to his wide reading in literature, philosophy, and history, and used without apology such phrases as "ontological necessity." Above all, he consistently invested the facts of navy life with meanings of universal implication, as he was shortly to do with the whaling life in *Moby-Dick*.

Few readers (judging by the reviews) seemed to detect any purpose in the book beyond diversion and reformism. It was "real," it was "poetic," it exposed an abuse. But that Melville was relating naval atrocities to the moral structure of civilization, few seemed to realize—or to care. One British journal detected in it a "dangerous . . . philosophy which ill accords with the truth of revelation"; and George Ripley of the *Tribune*, who had always been suspicious of Melville's doctrines, thought a good story somewhat spoiled by the "moral and metaphysical reflection he sets forth in bad Carlylese."

The scarcity of such serious responses suggests that Melville had gone far in developing techniques of disguise. ("What a madness & anguish it is," he wrote after he had finished the book, "that an author can never—under no conceivable circumstances—be at all frank with his readers.") His now-perfected microcosmic method left much to the imagination of readers not accustomed to using it, and his metaphors were deceptive. Accustomed to satires on clergymen, they probably did not mind Chapter XXXVIII on "The Chaplain," but they may well have missed the unobtrusive but excruciating metaphor of the ship (with its three mast-steeples) as church. Much "dangerous" reflection is buried in dialogues among sailors, in which pessimistic opinions are deceptively balanced against optimistic rejoinders. In Chapter XLV there is the "amusing incident" of the sailor-poet whose manuscripts were shot out of the cannon where he stored them. A commiserating shipmate recalls that once when he published a volume of poems "very aggressive on the world," his friends looked sheepish, and the "one or two who liked it were non-committal" (like some of Lombardo's friends in *Mardi*). As for "the addle-pated mob and rabble, they thought they had found out a fool." This last statement is promptly sterilized by Jack Chase, who makes a distinction between the public and the people: "let us hate the one and cleave to the other." The casual reader might probably have disposed of the passage by identifying himself with the people rather than with the public, but a careful reader might have noticed in the preceding chapter an ambiguous and ironic discussion of the capacity of "the people" (the name for the common sailors of a man-of-war) for self-deception on the subject of sin and sinners.

At about this time Melville bought a copy of Goethe's autobiography and marked this passage: " . . . Whenever we wish to speak of affairs of the soul . . . [we] withdraw from the crowd, and even from all society." He was discovering ways of speaking to, without withdrawing from, a public he was dependent upon.

10

Moby-Dick, Herman Melville's one unquestionably great full-length book, has never been properly understood as the work of a writer who was in a state of creative tension with a reading public whose limitations he had at last defined. Many of its devices, and to some extent its form and its greatness, can be explained in terms of that tension—a tension which was a crucial factor in the creation of Poe's major tales, Hawthorne's novels, Emerson's lectures, *Huckleberry Finn*, and *The Turn of the Screw*. All were products of a balance of the author's wish to express himself and yet to be bought and read and taken seriously. If this hypothesis seems to make the general reader in the nineteenth century a partner in the creation of some of America's greatest art, the compliment must be diluted by the fact that some of these works were commercial failures, that some were misunderstood, and some valued for the wrong reasons.

Certainly *Moby-Dick*, by all statistical standards of the time, was a public failure. At a time when, according to one knowledgeable publisher's man, a novel could not be counted a success unless it sold five thousand copies, only 2,915 copies of *Moby-Dick* were printed; and if the publisher had not suffered a fire, no new printing would have been necessary for twelve years. Our problem is why a novel which can still be read as a tale of nautical adventure, and was so read by many in its time, sold only 2,500 copies in its first five years, and only 2,965 in its first twenty, whereas the somber *Scarlet Letter* sold 10,800 and 25,200 in identical periods.

While he was still writing *Moby-Dick*, Melville explained his fate thus: "What I feel most moved to write, that is banned,— it will not pay. Yet, altogether, write the *other* way I cannot. So the product is a final hash, and all my books are botches." *Moby-Dick* was written *both* ways; and though some American critics considered it a botch, a majority of them did not, and some of the most favorable (if uncomprehending) commentary appeared in influential middle-class magazines like *Harper's*, *Graham's*, and *Godey's*.

The influence of the review in literary history is a perpetual puzzle. In the case of *Moby-Dick* there are four suggestive facts: (1) The earliest reviews were hostile. These appeared in powerful London journals (the English edition was published a month earlier than the New York), and some were reprinted in America. Many American readers responded more confidently to these than to the notices in clique-ridden American periodicals. That a majority of British reviewers (in London, Dublin, and Canada) attacked Melville's greatest book undermines somewhat the claim of British support of Melville's reputation. (2) Some American magazines like the *Literary World* and the *Democratic Review*, which had found something good even in *Mardi*, now turned against Melville, or radically qualified their praise. Melville's closest ally, E. A. Duyckinck, came close to labeling it a subversive book, and gave it scant attention in his authoritative *Cyclopaedia of American Literature* five years later. (3) Magazines of the South, now increasingly partisan and increasingly sure of Melville's hostility to southern institutions, condemned it. They could hardly have been pleased with a book in which the narrator and a savage made a "cozy loving pair" in bed, and in which a white is dubbed a "white-washed negro."

A fourth factor may have been decisive. It is an axiom in the book trade that word-of-mouth recommendation is a far greater influence on the fate of a book than reviews. By 1851 women had become the chief consumers of fiction in America, and it may well be that their mouths may have settled the fate of *Moby-Dick*. They could not have failed to notice that in Melville's last two books there was no place for women, or that there was unlikely to be one in a book about whaling. The *Dublin Review* spoke for them when it declared that in *Moby-Dick* there was "no love, no tenderness." Melville himself said that he knew only one woman who was pleased with it (Mrs. Hawthorne): "for as a general thing, women have small taste for the sea." The "Pequod" was wholly a man's world, embracing the male's interest in technology, male vulgarities about breaking wind, a male's tolerance for subjects like the whale's sperm and penis and viscera, and for mates who need to be told to "beware of fornication." Was it Melville's awareness of all this that

MELVILLE 243

explains his conspicuously increased attention to the female world in his next book, *Pierre,* and in his magazine stories of what has been called the "feminine fifties"?

These are matters of the book's immediate impact. Other novels as badly handicapped for the general market have achieved gradual acceptance after the first shock of annoyance or distaste has worn off. The great question is why *Moby-Dick* was forgotten when *Typee* was still remembered, and why it was not even rediscovered for thirty years after the author's death; why, indeed, in spite of its present exalted place, it still has hostile readers and is still capable of stirring up that latent "hatred of art" which Flaubert, in Melville's own time, declared to be universal.

Moby-Dick, as he first conceived it, was probably the same kind of compromise with his readers as the first part of *Mardi,* and *White-Jacket.* His first and premature sales letter to his British publisher described it as "a romance of adventure, founded upon certain wild legends in the Southern Sperm Whale Fisheries, and illustrated by the author's own personal experience . . . as a harpooneer." It would deserve handsome payment because of its "great novelty." He intended to "cook" this "blubber" into poetry by throwing in "a little fancy." Duyckinck, who read the manuscript thus described, pronounced it a "romantic, fanciful and literal and most enjoyable presentment of the Whale Fishery."

Melville must have revised this manuscript drastically to be able to describe the finished work as a "wicked book," the product of "my evil art," and for Duyckinck's pleasure in the first version to turn into deep disturbance over the second. Almost certainly, in the process of rewriting, Melville transformed a typical harsh whaling captain, such as had provided motivation for desertions in his earlier books, into a crazy superman whose heroic satanism infects not only the rabble crew but the narrator, Ishmael-Melville. Nevertheless, his sales letter accurately, if incompletely, describes the final version, and the general reader might have missed—often did miss, if we may judge by some of the reviews—the shattering implications of the role of Captain Ahab. It was still, potentially, for the superficial reader, an "interesting" book, and most of its surface was perfectly intelligible. Beneath the surface it was difficult (as two reviewers seemed to be aware), but no more difficult than *Hamlet* and *Lear* to the audience of that time, which, as Melville believed, went to Shakespeare for "the popularizing noise and show of broad farce and blood-smeared tragedy." (Melville's sense of what Shakespeare got away with in the popular market probably influenced his revision.)

He worked hard to make *Moby-Dick* interesting, intelligible—and saleable. The reviewer in *Peterson's*, a fashionable ladies' magazine, who said that if it had been compressed and all the "philosophical" and "transcendental" chapters deleted (he did not suggest, note, that Ahab be cast out), it "could [have been] decidedly the best sea-novel in the English language today," was asserting indirectly a truth that is too often ignored: that the "high art" of *Moby-Dick* is erected on a broad base of middling art—the art, practiced also by Poe and Hawthorne, of making prose easy and palatable for readers who do not wish to work too hard when they read. This fact was recognized both by the *London Spectator*, which sneered that Melville's medley of styles included that of "magazine article writing," and by the thoroughly "middling" *New York Home Journal*, which believed that in writing this book Melville must have been determined to "combine . . . all his popular characteristics."

These characteristics included Melville's "personal" tone ("[You] Call me Ishmael" has been subtilized, to use Melville's word, by modern interpreters, but it is rarely recognized as an example of the prevailing coziness of mid-century journalism); popular varieties of humor—the pun, the exaggeration, the incongruous; light handling of technical information—a journalistic

skill which runs unbroken from Poe and Dr. Holmes to Paul de
Kruif; and vivid, graphic description and action. The reviewers
praised all these qualities, and admiration of the last named was
all but unanimous.

Yet a majority of the reviewers felt that Melville had "spoiled"
(often this was the word they chose) a pleasing book. Much of
the criticism centered on one of two targets: the speculations of
Ishmael-Melville on God, man, and institutions; and the "horrors
and heroics of Ahab."

Under the first heading he was found guilty of "abuse of
society," of "sophistry," of a "piratical running down of creeds
and opinions," of violating "the most sacred associations of life"
—of being downright "dangerous." A good half of the reviewers
pretended that his speculations were simply irrelevant, that he
had intruded "gratuitous suggestions about psychology, ethics,
and theology," but we may suspect such a protest in a literary
culture which gladly tolerated authorial interpolations in works
of fiction. More characteristic of the time was the objection that
the speculations were unintelligible—that they were "abstruse,"
or "dreamy" or "transcendental."

Inasmuch as informal speculation or "reverie" was in this
decade becoming an established popular form in the work of
Donald Grant Mitchell, G. W. Curtis, and O. W. Holmes, we
may ask why Melville's speculations were either disliked, ignored,
or merely tolerated. It could not have been because the critics
thought him merely negative about contemporary beliefs, for
unless they were deaf they could hardly have missed such multi-
decibelled "affirmations" as Ishmael's celebration of "that democratic dignity which . . . radiates without end from God; Himself! The great God absolute!" Dr. Holmes in his popular *Break-
fast Table* series was to be even more critical about some aspects
of democracy and contemporary religious belief. But Holmes's
speculative devices had attributes which define the difference
between popular speculation and the intellectual processes of the

great Romantics. The comic device of the boardinghouse table relieved the reader of the necessity to take Holmes's elaborately casual, often obviously eccentric opinions too seriously. And, more important, he required of his readers no participation in his thinking processes except to affirm or deny, if they felt impelled to do either.

Melville, by contrast, was obviously serious, and—not so obviously—experimental. He opened doors, rather than closed them—tried to get readers to entertain propositions with him rather than to accept commitments. In a word, he wished his readers to join him in the search for truth, rather than demand of him confirmation of what they already believed.

To this end, he worked out a system to train the reader in imaginative, exploratory thinking. The characteristics of this method included, first, identifying himself with the reader; second, getting the reader interested in a fact or object, the nature of which invites speculation; third, "priming" the reader's mind by putting suggestions in the form of questions; fourth, sometimes stopping short after opening up a possibility and inviting the reader to draw the inference himself, as, for example, in Chapter LXXIV where a discourse on the relation of the size of the whale's eye to his sight ends in the invitation, "Subtilize it."

In Chapter I the object is water. The idea to be explored is the attraction of men toward the danger and the mystery which water represents. That "almost all men . . . cherish . . . the same feelings toward the ocean with me" is demonstrated by reference to the habits of men, to preoccupations of painters, to the myth of Narcissus, and to the "universal itch for things remote."

His task here was simple compared to that in the chapter on "The Whiteness of the Whale," where his objective is nothing less than getting the reader to entertain the *possibility*—not the certainty—that behind the immensities of the universe there is a blank void of nothingness—of no-God—from which emanate terrors beyond our comprehension. The strain of this effort is

evident in his almost frantic appeals (five of them) to the reader
to stay with him and give careful attention: (1) Unless I "explain
myself" this book might be meaningless; (2) "Let us try. . . .
[for] without imagination no man can follow another into these
halls"; (3) "What I mean . . . may perhaps be elucidated by
the following examples"; (4) But, you say, I am being a coward;
(5) "But not yet have we solved the incantation of this
whiteness. . . . "

The climactic paragraph, in which the appalling proposition is
put, is not assertion but question. We are told not that evil is
absolute but that *if* we grasp imaginatively all the associations
of whiteness, and all that history and science can tell us about it,
then we are in a position to understand Ahab's "fiery hunt" for
the source of evil. But we are also warned that he who sees
nothing but the whiteness is a "wretched infidel" who "gazes
himself blind."

As Melville rightly says, unless this chapter succeeds, the whole
book may be meaningless, for if the crazy captain is to be anything more than a Gothic monster or a medical curiosity, all
our stock responses to the facts of his situation and to the whale
must be broken down. Melville is trying to do here what every
major poet since 1800 has had to do: break down stock responses
to images and types. The stock responses are not wrong, he
assures us (in a sentence forty-four lines long, the first thirty-
nine of which are subordinate clauses conceding the accepted
benign associations of whiteness); they are merely one-sided and
oversimple. To a generation of readers still predominantly governed by Scottish common sense with its official catalogues of
approved responses to poetic stimuli, such a chapter offered training in a new kind of reading. But there is little evidence that
the instruction was welcome, and we can assume that because
it involved the reader in creative process, it was rejected.

The second major objection was to the character and speech
of Ahab. Fewer than half the reviewers even bothered to mention
him, and most of those either dismissed him as a crazy bore or

condemned his speech as extravagant and bombastic. Clearly, the method of Shakespearean tragedy with which Melville invested the Ahab story and the rhetoric of the Renaissance stage which he imposed on Ahab's speech were generally considered a violation of verbal realism.

The public failure of *Moby-Dick* remains, to some extent, inscrutable. It appeared in a decade when public resistance to serious fiction was relaxing. It contained much that was of approved attraction to the general reader. Its uninteresting or unintelligible parts might easily have been skipped by the many readers who confessed to being fascinated by the natural history, the technology, the description, and physical action with which the book abounds.

We must turn to one of the most perceptive and sympathetic of Melville's readers for some clue as to why a book with such attractions had such a brief public life. Evert Duyckinck thought that *Moby-Dick* was an important event in the world of fiction, which was "crowded with successful mediocrities," and thought it an honor to be in the company of such "nobler spirits" as Melville. Yet, he declared, "a fourth of the volume" is given over to a "vein of moralizing" and "extravagant daring speculation" in which there is a "piratical running down of creeds and opinions" and a violation of the "most sacred associations of life." He concedes that such speculation is not actually "dangerous" in this believing world, but it is "out of place and uncomfortable." "Uncomfortable" becomes a revealing word when we note that it refers, in the same sentence, to what he calls the "conceited indifferentism of Emerson." "Indifferentism" presumably describes both Melville's and Emerson's aloofness from the world's commitments—their ability to understand and share man's faith while rejecting the worldly context in which faith usually operates. But the most significant word is "conceited." In using it Duyckinck was in harmony with Melville's worst enemies, particularly the *Democratic Review*, which asserted that his failure was due to his "vanity," his "morbid self-esteem," his determination to "centre all attention upon himself." Such charges are incredible to modern readers who recognize (as no contemporary reviewer did) that the central theme of *Moby-Dick* is love and sympathy. But what Duyckinck really meant by conceit was introspection. He and the few who bothered to read *Moby-Dick* carefully enough even to feel "uncomfortable" about it were unconsciously but resentfully perceiving that fiction was beginning to be, like poetry, a potential means of self-exploration for the writer. This is a function of literature which the common reader has never accepted unless it is so disguised that he need not contend with it. No one recognized Ahab as a product of Melville's self-exploration, and therefore, though he was thought repulsive by most reviewers, he was not resented. It was Ishmael-Melville who, through introspection, came to understand and sympathize with Ahab and caused discomfort.

II

Like a man marching to his doom, Melville began writing his worst professional failure before *Moby-Dick* reached the bookstores. *Pierre* was unanimously damned by reviewers, and sold only 1,856 copies (of an edition of 2,310) in thirty-five years. So offensive was it to the novel-reading public that biographers have often thought it Melville's deliberate affront to an ungrateful public. It was not. Although it was one of his most serious books, he conceived it as a market novel, and, moreover, as only the first of a series in a "new field of productions" which were to be "not unprofitable business adventures."

To understand his developing hope that he could write books both profound and popular, we must consider his state of mind in the summer and fall of 1851 when he finished *Moby-Dick* and began *Pierre*. He saw much of Hawthorne, and they had long talks of "things of this world and of the next, and books and publishers." In long letters he poured out his heart on the subject of the writer's fate in his own time. He had already decided that Hawthorne was the one indisputable American genius of his day. When, that summer, he witnessed the popularity of *The House of the Seven Gables* and the successful "promotion" of Hawthorne by his publishers, he had reason to believe that in the nineteenth century it was possible, as it had been for Shakespeare, to plumb the depths of mind in "black" books which nevertheless had popular appeal. He himself was attempting precisely that in *Moby-Dick*, and when in November he learned that Hawthorne understood his book, he had a feeling of "unspeakable security"; he was comprehended by a man who, in successful books, said "No! in thunder." The first sales of *Moby-Dick* looked promising —1,500 the first month. But he had a new child in the house, and he was $700.00 in debt to Harper. "Leviathan is not the biggest fish;—I have heard of Krakens." Krakens was *Pierre*. By Christmas he was working at it with almost manic concentration.

All that we know at this stage about his strategy for opening the "new field" is that the new work was not a "chalice" of salt water, but a "rural bowl of milk." The first five-eighths of *Pierre* (through Book 15) is decidedly rural, if not all milk. In idyllic country a rich, handsome, charming young squire woos a rich, beautiful, blonde girl, with the blessing of his haughty, aristocratic, widowed mother. A melancholy brunette spoils the picture by turning out to be the illegitimate daughter of Pierre's revered father. Immolating himself for the sin of his parent, Pierre jilts Lucy and takes Isabel under his protection in the simulated role of husband. Cast off by his mother, he takes Isabel to the big city.

At this point the scene becomes and remains urban. Living in abject poverty in a tenement, the pair are joined by Lucy and a "ruined" girl from home named Delly. A villain enters in the form of Pierre's rich, effeminate city cousin Glen, who is to supplant him as heir. In a whirlwind finish, four characters die. Pierre murders his cousin, and in prison he and Isabel commit suicide as Lucy dies of heartbreak.

So far as these bare bones of plot reveal, the formula, except for the unhappy ending, derives from current melodrama and the "misery novel" as developed by Mrs. Rowson and her imitators. Isabel's history serves as the theme of the long-lost child. There are overtones from current mass fiction; the "wholesome country-wicked city" myth, the theme of the permanent "ruin" suffered by the once-seduced girl. And occasionally Melville's language rhythms drop to the level of popular melodrama. Delly is "forever ruined through the cruel arts of Ned," thinks Pierre; and "Her father will not look upon her; her mother, she hath cursed her to her face," says Isabel.

In the light of these characteristics of the book, we can understand Melville's sales letter to Bentley: "My new book [possesses] unquestionable novelty, as regards [i.e., in comparison with] my former ones, treating of utterly new scenes & characters; and, as I believe, very much more calculated for popularity than anything you have yet published of mine—being a regular romance, with a mysterious plot to it, & stirring passions at work, and withall, representing a new & elevated aspect of American life. . . . " The implication of the word "regular" and emphasis on "plot" indicate the area of his compromise with public taste, and the phrase "elevated aspect of American life" indicates the basis for a serious treatment of a popular form. The book itself shows that Melville intended to raise the "misery" formula to the status of Renaissance tragedy. By presenting Pierre and Lucy as members of the agrarian aristocracy at the top of the American social pyramid and making them sacrifice place and material comfort to higher values; by making a gaudy plot a vehicle for profound psychological revelations; by making his hero as intellectual and introspective as Hamlet; and by raising his prose to the pitch of poetic tragedy; and by letting the plot follow its own logic to a tragic ending, Melville hoped to invest the common formula with dignity and meaning.

The story of Pierre-as-author has two lines of significance. In the first place, it contributed heavily to the unpopularity of the book, and was specifically attacked by many critics. In discussing the problems and the status of the artist, Melville once again tried to involve his readers in the creative process. And in describing Pierre's conflict with the publishing and reading world, he made the author the hero and the reader the villain. One notes that genuinely commercial writers sometimes flatter the public by reversing the formula: in our own time the fictional villain is often an "aesthete" or an "intellectual."

Melville here seems to take perverse satisfaction in abusing, satirizing, and insulting the reading public and its representatives—editors and publishers. He excoriates the kind of novels that they make popular. He accuses them of "unforgiveable affronts and insults" to great authors like Dante in the past; of missing the "deeper meanings" of Shakespeare; of judging literature as they do morals; of praising an author's worst books, or liking his best ones for the wrong reasons. The publishers who serve them are thievish illiterates. In short, "though the world worship Mediocrity and Common Place, yet hath it fire and sword for all contemporary Grandeur." But bad as the present is (it is a "bantering, barren and prosaic heartless age," which will not tolerate the serious), the future will be worse, for it will see "the mass of humanity reduced to one level of dotage."

Concomitantly, the author-hero is presented as a full-blown example of the Genius temperament. For this aspect of *Pierre* Melville disinterred Lombardo from Chapter CLXXX of *Mardi*, reappropriating many of the latter's concepts of art and authorship. Using some of Lombardo's phraseology, he made *Pierre* his nineteenth-century counterpart—a youth dedicated, lonely, divinely inspired, poverty-stricken, suffering, misunderstood, ruining his health by long hours of exhausting creativity in an ice-cold room. That a character as morally and morbidly diseased as the reviewers thought Pierre was, should also have been a genius, set apart from and above the stupid public which crucified him, did little to improve the reader's already pejorative image of the creative writer.

The second significance of this extension of the story is that it is symbolic representation of Melville's own transformation from journalist to philosopher-poet. We need not hesitate to identify the narrator with Herman Melville. Though the book starts off in the mode of authorial omniscience, it is not long before we are aware of intrusions of authorial personality. Nor need we be put off by superficial differences between Pierre's career and Melville's. The country boy of eighteen who is a well-known amateur author of sonnets and fugitive pieces, and a magazinist rather than a book-writer, is not the Melville who, after roaming the seas, became a professional writer of travel works at the age of twenty-seven. Nor does the genteel, respectable, pious country boy correspond to the skeptical, roughneck sailor. But these contrasts represent necessary compromises with the given facts about Pierre. Everything else about his career could have been drawn from Melville's observations of the literary world in New York; and the "world-revelation"—the moral shock which transforms Pierre from a dilettante to a serious writer—corresponds to Melville's discovery, during the writing of *Mardi,* which transformed him from a journalist to the author of *Moby-Dick.* The distance between the celebrated country gentleman-amateur and the Pierre slaving at his Honest Book in New York is the same distance as that between the author of *Typee* and the author of *Mardi.* Through Pierre, Melville is looking back at his experiences with himself and with the literary world between 1846 and 1849. Opinions in this book about readers, critics, publishers, the exploitation of the newly popular writer, writing schedules and writing habits correspond to Melville's opinions in previous works and in letters and journals.

At the center is Melville's memory of his experience with *Mardi*. Pierre's book, like *Mardi*, is "comprehensive and compacted" and is intended to "surprise and delight" the world. Like Lombardo's Koztanza it was born of the double need to "deliver . . . Truth" and pay the rent; it was written under the excessive dependence of newly discovered great minds of the past. Some samples from Pierre's book, "directly plagiarized from his own experiences to fill out the mood of his apparent author-hero, Vivia," suggest the tone and mood of *Mardi* and its author-hero Taji, who, we remember, fainted and slaved in his writing cell as Pierre did in his New York flat. Pierre's revulsion against that "vile book" after he finishes it reminds us of Melville's thanking God when *Mardi* was "off [his] hands." When Pierre is "stabbed" by the publisher's letter in which he is accused of swindling them out of a cash advance "upon the pretense of writing a popular novel for us" which, instead, turns out to be a "blasphemous rhapsody" filched from "vile Atheists," we think of the outraged reviewers of *Mardi* who had expected another *Typee,* and of Melville's cry to Duyckinck that "that thing was stabbed."

By 1852 Melville's professional attitude was a mixture of perversity, innocence, and desperation, and a tendency both to overrate and underrate the general reader. And the cause of his confusion, in part, was his hope that he could, like Shakespeare, and by using some of Shakespeare's methods, contrive to be at once profound, tragic, and popular. To the groundlings, he thought, Shakespeare offered "the popularizing noise and show of broad farce and blood-smeared tragedy," and other effects of the "tricky stage." So in *Pierre,* Melville offered violent renunciations, hypocrisies, treacheries, murder, suicide and high-pitched Renaissance dialogue. But just as Shakespeare craftily put into the mouths of his "dark" characters things so "terrifically true" that no "good man, in his own proper character" can "even hint of them," so Melville, like his own Pierre, hoped to translate atheism into "godliest things," disguise misery and death in forms of "gladness and life," and conceal "everything else . . . under the so conveniently adjustable drapery of all-stretchable Philosophy." Thus he might "egregiously deceive the superficial skimmer of pages."

Such deceptions had a chance of success in *Moby-Dick*, where, by keeping his story in the foreground, he rendered the intellectual and symbolic framework invisible or inconspicuous to readers who wished only to be diverted by action and description, and instructed about whaling. And if Ishmael is Melville, he is also within the drama as a guide necessary to the reader's understanding of the action and of whaling. But in *Pierre* the narrator is an intrusive nuisance. And he is most intrusive in the sections on authorship where he pretends to be exhibiting his hero's unspoken reflections on the creative life. In his artificial attempt to connect the story of Pierre's disillusionment as moral man with the story of his writing career, he commits the final perversity of rendering him disillusioned about the art of fiction. For the young author's despairing conviction that his finished book is a stacked deck ("he was but packing one set the more"), he was inviting the reader to share what was apparently his own loss of faith in fiction itself. If, as Charles Feidelson has argued, Melville wrote himself out of his belief in his craft, Pierre's suicide can be taken as a symbol of Melville's professional self-destruction.

Melville's reputation never recovered from this episode, and reviewers of his later works persistently reminded readers that they were by the author of *Pierre*. But his professional fate had already been sealed by his publishers. The wording of the contract for that work suggests that the Harpers had not read the manuscript when they accepted it, but they were by then so doubtful of his ability to please that for the first time they put the whole financial risk on him by exempting the first 1,190 copies from royalty. When he offered the work to Bentley, he was informed that the latter had lost a total of £453 on his works. Because in *Mardi* and *Moby-Dick* he had not "restrained [his] imagination"; had not "written in a style to be understood by the great mass of readers"; and had "offended the feelings of [the] sensitive," Bentley refused to accept *Pierre* unless he was permitted to make "such alterations [i.e., 'revisal and occasional omission'] as are absolutely necessary to 'Pierre' being properly appreciated here." Negotiations broke down, and the British edition that appeared was made up of imported sheets.

12

Nevertheless, he continued as professional for another seven years, for his problem in adversity was that of Pierre: "What else could he do?" The following table will suffice to dispose of the old theory that he bid farewell to his public in *Pierre*.

1852   Began a novel, "Agatha" (unpublished).

1853   Began a book on "Tortoises and Tortoise-Hunting" (unpublished); contributed prose to three issues of monthly magazines.

1854   Contributed prose to thirteen issues of monthly magazines; another piece was rejected and was unpublished in his time.

1855   Contributed to nine issues of monthly magazines; published *Israel Potter*, which had been serialized.

1856   In spite of seven months of travel, contributed to four issues of monthly magazines; published *Piazza Tales* (all of which except the title piece had appeared in magazines).

1857   Planned book, "Roman Frescoes" (probably to be derived from his travel journals, but never published). Published *The Confidence-Man*. Gave eleven professional lectures.

1858   "Busy on a new book" (perhaps "Roman Frescoes,"
       or a sequel to *The Confidence-Man,* or a volume of
       rural sketches). Gave eleven professional lectures.

1859   Gave nine professional lectures. Prepared a book of
       verse, which he completed in 1860.

Inasmuch as almost all of the completed prose works (except
his uncompromising, strictly non-commercial novel, *The Confidence-Man*) were printed in middle-class magazines (*Harper's
Monthly* and *Putnam's Monthly*), this coda to Melville's professional life looks like the weary capitulation of a defeated man to
the general reader, or a mopping-up of his leftover materials from
his life in the Pacific, the Berkshires, and New York, and his
travels in Europe. Certainly there is defeat in his "guarantee,"
when he submitted the manuscript of his historical novel *Israel
Potter* for serialization in *Putnam's,* "that the story shall contain
nothing of any sort to shock the fastidious. There will be very
little reflective writing in it; nothing weighty. It is adventure. As
for its interest, I shall try to sustain that as well as I can."

That he was trying to come to some sort of terms with the
common reader is suggested by the subject matter of his shorter
pieces: three are returns to the romantic Pacific; nine have rural
settings, and seven deal with the popular subject of home and
woman. Under the circumstances he might have felt a wry
satisfaction if he had known that a magazine expert, G. W. Curtis,
thought his "I and My Chimney" "capital, genial, . . . thoroughly magazinish." And other contemporaries called "Cock-a-
doodle-doo!" "lively and animated"; "Bartleby" "lifelike," "quaint
and fanciful"; "Benito Cereno" "thrilling"; "The Encantadas"
"charming." Yet when we examine these eighteen shorter works,
we find that only three do not deal essentially with some kind of
loss, poverty, loneliness, or defeat. We may suspect that the old
Melville was still at work, but that his techniques of disguise and

concealment were so successful that these works were considered suitable for a magazine audience.

The three ostensibly "happy" pieces are among the most suspect. They may have been part of an abortive plan for a book of country sketches, centering in Melville's Pittsfield farm, which he had had in mind as early as 1850. ("H. M. knows every stone and tree, and will probably make a book of its features," wrote his intimate friend E. A. Duyckinck in that year.)

"The Apple-Tree Table" and "I and My Chimney" have the same characters: the narrator, his aggressive wife, his two daughters, Julia and Anna, and a servant, Biddy. Inasmuch as they all turn up again in "Jimmy Rose," a story of the city to which the narrator moves from his country place, it is possible that Melville intended to link city and country stories in one collection. A country-gentleman narrator and a country community also figure in "The Lightning-Rod Man," "Cock-a-doodle-doo!" "Poor Man's Pudding," and "The Piazza"; and "The Tartarus of Maids" records an excursion from such a house in the Berkshires.

Two of these—"I and My Chimney" and "The Apple-Tree Table"—are in the form of domestic comedy, the narrator-husband putting up a semicomic defense of the values of country things and traditions which are threatened by the forces of modernism and efficiency (represented by the wife), a theme both common and popular in a culture which was changing too rapidly for comfort. Yet under the surface, these stories move away from the customary sentimentalism of the theme and become devastating commentaries on the idea of progress and the defeat of individualism and the imagination. The theme of "The Lightning-Rod Man" is similar, but here Melville's satire comes close to the surface: the salesman avoids "pine-trees, high houses . . . upland pastures" and "tall men," and threatens to "publish" the narrator's "infidel notions." Several reviewers condemned this story without saying why. The "lively and animated" "Cock-a-doodle-doo!" reads, a hundred years later, like an impudent takeoff on the popular "sunshine and shadow" theme then so popular in the pages of *Harper's,* where this sketch was published. The narrator's "doleful dumps" are cured by the optimistic crowing of a magnificent rooster. He traces the bird to a miserable hovel where its owner, his wife, and their three children cheerfully die of sickness and starvation. The rooster then crows itself to death in an ecstasy of affirmation.

"Poor Man's Pudding" (which was twice reprinted in other periodicals) seems to affirm the dignity and pathos of the American poor; but it is essentially a rejection of the sentimentalization of poverty practiced by the poet Blandmoor and his ilk, who "speak prosperously" of what is and "ever will be" the "misery and infamy of poverty." The title phrase of the story (the point of which is that "through kind Nature, the poor, out of their very poverty, extract comfort") reappears in "Jimmy Rose," where a ruined rich man, turned parasite, but holding to his status as gentleman, indignantly rejects the comforts which are extended to paupers.

As little inclined as ever to accept popular slogans, Melville summed up explicitly in one of these stories of poverty his bitter conviction that "those peculiar social sensibilities nourished by our own peculiar political principles . . . do but minister to the added wretchedness of the unfortunate."

He rightly omitted most of these pieces from *The Piazza Tales:* they are interesting now just to the extent that we are interested in Melville. And to the credit of his public, the then most widely admired stories in that volume were his best—"Bartleby," "The Encantadas," "Benito Cereno," and "The Bell-Tower." Yet the point of his poverty sketches is retained in his prefatory sketch, "The Piazza." From his piazza the narrator sees on a mountainside a sunlit cottage which seems a house in fairyland. But after he has journeyed to it, it turns out that the radiant windows are fly-specked, and that behind them lives, in solitude and poverty, weary, pale-cheeked Marianna. Hereafter, "I stick to my piazza," knowing that the truth comes in not with the sun but "with darkness": "I walk the piazza deck, haunted by Marianna's face, and many as real a story." If the reviewers noted this unpromising preface to Melville's "real" stories, they did not mention it.

"Dark" as these stories were, they were moderately admired, and there were only a few complaints about Melville's unintelligibility and "peculiarity." In learning to write for the magazines he seems to have put into practice a principle he stated broadly in *Mardi* and in *Pierre*: "It is impossible to talk or write without apparently throwing oneself helplessly open." He now took protection in what might be called strategy of omission. In the Hunilla section of "The Encentadas" he asserts that he omits two crucial episodes in the widow's story because "I will not file this thing complete for scoffing souls to quote, and call it firm proof upon their side. . . . In nature, as in law, it may be libelous to speak some truths." From the context one judges that the island on which the widow, a half-breed Indian woman, was stranded was visited by whalemen who subjected her to unspeakable atrocities. This guess is supported by the last sentence of the story: as Hunilla, bearing her destroying grief, rides away "upon a small gray ass . . . before her on the ass's shoulders, she eyed the jointed workings of the beast's armorial cross." We remember that at the end of "Benito Cereno," the dead eyes of the executed slave, Babo, "met, unabashed, the gaze of the whites; and across the Plaza looked towards St. Bartholomew's church." And then we remember Melville's long obsession with the history of white, Christian corruption and abuse of primitive peoples in the Pacific, and the public's protests against his exposure of the Western civilizers in *Typee* and *Omoo*. His attack continues in these late stories, but the libelous truth is almost inaudible.

Melville's practice of deletion reflects also, perhaps, the tendency of serious novelists in the nineteenth century to thwart the common reader's tendency to identify the external action of a story with the story's meaning. He did this by suppressing story elements which might deflect the reader's attention from the story's real purpose. Thus Hawthorne suppressed the "facts" of the crime in which Miriam is involved in *The Marble Faun* lest they be taken as an explanation of Miriam. Thus, in "Bartleby," a history of the events leading to Bartleby's withdrawal might have been mistaken for the meaning of his withdrawal. Thus, in "The Fiddler," an explanation of Hautboy's resignation from the status of genius would have deflected attention from Melville's real subject, which was the quality of wisdom in a man who has renounced ambition. The practice of deletion reaches its climax in Henry James, who at times almost achieved the objective (stated by Flaubert, a self-declared enemy of the common reader) to write a story "about nothing at all." *

---

* The conclusion of this essay has been omitted because it is too fragmentary to be useful.—Ed.

CHAPTER THIRTEEN

Melville and the Common Reader*

M ELVILLE'S career in fiction reflects almost all those tensions between the artist and society which sometimes make literature and sometimes mar it. He was, first of all, out of harmony with a predominantly female fiction-reading public. It is a crude but not misleading index to taste in his time that *Moby-Dick*, a thoroughly masculine book which few women have liked, sold only 2,500 copies in its first five years and less than 3,000 in its first twenty, whereas *The Scarlet Letter*, in identical periods, sold 10,800 and 25,200.

Second, Melville's effective career came to an end at an unfortunate moment. Though the fiction-reading audience on the Atlantic coast had begun to stratify in the 1840's, it was a decade before reader levels in the national market were clearly defined. Melville's proper level was the upper middle class, where, in the 1850's, literary taste was beginning to be interpreted and guided by the editors of national monthly magazines like *Harper's* and the *Atlantic*. Central to Melville's problem was the fact that he entered this magazine world only in 1853, when his reputation was already ruined. All his earlier work was published in book form,[1] and was offered to an undifferentiated audience of men, women, and children among whom there was, of course, a fantastic range of sophistication and seriousness. Thus it was possible for a leading critic to label *Typee* and *Omoo* as "vendible," "venomous," and "venereous," and for a Cleveland bookseller to advertise the same titles as "Books for Little Folks."

I shall be using the term "common reader" glibly, realizing that it refers to mentalities as different as "the superficial skimmer of pages" (Melville's phrase) and what Albert Guérard calls "the alert non-professional reader." In Melville criticism one locates the common reader by ear, as it were. His professional readers are more easily identified. They were not university men for whom, as in our time, literature exists in its own right, but reviewers for newspapers and magazines whose first allegiance was not to art but to the immediate interest of society. In other words, the great majority of Melville's responsible critics functioned precisely as does the Henry Luce reviewing staff today.

The difference between his common readers and his critics emerges clearly in their responses to his public personality. From first to last, Melville was known by friend and foe alike as a vibrant, fascinating stylist whose moods, ranging from the gay, fanciful, playful, funny, and impudent, to the somber and meditative, were those of a living, colorful person. Because it was an intimate style, the common readers took it to be an expression of all that Melville was, and typed him as a free-wheeling bachelor-sailor with a gift for narrative. It was inevitable that they should have tried to exploit his personality ("Typee Melville" and "Mr. Omoo" were common nicknames, to his shame and annoyance), just as Wolfe and Hemingway and Dylan Thomas have been exploited in our own time. The critics, on the other hand, were worried precisely because this intimate style was so palatable to readers who could be corrupted by the subversive thinking which was masked by that style. They need not have worried. All the evidence indicates that common readers skipped or ignored his persistent criticism of institutions, and did not buy those books in which thinking crowded the narrative.

Melville's public personality became a debatable issue in the first paragraph of his first book. *Typee* begins with the words, "Six months at sea! Yes, reader, as I live, six months out of sight of land. . . . " This is the cozy, person-to-person style of the journalism of the forties, which Melville was to develop so miraculously in the book beginning "Call me Ishmael." But readers of the first edition might have noticed that, in a sentence he wisely deleted later, he fenced himself off almost at once by belligerently identifying himself with "good-for-nothing tars" who disturb the luxuriating "state-room sailors." British reviewers promptly charged that no common sailor could write so well, and that therefore Melville must be a gentleman-Munchausen fabricating adventures for the mob. American readers, knowing that gentlemen sometimes sailed before the mast, either accepted his adventures as truth, or lovingly dubbed him the "American Defoe." To the end of his life his readers wished him to remain just that.

Serious critics, however, suspected his sympathy with a dispossessed class and his hostility to the civilized world, and typed him as a dangerous malcontent. Still worse, not liking his ideas, they were able to attack his morals because in *Typee* he failed to put a protective distance between himself and his materials. Neglecting even the pseudonymity with which most American travel writers sheltered themselves, Melville declared himself a Melville on the title page, a Gansevoort in the dedication to his uncle, and a purveyor of the "unvarnished truth" in his Preface. Part of the "truth" which the critics seized upon was a drunken sexual orgy of the sailors with a crowd of native girls. Though, authorially, he specifically deplored this corruption of natives by their white "civilizers," nothing in the text suggests that, as sailor, he absented himself from these festivities. In fact, technically, he made the episode disastrously personal by saying of his naked visitors, "What a sight for us bachelor sailors! how avoid so dire a temptation?" With similar clumsiness, he alluded in Chapter XX to half-naked girls dancing in the moonlight, "all over, as it were," in a way that was "almost too much for a quiet sober-minded young man like myself."

Deletions in the second edition of *Typee* corrected some of these errors in point of view; and in *Omoo* he managed a detailed description of a wildly phallic native dance without seeming to be in the middle of it.[2] Though the Victorian age had begun, common readers seem not to have been offended by the voluptuous dances of his "naked houris," his cohabitation with Fayaway, or his sailor orgies—or perhaps they thought it was all fiction. Margaret Fuller of the New York *Tribune* spoke as common reader rather than as critic when she recommended *Typee* for its "pretty and spirited pictures," and declared that the "sewing societies of the country villages [would] find this the very book they wished to . . . read while assembled at their work." But the critics were appalled. Miss Fuller's employer, Horace Greeley, who saw the problem of an unstratified literary market, thought Melville a "born genius," but *Typee* and *Omoo* are "dangerous reading for those of immature intellects and unsettled principles. Not that you can put your finger on a passage positively offensive; but [these books] are "diseased in moral tone." Evidently Mr. Greeley had found something offensive to put his finger on by the time of Melville's marriage, for the *Tribune* reminded the bride of Fayaway in Melville's past. We need not wonder that Melville was excluded, like Poe and Whitman, from the nineteenth-century hall of literary fame, to which the academy admitted only those writers who had led blameless lives.

There is no evidence that Melville cared that his morals had been impugned except that he did not again, authorially, participate in the romps of sailors. But he at once set about altering the public's conception of him as a *common* sailor. In *Omoo* he carefully sets himself up as the only educated man in a crew of "reckless seamen of all nations." Early in *Mardi* he reports that his mates spotted him as a gentleman by his language, his table manners, and his "unguarded allusions to *Belles-Lettres* affairs."[3] White-Jacket–Melville emphasizes his place among educated writers by referring to "my friend Dana" and "my fine countryman, Nathaniel Hawthorne." And Ishmael-Melville is a seagoing encyclopedia of the humanities, fine arts, and sciences. At the same time, though he retained his tones of journalistic intimacy, he broke through the restrictions of the journalistic vocabulary and drew more and more freely on philosophical terminology and on the imagery and diction of the Hebrew, classical, and Renaissance literatures. It is possible, indeed, that Melville became the most richly and learnedly allusive of romantic novelists partly in reaction against the label of "good-for-nothing tar" which he had pinned on himself. For such apostasy he paid the inevitable penalty: the journalistic world said his later work "smelled of the lamp," and called him "pretentious" and "pedantic." But he had escaped from his pigeonhole.

Nevertheless, as a professional writer, chronically in debt, he not only desperately needed the common reader but actually hoped—and for a while, believed—that it was possible "to suit at once the popular and the critical taste." The words are Poe's, and I take the latter phrase to mean, not the taste of critics (Poe knew better), but the taste that is critical—that is, the taste of the writer himself and of the few who understand him. An oft-quoted passage by Melville seems to contradict this hope: "What I feel most moved to write, that is banned,—it will not pay. Yet, altogether, write the *other* way I cannot. So the product is a final hash, and all my books are botches." The important word here is not *botches*—his books may or may not be that—but *hash,* which asserts that he tried to write both ways at once. In more optimistic moods he believed that he could do so successfully. It was a hope which he shared with all his great contemporaries, including Emerson, Thoreau, and Whitman, and which even Henry James did not relinquish until the turn of the century. If it seems to have flickered out in our time, there are Hemingway and Faulkner and R. P. Warren to prove its viability. Melville seems to have given it up only in his last novel, *The Confidence-Man*; but even here we cannot be sure, for he seems to have planned a sequel to this, the most baffling of his books, after both his American and his English publishers had abandoned him as a failure.

Melville's two ways of writing can be defined by analysis of the three works which he first conceived as popular books (written, that is, "the other way"), and then drastically reconceived so as to include also what he was "most moved to do." These were *Mardi*, *Moby-Dick*, and *Pierre*. In the finished forms of all three, the popular materials remain either as a base or a starting point for the more private material which he imposed on them. I pause here to point out the impossibility of reading books so composed in the way many Melville critics try to do— that is, as structurally organic wholes all the parts of which can be schematically related to all the other parts. Melville's gift was not for unity, or integrated structure, but for diversity and digression, and he took advantage of all of what has been called the "novel's liberties and privileges."

In the three rewritten works, the two that he first conceived as forms of travel, *Mardi* and *Moby-Dick,* are based on precisely those popular materials which predominate in his four successful travel works—loose, episodic, anecdotal narrative; information; and informal, intimate commentary. These materials the readers liked and the critics praised, even though they rejected the two books as wholes. What he was "most moved to write" he added, to *Mardi,* in the shape of intellectual allegory; to *Moby-Dick,* in the Ahab drama. And it was the allegory and the drama which the public disliked. The rejection, it appears, was due primarily to Melville's shift from direct commentary to forms of thinking which the public found repulsive.

The forms of thought and opinion in fiction have been a major problem for American writers from Charles Brockden Brown to William Faulkner. In writers whose thinking was generated mainly by conflicts between themselves and public beliefs and values, e.g., Cooper, Howells, and Sinclair Lewis, ideas are usually

presented through the dialectic of characters who represent different social classes, occupations, races, regions, or sexes. By and
large, this form of thought has been the safest, so far as tensions
between writer and reader are concerned, partly because it is so
easily skipped by the reader who is anxious to get on with the
narrative, partly because it is potentially so deceptive even for
the critical watchdog who seeks to identify what the author
thinks with what his characters say. Such writers are most likely
to get into trouble when they make direct authorial statements,
or indirect ones through thin disguises, like Cooper's Major
Effingham or Lewis' Arrowsmith. But if we can judge from the
sales records of Cooper's novels, the common reader will stay
with the author, no matter what he thinks, as long as narrative,
information, and other diverting elements heavily outweigh the
thinking. Cooper's readers rejected only those novels in which
thought and opinion predominated.

Cooper's and Howells' characteristic dialectical thinking offers
the reader choices: he can take sides in the argument, or accept
it in suspension, or simply ignore it. The same is true of Melville's
thinking in his first two books. Moreover, in these, his thinking
was chiefly about primitivism. Though some critics resented his
attacks on institutions, by the 1840's the subject was being
argued more sentimentally than seriously. But when in *Mardi*
Melville began to generate ideas out of contradictions within
himself, he shifted to a kind of internal dialectic which gave
the reader no choice. He involved him in the very processes of
thought, made him collaborate in exploratory, speculative thinking which is concerned not with commitment but with possibility.
It is the one kind of thinking that the general reader will not
tolerate, and the nineteenth-century critic, when he detected it,
declared it subversive.[4]

Melville began *Mardi* as "another book of South Sea Adventure (continued from, tho' wholly independent of 'Omoo')," and
was so sure that it would be a "hit" (his word) with the general

reader that he asked of his London publisher an advance double that he had received for *Omoo*. His original intention survives, if at all, only in the first forty chapters. This portion differs from the earlier travel works in two respects. First, though the narrative is characteristically episodic and in the first person, it is somewhat more fictionalized. Second, and more important, there is a new quality in the non-narrative elements. In this part of *Mardi* he develops what he later perfected in *Moby-Dick*—the popular art of clear and charming exposition of natural and technological fact; and for the first time, he uses fact as a vehicle of meaning. Fact becomes occasion for meditation: the doctrinaire and contentious commentary of *Typee* becomes deeply personal reflection. This change in his style was widely admired as a way of combining "fact and fancy."

After this beginning, however, flesh-and-blood narrative fades into the patently allegorical story of the discovery, the loss, and the search for the maiden Yillah. In terms of the intellectual purpose of the book, that search means little: in long stretches Yillah is forgotten completely. She is not what the book is about. I suspect that she is the product of one of Melville's miscalculations of the common reader—that he invented her to provide a story-line to carry the reader along with him, and that the pursuit is about equivalent to Cooper's Indian chases, which keep the reader busy while the author interpolates materials which are of primary interest to himself. The substance and the essence of *Mardi* are in the discourse of the characters—in Melville's dialectic with the world and with himself.

He was, of course, deserted by readers as soon as they realized that the Yillah story was bait to lure them into an intellectual jungle. In England, where, to Melville's disgust, *Mardi* was printed in three volumes for circulating libraries in the format of the novel, defrauded readers were indignant, and the exasperated publisher, who lost money on it, reported that "the first volume was eagerly devoured, the second was read," but the third was so ill-adapted to "the class of readers whom . . . the First Volume . . . gratified" that it virtually "stopped the sale of the book."[5]

In the allegory, which was what Melville was "most moved to write," he met head-on—and disastrously—the problems of authorial identity and of dialectical speculation. As long as the narrator in Volume One has a definable personality—that of a lively, learned, meditative adventurer, like White-Jacket or Ishmael, Melville's touch is sure. But after Chapter XL, when he is given the name of Taji, the narrator disintegrates. As the pursuer of Yillah he becomes a mere function of the perfunctory plot, takes no part in the discourse, and is often forgotten. The "I" of the first part tends to become "we" in the allegory, and even the "we" often disappears in a fog of authorial omniscience. Sometimes, within a brief space, Taji speaks as "we," is addressed by the author as "you," and is referred to in the third person by his companions as if he were not there. Once, even though Taji is supposed to be in the middle of the Pacific, Melville shoves him aside, and, speaking from his New York house, says, "My cheek blanches while I write . . . while I slave and faint in this cell."

Though, in terms of the story, the narrator becomes Taji, in terms of the intellectual content of the book he is displaced by a set of characters who represent the component parts of Melville's new creative personality. The journalist survives as Mohi the chronicler, the purveyor of mere fact,[6] who, though he sometimes spins yarns, is treated with contempt. Yoomy is the poet in the new Melville, a tender-minded believer, impatient of raw fact, "capricious . . . swayed by contrary moods—made up of a thousand contradictions . . . [and] no one in Mardi comprehended him." The dominant character and chief talker in this trio is the philosopher and critic, Babbalanja. He is the seeker after meaning, the believer in "polysensuum," or many meanings, the enemy of the "armed and crested lies" of the world and of

Philistinism. In a further fragmentation of personality, Babba-lanja, whenever his discourse reaches the limits of intelligibility, is possessed by his demon, Azzageddi, who talks gibberish. In these four entities, from the factual historian to the inarticulate demon, with the poet and the militant philosopher between, we get the full range of Melville's conception of creative self.

Mardi was a necessary laboratory job for Melville[7]—an explo-ration of his mind at precisely the moment that the able journalist was becoming an artist. As a market book, however, it was an impossibility, for it cannot be read as story—it must be studied, and the content is meaningful not for the results of thought but for the process of thinking. The book was declared, all but unanimously,[8] to be unintelligible, and it took Harpers seven years to get rid of 3,000 copies. Melville said bitterly that *Mardi* was "stabbed," meaning that the critics attacked not the book but the author. He and the critics were both right, for they perceived that the book *was* the author in a sense that fiction should never be.

Moreover, the critics sensed that the book was hostile to them, to the general reader, and to the world. It is sometimes wrongly stated that it was the critical attack on *Mardi* that caused Melville's increasing hostility to the public. The reverse is true, for the hostility is in the book and antecedent to its failure. Its immediate source was his humiliation that *Typee* and *Omoo,* which he had outgrown by the time he finished the latter, should have earned him such cheap notoriety. He had begged his London publisher to omit "by the author of *Typee* and *Omoo*" from the title page of *Mardi.* Babbalanja declares that there is "more likelihood of being over-rated while living than of being under-rated when dead." And when Yoomy sings an immortal but anonymous song, the philosopher says, "This were to be truly immortal; to be perpetuated in our works, and not in our name. Let me, oh Oro! be anonymously known!" He implies that by exploiting the writer as person and trying to keep him down to the level of his poorest work, the world gives him contemporary reputation at the expense of ultimate fame. "Does not all Mardi by its action declare it is far better to be notorious now than famous hereafter? . . . To insure your fame, you must die." It was to be his bitterest pill from now on that Typee and Omoo kept on selling while his better works languished, and he predicted (what was to be true until 1920) that he would go down to posterity as a "man who lived among cannibals," and that Typee would be fed to babies along "with their gingerbread."

But the deepest source of his alienation was his sudden[9] discovery of the meaning of genius and his affinity with it, and his belief that the world resents genius until time and death sterilize it. The word was used ambivalently in contemporary criticism. Though it often served as a mere compliment to the individuality of Melville's style, it was more commonly qualified by the word "but," in a context meaning that such individuality as his was not to be trusted socially. And he was all the more distrusted because in Mardi and Pierre he not only identified himself with genius but put it in invidious contrast with the common character. "Men like you and me," he wrote Hawthorne, form "a chain of God's posts round the world," and in the "boundless, trackless, but still glorious wild wilderness" which is the domain of genius, we are attacked by "Indians [who] do sorely abound, as well as [by] the insignificant but still stinging mosquitoes." The mosquitoes sting in Chapter CLXXX of Mardi, where Babbalanja is the spokesman for Lombardo, a mythical great artist of the past who received "coppers then, and immortal glory now." In a dialogue about Lombardo's masterpiece, the Koztanza, Melville's belief that genius is hated must have been plain to any attentive reader. Abrazza, an arch-Philistine, utters stupid and spiteful platitudes about genius that are still current. Babbalanja's attempts to correct him are futile, for it is clear that Abrazza resents not literature but writers: when he has finished attacking the Koztanza, he confesses, "I never read it." Equally obvious is the soaring egotism in the chapter, "Dreams," in which, shaking himself free from all his spokesmen and writing as Melville, he allies himself with the great community of genius of all time: "In me" the great writers "recline and converse." "Blind Milton sings bass to my Petrarchs . . . and laureats crown me with bays." This egotism is capped with romantic self-pity as he speaks of "the Dionysius that rides me," so that he is "less to be envied, than the veriest hind in the land." In a dozen furious reviews of *Mardi,* the crucial word was "conceit."

From Irving and Longfellow to James and beyond, one of the symptoms of friction between the American writer and his public has been his tendency to write about writing—to write poems about poems and fiction about novelists. Though such works vary widely in tone from defensiveness to a guilty deprecation of art itself, they all derive from the sense that the writer is different from people and that people resent him for it. He has often attempted to minimize that difference, as Poe did when he described the writing of "The Raven" as a purely rational process. Just as often he has allied himself with people against writers. It is a sure sense that impels a James Whitcomb Riley to attack poets in his verse and a Herman Wouk to make villains of artists and intellectuals.

Melville, like Henry James in his short stories of the nineties, took the offensive, and, particularly in *Pierre,* made the embattled genius a hero and a martyr. This is the book which shut him off from any further serious consideration by contemporary critics, and the public's rejection of it was conclusive: it took Harpers 35 years to sell 1,800 copies. Considering Melville's original intention in writing it, it was an incredibly blundering and perverse performance for a professional writer. His intention is plain: he conceived it as a market novel, based solidly on the formulas which mass fiction had been exploiting since the days

of Mrs. Rowson, and which in Melville's time were the chief
staple of Robert Bonner's mass story paper, the *New York
Ledger*. Here is the plot:

In idyllic country a rich, handsome, charming young squire
woos Lucy, a rich, beautiful blonde, with the blessing of the boy's
haughty, aristocratic, widowed mother. A melancholy brunette,
Isabel, spoils it all by turning out to be the illegitimate daughter
of Pierre's revered father. Immolating himself for the sin of his
parent, Pierre jilts Lucy and takes Isabel under his protection
in the simulated role of husband. Cast off by his mother, he takes
Isabel to New York City. Living in abject poverty in a tenement,
the pair are joined by Lucy and a ruined servant girl from home.
The villain enters in the person of Pierre's rich, effeminate city
cousin, Glen, who is to supplant him as heir. In a whirlwind
finish, four characters die: Pierre murders his cousin, and in
prison he and Isabel commit suicide, as Lucy dies of heartbreak.
Except for the unhappy ending, this is the stuff of mid-nineteenth-
century misery fiction and melodrama. Here also is the popular
myth of the wholesome country vs. the wicked city, and of the
permanent "ruin" suffered by the once-seduced girl. Occasionally
Melville even lapses into the language of melodrama: "Her father
will not look upon her; her mother she hath cursed her to her
face," and Delly is "forever ruined by the cruel arts of Ned."

This work he described to a publisher as a "regular romance,
with a mysterious plot to it, & stirring passions at work." It
would, moreover, be the first of a "new field of productions,"
which would enrich both him and his publishers. That he wished
its popularity not to be damaged by association with his previous
works is evident in his request that it be published anonymously.
Poverty and debt had forced him into the mass market.

But beneath—or above—this intention lay another. He was
coming to believe that "the tribe of 'general readers'" (his
words), who would not tolerate the unpleasant truth, could be
deceived. The artist could be as profound as he wished without

being resented if he concealed his profundities under a pleasant
or sensational narrative surface through which the reader looking
for mere diversion could not penetrate. Thus greatness could be
achieved in the public art of fiction in the nineteenth century,
as it had been in Shakespeare's theater. The idea is hinted in
Mardi, when Media, warning Babbalanja of the Abrazzas of the
world, shuts off the philosopher's undisguised speculations on
religion with the words, "Meditate as much as you will, but say
little aloud, unless in a merry mythical way." He had practiced
the merrily mythical in *Moby-Dick,* with some success, if one
may judge by reviews which admired the surface and nothing
else. He brooded about how Shakespeare, beneath the surfaces
of "popularizing noise and show of broad farce and blood-
besmeared tragedy," "craftily" puts into the mouths of dark
characters like Hamlet and Timon "things which we feel to be
so terrifically true, that it were all but madness" for any writer
"in his own proper character, to utter, or even hint of them,"
and how this "madness of vital truth" is undetected by the public
which burns its "tuns of rancid fat" at Shakespeare's shrine.

In the summer of 1850 he discovered in Hawthorne the
darkness and the depth of Shakespeare, and was convinced that
his neighbor was not only, like Shakespeare, "almost utterly
mistaken" by his readers, but that he deliberately courted misunderstanding in order to protect himself. Indeed, this genius
"takes great delight in hoodwinking the world," partly by giving
his dark stories innocent titles (like "Young Goodman Brown")
which are "directly calculated to deceive—egregiously deceive,
the superficial skimmer of pages." In 1851, when he was finishing
Moby-Dick and beginning *Pierre,* he had long talks of "things
of this world and of the next, and books and publishers" with
Hawthorne, who, for the first time, was reaching a large public
with serious fiction. It was at this point that Melville deserted
the adventure narrative and conceived a domestic thriller in
which, under a surface of popular formulas, he would dive to

greater depths than he had reached in *Moby-Dick*. "Leviathan is not the biggest fish," he wrote as he began *Pierre*; "I have heard of Krakens."

The result of all this scheming was an out-and-out attempt to invest the sensational love novel with the dignity and profundity of Shakespearian tragedy. Pierre and Lucy are presented as agrarian aristocrats and are put at the top of the American social pyramid in order to provide for the classic tragic "fall." The gaudy plot is a vehicle for profound psychological perceptions. The country-boy hero is an intellectual and introspective as Hamlet. The language and dialogue, a combination of Shakespeare and Mrs. E. D. E. N. Southworth of the *Ledger*, are elevated right out of the realm of recognizable English speech. And the plot, which a *Ledger* writer would have twisted into a happy ending at the last moment, is allowed to follow its natural course to a catastrophe which kills off the good and the bad alike. He puts into Pierre's mouth the "vital truth" which it would be "madness" for him to utter "in his own proper character"—but not "craftily" enough. The reviewers promptly identified Pierre with Melville and found him both mad and socially dangerous.

Once more, the fault lay partly in Melville's bad handling of speculative commentary and of technical point of view. Much as readers either disliked or ignored the speculation in *Moby-Dick,* he had tried to lead them gently into it—indeed to train them in speculation. In the chapter on "The Whiteness of the Whale," for example, his object was to get the reader to entertain the *possibility—not* the certainty—that behind the immensities of the universe there is a blank void of nothingness, of No-God, from which emanate terrors beyond our comprehension. Aware that a generation which had been taught to read by the Scotch rhetoricians tended toward stock responses to images, he worked patiently to complicate these responses without destroying them. After a long list of the accepted benign associations of whiteness, he tried to lead the reader, example by example, to the realization that white is also the symbol of terror, and that therefore malignity and benignity are inseparably one. The climactic paragraph, in which the appalling proposition is put, is not assertion but question. The reader is told not that evil is absolute but that *if* we grasp imaginatively all the associations of whiteness, then we are in a position to understand a madman's "fiery hunt" for the source of evil. But we are also warned that he who sees nothing but the "colorless, all-color of a-theism" is a "wretched infidel" who "gazes himself blind." Again and again, in this chapter, Melville begs the reader to concentrate and to collaborate with him. "Let us try," he says at one point, "for without imagination no man can follow another into these halls." Note the community between writer and reader that is implied or invited by the *us* and by the use of "another" (man) instead of the divisive pronoun "me."

This sense of community is wholly lacking in the speculations in *Pierre*. No collaboration is invited, and the reader gets no guidance toward possibility. Properly guided, he might, perhaps, have understood that Pierre's progress toward disbelief in virtue (which is the theme of the book) is a necessity of *his* character, not of Melville's; that what was necessity for Pierre was possibility for Melville; that the denouement does not prove that Melville thinks Pierre is right—only that the possibility of a man's thinking like Pierre constitutes the "tragedy of mind." We recall that, in the denouement of *Moby-Dick,* a regenerated, believing Ishmael survives not only shipwreck but his own speculative thinking.

Much of Melville's blundering in *Pierre* may have been due to his having radically reconceived and rewritten it during the course of composition. On January 8, 1852, he wrote Mrs. Hawthorne, "I shall not again send you a bowl of salt water. The next chalice I shall commend, will be a rural bowl of milk." On February 20 he signed a contract with Harpers for a book of about 360 pages. On April 16 he wrote his English publisher that his book could be about 150 pages longer than the one he had first proposed. In the finished book the first five-eighths (to Book 16) is rural; the rest is urban. Nothing in the rural part prepares us for the revelation in Book 17 that the country youth is a popular author deeply involved in the literary commerce of the big city; in fact, Melville belligerently concludes a lame apology for this surprise by saying, "At any rate, I write precisely as I please." This is only one of the many places where Melville is an intrusive nuisance, who talks over his hero's shoulder or patently puts his own thinking, with which his critics had long been familiar, into Pierre's head.

In revision, then, Melville added a story of authorship, which ends in defeat, to a tragedy of morals. The denouements of both are artificially—almost comically—synchronized. I conjecture that, finding his initial plot inadequate to motivate the catastrophic change in Pierre's moral thinking—from complete innocence to a knowledge of evil—Melville arranged for him to find himself and clarify his problem by writing a book. This was a mistake. For not only is the hero a writer, an intellectual, and a full-blown example of the "misunderstood Genius," as cordially detested by the public then as he is now, but the public, as readers and publishers, become villains who crucify the Genius. Even in the rural story Melville as narrator had gone out of his way to excoriate the popular novel and those who read it; to accuse the world of "unforgiveable affronts and insults" to poets like Dante; of missing the "deeper meanings" of Shakespeare. Now, with the sufferings of Pierre as author to spur him on, he accuses his readers of judging literature as they do morals, of praising an author's worst books, or liking his best ones for the wrong reasons; and pictures the publishers who serve them as thievish illiterates. In short, "though the world worship Mediocrity and Common Place, yet hath it fire and sword for all contemporary Grandeur." And the future will be worse, for authors will be as "scarce as alchymists" and the "mass of humanity reduced to one level of dotage." The world repaid Melville in kind for these compliments, and his reputation never recovered from the attack on *Pierre*.

One would expect this to have been the climax of Melville's quarrel, but it was not. He continued as professional author for seven more years—to 1859—chiefly as an anonymous magazinist. Ironically enough, it was in magazines that he practiced most successfully the deceptions he had intended in *Pierre*. In two books and fifteen magazine pieces he did some of the darkest and bitterest writing of his life. But he had learned his lesson, as he explicitly admitted when he submitted *Israel Potter* for serialization: in apparent capitulation, he promised the editor that it would contain "very little reflective writing in it; nothing weighty." He continued, in other works, to be reflective and weighty, but his thinking is so solidly embodied in situation, or so well disguised in the dialogue of deceptively cheerful or dull-witted or eccentric characters that it cannot often be imputed to him. Occasionally the old embattled Melville rises to the surface. Even *Israel Potter*, in its ironical dedication to the Bunker Hill Monument, contains some thinly covered bitterness about fame in America. And in "The Encantadas" he has the enemy in mind when he declares that he omits two crucial episodes from the widow's story because "I will not file this thing complete for scoffing souls to quote. . . . In nature, as in law, it may be libelous to speak some truths." But on the whole he masks his rejections of public values and slogans so skilfully that, although twelve out of fifteen of his magazine pieces deal essentially and unsentimentally with some kind of loss, poverty, loneliness, or defeat, some of the blackest of these were praised as "quaint," "fanciful," "lifelike," "genial," and "thoroughly magazinish." His most impudent piece of deception was a takeoff on the popular "sunshine-and-shadow" theme. "Cock-a-doodle-doo!" appeared in *Harper's Magazine*, which its founder had dedicated to "the plain people . . . not philosophers and poets." The narrator in this story is cured of a case of the "doleful dumps" by the inspirational crowing of a distant rooster. Tracing the bird to a miserable hovel, he finds its owner, his wife, and their three children cheerfully and optimistically dying of sickness and starvation. The rooster then crows itself to death in an ecstasy of "affirmation." Today this piece would not fool even a *Life* magazine editorial writer, but a contemporary reviewer called it "lively and animated."

Yet, if I interpret correctly one of Melville's most enigmatic stories, he had finally come to terms with himself as a writer, in his time, and in America. "The Fiddler" (1853) is a parable about genius, reputation, and fame. In *Harper's*, where it appeared, it seemed to harmonize comfortably with popular middle-class writings, like G. W. Curtis' *Prue and I*, which deprecate ambition and celebrate simple contentment. The fiddler, Hautboy, is a former English prodigy, who, at the age of twelve, had received the homage of the crowd on the London stage. For reasons not given, he had resigned from his status as genius, and now, at forty, he is an American who teaches fiddling for a living, walks Broadway "happy as a king"—and "no man knows him." The narrator, Helmstone, is a poet, whose classical tragedy has been attacked by the press. At the circus, watching the crowd's enjoyment of the clowns, he thinks bitterly of the rebuff he would get if he were to read to such people one of his "sublime passages."

So far, analogies with Melville's career, past and future, are obvious. His serious work, too, had been attacked, and he also was to resign and to walk Broadway unknown until his death. But we hear a new note when, at the circus, the poet is struck by the genius's innocent delight in the clowns, and his capacity to share simple pleasures with the crowd. Hautboy's "honest cheeriness disdained my disdain. My intolerant pride was rebuked." The fiddler is again at one with the crowd when, at home, he plays "Yankee Doodle" and other common tunes. Yet the listening poet is "transfixed by something miraculously superior in the style," and his "whole splenetic soul capitulated

to the magic fiddle," to the "bow of [this] enchanter." And as
he plays, the fiddler has a "divine and immortal air, like that
of some forever youthful god of Greece."

When a third character tells the persecuted poet that
"neglected merit, genius ignored, or impotent presumption" are
all much the same thing, we come close to the meaning of the
story. I take this to be that no writer can know whether his
productions are the stuff of immortality, or rubbish. What is
durable is not the Epic—the Big Job—in itself; this can fail
precisely because it attempts something beyond mortal achievement. But style, which is the expression of character, is immortal.
And the real fruit of genius is not the epic it attempts but the
character which genius achieves while creating. Hautboy's reward
lies in his mature capacity for life itself. His good sense and good
humor enable him "intuitively to hit the exact line between
enthusiasm and apathy," "to see the world pretty much as it
[is]." Yet "he did not theoretically espouse its bright side nor
its dark side. Rejecting all solutions, he but acknowledged facts.
What was sad in the world he did not superficially gainsay; what
was glad in it he did not cynically slur; and all which was to
him personally enjoyable, he gratefully took to his heart."

Can we say that this version of genius and this truce with the
insensitive public was the final settlement of Melville's long
quarrel with readers? One never knows with him. "The Fiddler"
seems to anticipate the studied resignation in *Billy Budd,* which
he did not publish. The conclusion of his career in print was
logically perfect: two volumes of verse privately printed, in
editions of twenty-five copies each.

*Read before the English Institute on September 3, 1957.

1. That four of his most popular books are slightly fictionalized autobiographical
travel rather than novels makes his case the more significant; for it is precisely in
this borderland between forms of fact (that is, travel, history, and the literal
representation of manners) and forms of fiction that the American novel became
a respectable literary genre (respectable, that is, in the eyes of the cultivated
contemporary reader) during the first sixty years of its existence.

2. Chapter LXIII. Melville reports this not as a "modest young man," but as an observer with a touristic and anthropological interest in the "heathenish games and dances which still secretly lingered in the valley." He watches from a hiding place, and the girls are guarded by "hideous old crones who might have been duennas." Rather perversely, however, he points up the sexual symbolism of the dance by recording that it was with difficulty that he restrained his companion from "rushing [out of the bushes] and seizing a partner." The dance was at first a part of the manuscript of *Typee*, from which he excluded it because, possibly, in that context it would have been more personal than in *Omoo*. Melville to John Murray, January 29, 1847: "You will perceive that there is a chapter in the book which describes a dance in the valley of Tamai. This description has been modified and adapted from a certain chapter which it was thought best to exclude from *Typee*."

3. Chapter III. The whole chapter is an elaborate exposition of his social status and identity in relation to the character of the common sailor.

4. See a representative comment by Melville's friend, E. A. Duyckinck: In *Moby-Dick* (which Duyckinck greatly admired) Melville's "extravagant daring speculation is out of place and uncomfortable," and it violates "the most sacred associations of life."

5. Compare the autobiographical passage in *Pierre*, where the publishers write the young author, "Sir:—You are a swindler. Upon the pretense of writing a popular novel for us, you have been receiving cash advances from us, while passing through our press the sheets of a blasphemous rhapsody, filched from the vile Atheists, Lucian and Voltaire" (Book 26, sec. iv).

6. This was now Melville's view of his earlier works. In explaining to John Murray why he changed *Mardi* from a continuation of *Omoo* to a work of fancy, he said, "Well: proceeding in my narrative of *facts* I began to feel an incurable distaste for the same; & . . . felt irked, cramped & fettered by plodding along with dull common places . . . " (March 25, 1848).

7. See his comment less than a month after it appeared: " . . . My mood has so changed, that I dread to look into it, & have purposely abstained from so doing since I thanked God it was off my hands" (April 5, 1849). If one accepts Pierre's writing of his magnum opus as analogous to the writing of *Mardi,* the second paragraph of Book 21, sec. i, in *Pierre* suggests that Melville had some regrets about having loaded *Mardi* with undigested reading.

8. A unique exception deserves to be remembered: " . . . Other parts [of *Mardi*] require a wide-awake application, or, as in 'Gulliver's Travels,' one half the aroma will be lost. . . . The book invites study, and deserves . . . close investigation" (*Albion*, April 21, 1849).

9. Nothing in *Typee* and *Omoo*, and nothing in all the documents printed in Jay Leyda's *Melville Log*, suggests that Melville thought about his writing in terms of genius, or in anything but commercial terms, before January 1, 1848. But on March 25 of the same year he wrote the famous letter to Murray announcing the newly conceived *Mardi*. Thereafter, the concept of genius pervades his writings and his correspondence with Hawthorne.

CHAPTER FOURTEEN

Literary Economics and Literary History

O NE OF THE most interesting reactions to the *Literary History of the United States* has been a demand for a revision of the methods of literary history. Discussing the work in a recent issue of the *Kenyon Review*, Professor René Wellek declares that the way out of the problem of literary history "can only be through a definition of its subject matter, through a development of a clear methodology, through a conception of what is meant by history and what is meant by literature." I agree on all counts. It is easy to agree also with the opinion quite evidently held by Wellek and Warren, in their distinguished book, *The Theory of Literature,* that literary history is not sufficiently literary. I believe that it is equally important to recognize, however, that much literary history is arid because it is not historical enough. It is a safe estimate that 95 per cent of all past literature, by any definition of that word, has little or no intrinsic value for the intelligent, non-academic, non-scholarly reader of today. The real present value of books that once interested readers is historical, the same kind of value that we attach to a past election, revolution, railroad system, school law, or system of ideas. Literary historians sometimes try to persuade us that a dead book is really still alive because it embodies an idea or exhibits a form that is still current. One might as well argue that grandfather is still alive because he was a Republican or a yogi. Literary history has been much too busy trying to prove that past writers shouted loud enough to be heard by posterity. We should be more interested in knowing how far their voices carried in their own generation, and—equally important—whether their generation talked back.

It has been recognized often enough that the relation between the writer and society is reciprocal. But recognition is not enough; we need more demonstration. The tendency is to assign a dynamic role in this relationship to the author only, and a merely passive one to society as represented by the reader. Still worse, most scholars assume that literary history can be adequately represented by a line—with the writer at one end and the reader at the other. Actually, instead of being merely linear, the pattern is triangular. Opposite both the writer and the reader stands the whole complex organism of the book and magazine trade—a trade which for the last two centuries, at least, has had a positive and dynamic function in the world of literature. In this triangle, cultural force or influence runs in both directions. The book trade is acted upon by both writer and reader, and in receiving their influence the book trade interprets it and therefore transmutes it. Correspondingly, writer and reader dictate to, and are dictated to by, the book trade.

These reciprocal influences are complex, and our instruments for determining and evaluating them are, to say the least, inadequate. Current criticism and anthropology are attempting to illuminate them through the concept of "myth." According to Wellek and Warren, the imaginative artist's "need" for myth is "a sign of his felt need for communion with his society, for a recognized status as artist functioning within society." Certainly the concept of "myth" is a rich and rewarding one for literary study. But though critics identify past myths readily—and recklessly—enough (recent articles on *The Confidence-Man* and *Billy Budd* are examples), how do they know whether or when the artist *succeeded* in communing with society by means of myth? Surely the question is relevant. Until we know more about public response to myth, myth-hunting will remain what it is at present

—a playground for the critical imagination, rather than a branch of cultural history. A writer's success in communing with society cannot be determined by guesswork. The critic and historian both need instruments: publishers' records; the correspondence of authors and editors (much of it still unpublished); facts about the circulation of magazines and sales of books; and—most difficult of all to find—reliable evidence of reader response.

I propose from this point on to explore some reader-writer-book trade relations in America between 1800 and 1860, with the purpose of suggesting methods for getting at some of the neglected realities of cultural history. I hope to show that recognition of the triangular pattern I have suggested will contribute a better understanding of the ways in which writers have produced and communicated.

The book trade first. We recognize at once that through the book trade the whole economic life of the nation was brought to bear upon literature and literary life. The rise and decline of literary centers is to be explained not by theories of "culture cities" but by the facts of transportation. In one period a new and regular packet line to England gave Philadelphia priority in the reprinting of Scott and Byron, thus enabling that city to dominate American literary publishing for two decades. The geographical isolation of Boston kept it from being the literary center it is generally supposed to have been until mid-century, when a railroad line across the Berkshires enabled its publishers to compete in the western market. But a deep harbor and the Erie Canal insured the eventual and permanent leadership of New York in literary publishing.

Other economic facts were equally compelling. Any depression, any spurt of wildcat banking, an early freeze on the inland waterways, might result in a writer's being told, "We are accepting no new books," or "Yours must wait two or four or six months." Improvements in technology, leading to cheap printing, helped to kill the American novel temporarily in the forties because the market was flooded with ten and twenty-five cent editions of British novels. Publishers then said to American writers, "Stop writing novels and turn out short stories for magazines." But competition killed off the reprinters of foreign works, and publishers said, "Give us novels again." Stereotyping was perfected, and books that might have died in a year were kept in circulation for ten or twenty.

Then, too, we have never recognized the effect of discount policy upon the sale and circulation of books, upon the American writer's prosperity, and ultimately upon regional culture. In the 1820's, for example, native novels retailed in America for the same price as British novels—about two dollars; but Cooper had to be paid and Scott did not, and Cooper's royalties had to be squeezed out of discounts. A Philadelphia bookseller got a 45 per cent discount on Scott in quantity; a maximum of one-third on Cooper. His profit on a Cooper book was adequate when he sold it at retail in Philadelphia, but when he sold it to book-shops in the interior he had to split the discount, and half of one-third was not an attractive profit for either wholesaler or retailer. Therefore, in a Pittsburgh bookshop Scott had an advantage over Cooper that had nothing to do with literary quality. As a result, American literature in the twenties had an adequate circulation in Atlantic urban centers, where distributors could take the whole discount; but for obvious reasons its circulation in the interior was limited. On the other hand, British literature flowed west in much greater quantity. This fact, of course, has some implications for cultural history.

Until mid-century Emerson's essays were not widely sold outside New England because he would not let his publishers discount his books at more than 10 or 20 per cent. When a new race of enterprising Boston publishers took over his books in the fifties, his work was for the first time made easily available to a national audience. Literary history tends to place Emerson's audience and influence in the thirties and forties, which is correct as far as his relations with contemporary writers is concerned. But he did not have a national audience or a national response until the second half of the century.

Other economic factors also influenced literary form. When Scott began to write his romances, the booksellers of Great Britain had established the three-decker as the most profitable form for the publication of fiction. By 1820 new Waverly romances were selling at thirty shillings a set. Scott's share of this was one-sixth, and his return on the first issue of *Ivanhoe* was $15,000 (about $60,000 in terms of modern money). At that rate Scott could not afford to worry about functional or organic construction. The material for every novel was poured into the three-decker like so much concrete into wooden forms. But, as the American market could not absorb the expensive three-volume set, Scott was republished here in two-volume, two-dollar sets. When Cooper began writing in 1820, the two-volume novel was his predetermined form. For thirty years, no matter what his theme or plot, he padded and stretched and invented incident to fill two volumes of four hundred pages each. So did his contemporaries—Neal, Kennedy, Sedgwick, Simms. Any study of the form of novels in that period ought to begin with recognition of this crude fact.

As economic pressures had formed the two-volume pattern, so, in the 1840's, other economic pressures broke it. In the violence of American competition for British books, our publishers were forced to print novels in one volume, because that form was cheaper, and to charge according to length. Now a novel in one volume could be as short as *The Scarlet Letter* or as long as *Moby-Dick*. We discern organic form in both works. We should remember that both were published during a brief era when the book trade did not dictate some aspects of form to the professional novelist.

In the late fifties a new economic influence on the form of the novel took up where the old one left off. Magazine serialization of fiction had been going on sporadically since the eighteenth century, but in 1850 *Harper's New Monthly Magazine* established permanently the lure of the words "to be continued." Because from then on the novelist could sell his books at least twice, it was a foregone conclusion that the novel would become the dominant literary form for professional writers. But the novelist paid for his new prosperity by submitting to a new tyranny. Editors began to dictate the length and number of instalments, and instalment publishing itself predetermined form to a certain extent. A writer could not simply send an editor thirty pages of his manuscript for the March issue; he had to finish off the instalment as a unit, and, if possible, make the reader look forward to April. Can there be any doubt that the form of the novel after 1850 was affected by the economic fact of serialization? Much criticism of the form of James and Howells is simply naïve because of a failure to look at their work as it appeared serially in magazines, and at the correspondence (most of it unpublished) in which they quarreled, sometimes bitterly, with editors over problems of instalment publishing.

Poetry was not exempt from such material pressures, as a rather appalling episode of 1845 shows. *Graham's Magazine* is mentioned in all the literary histories, but one is rarely taken into its inner sanctum where literary history was made. The editor had agreed to pay Longfellow fifty dollars a poem on condition that he publish in no other magazine. Longfellow consented, but one of his contributions drew a protest from Graham. The poet had charged fifty dollars for a sonnet. This, hinted the editor, was cheating: it raised the cost of verse to almost four dollars a line, and did not fill enough space for the money. The editor's economy was not the poet's. Graham operated on a budget—so many pages to be filled, so much cash to be paid for filling them. But, as Thoreau had pointed out, the poet has an economy too. From Longfellow's point of view, a sonnet might cost as much in time, work, and inspiration as forty lines of quatrains. One can assume a connection between this episode and the fact that, before the fifties, Longfellow, an excellent sonneteer, wrote few sonnets but many poems in space-consuming quatrains. The foregoing examples and episodes indicate, I think, that the role of the book trade in American literary culture was anything but passive. We are only now beginning to write the history of that trade; but the findings of such scholars as W. S. Tryon, Rollo Silver, and Walter Sutton,* when made available, will contribute to a much needed revision of our literary history.

So much for the place of the book trade in the pattern. We are perhaps even more ignorant of the reader as a force in literary culture. Here the problem of method is particularly troublesome. Theoretically there can be no complete account of the reception of a work of literature until every reader's reaction to it has been polled and classified, and this, of course, is impossible. Actually there are many little used shortcuts which offer acceptable clues to reader response. Publishers' sales records, of course, are primary evidence. So are the library circulation reports which began in the seventies and which were printed in the book-trade journals. Otherwise, the most valuable evidence lies scattered in the correspondence of authors, publishers, and editors.

To return to the unpublished Longfellow-Graham letters for illustration. Before the Graham era of economically efficient literary magazines, American poetry was seldom paid for, and editors did not think it worth while to copyright the contents of their issues. As a result, newspapers throughout the country clipped freely from the magazines such poetry as most pleased their readers. For this reason, by 1840, some poets were beginning to enjoy a national reputation even before the advent of national magazines and publishers. It is probably safe to say that the

---

* See Walter Sutton, *The Western Book Trade: Cincinnati as a Nineteenth-Century Publishing and Book-Trade Center* (Columbus, Ohio, 1961) ; W. S. Tryon, *Parnassus Corner* (Boston, 1963) ; and Rollo Silver, *The American Printer, 1787–1825* (Charlottesville, Va., 1967).—ED.

rise of a truly popular national poetry was directly connected
with this neglect of editors to take advantage of copyright law.
After Graham had built up a circulation big enough to permit
high payment to authors, he used the statistics of newspaper
reprints as a measure of a poet's popularity and rate of pay.
Thus Graham wrote Longfellow in 1844, explaining why Lowell's
poems were worth only twenty-five dollars: "I know the test of
general popularity as well as any man—and he [Lowell] has
it not. He is well-known in New England and appreciated there
but has not a tythe of the reputation *South* and *West* possessed
by yourself and Bryant. This, of course, I *know*—it is no guess
work, for with a thousand exchange papers scattered all over the
whole Union I should be a dolt in business not to *see* who is most
copied and *praised* by them." Graham was right, and the records
of Ticknor and Fields, Lowell's publishers after 1848, confirm
his judgment. Here is evidence of reader response which should
not be overlooked by historians.

Nothing better demonstrates the dilemma of literary history
than its uncertainty about what to do with popular writers in
general, and with the fireside poets—Bryant, Longfellow, Whittier, Lowell, Holmes—in particular. In every new history the
space devoted to them shrinks. The shrinkage may be justified
on critical, but hardly on historical, grounds, for the importance
of these poets in their own century cannot decrease. We err,
as historians, in allowing the taste of the modern reader to
nullify the taste of the nineteenth-century reader. It is as if
the political historian were to ignore the administration of
Grant because it was not in accord with the social principles of
Franklin D. Roosevelt.

The error, I think, arises in part from our persistent neglect
of the reader as a force in literature. The more we neglect him,
the more we lose in historical perspective. And I suggest that
we do not gain perspective by relying on the contemporary
critical reception of a writer as an index to his standing with

his readers. We have had a good many "reception" or "reputation" studies in recent years, and historians have drawn upon them heavily. A doctoral candidate faithfully and tiresomely quotes from all the contemporary reviews he can find, adds them up, and says, this book was successful in its time, this one was not. The method is unrealistic and misleading, because it ignores certain practices of the book trade. In some periods the favorable tone of most book notices means simply that periodicals wished to be kept on the publisher's free list and to receive complimentary copies of his expensive books along with those which he simply wished to plug. Sometimes publishers put reviewers on their payrolls as professional readers and enjoyed, as a result, a certain amount of immunity or privilege. Often, favorable reviews originated in the publisher's office; or the publisher clipped a good notice from a journal, copied it, and sent it around to all the other journals where the reviewers were too busy, or too tired, to read all the books they discussed. In some periods criticism reflected inter- or intra-urban literary gang squabbles. In the era of the gentleman-author, well-known writers had friends in practically all the leading magazine and newspaper offices. We cynically recognize that many of these facts are operative in the publishing world of today. Why do we become credulous when as literary historians we make use of past criticism?

But beyond all this stands the fact that the reviewer, or critic, was and is simply another reader. His thinking may have represented that of a group or a class, but so did that of the individual reader. Particularly before the establishment in the 1850's of regular signed book-review columns, which bore the stamp of professional and predictable critics like George Ripley, a book notice might represent the opinion of a thousand, a hundred, or no readers at all—except the critic. Consider the hostile critical reception of Cooper's *The Bravo,* and then note that sales records show this to have been one of his most popular books. Cooper himself early decided that sales figures were the only true index to his standing with the public, that there was no necessary correlation between critical response and reader response. Publishers have always recognized the unreliability of critical opinion as a trade index. They do not care what a critic says as long as he says it. In the book trade it is not criticism that matters but publicity. To the historian, past criticism, though sometimes useful as a clue to the thinking of the segment of society that produced it, is almost valueless as a guide to reader taste.

Turning finally to the place of the writer in the pattern, we recognize at once that in so far as he was dependent upon, and influenced by, the reader and the book trade, he was not only artist but economic man, and that his artistry and economics were usually at war with each other. As artist he had his private vision, his values, his aesthetic or intellectual or spiritual mission, which rarely corresponded exactly with the values and ideals of the society in which he lived. Inevitably he was alienated from much of society part of the time, and from some of it all the time.

This alienation was intensified by his sense of his social place as an artist. Historically, the creative writer was not a worker or producer, but a gentleman-amateur who exhibited his talent to his social equals but did not depend upon it for a living; or he accepted the patronage of a social superior, and was still independent of buyers and readers. He wrote when the spirit moved him, endured none of the pressures of commerical time and the market, sought reputation— "fame" in the Renaissance sense—but not publicity. In a pecuniary society under democratic patronage, this proud and independent attitude was an anachronism, but vestiges of it survived until 1850 and later. We recognize the typical attitudes of the patrician writer in the literary magazines of early decades, like the *Monthly Anthology*, which, according to their title pages, were edited by "societies of

gentlemen"—and not for profit. We perceive them in the letters
of Jefferson, William Wirt, Hugh Swinton Légaré, Francis P.
Gilmer, and young Emerson, who conceived of the "literary
profession" as a life of study and scholarship to be pursued by
gentlemen of independent income. Long after Byron and Scott
had proved that a gentleman could write for money, we see
the mark of the patrician in the American writer's demand
for privacy, for dignity in his commercial relations, and in his
resistance to commercial exploitation. Gentleman psychology
largely explains the persistence of literary anonymity—the fact
that Cooper and Irving kept their names off their title pages until
the early forties. Irving in 1820 even hesitated to send out review
copies to strangers lest he seem to be courting the favor of the
market; Longfellow in the forties objected to the use of his
name on the mastheads of magazines to which he contributed;
Emerson in the fifties severely restricted the advertising of his
books—at the very moment when Barnum, Beecher, and Bonner
were inventing the modern art of ballyhoo. But such reticences
were doomed. Books had become articles of commerce, as Cooper
frankly recognized. Authors' names were brand names; to be
sold, goods must be "promoted." And of what avail was an
anonymous title page when copyright law required that the
owner of a work put his name on the back of that page?

Under these conditions the fastidious attitudes of gentleman
authors could not survive. During the twenties and thirties
writers like Irving, Cooper, and Emerson, who began as patrician
amateurs, were transformed into hard-working professionals, but
they never ceased resenting the forces that brought about that
change. Yet the American author of the period was resourceful
in protecting his integrity from the pressures of the market and
of democratic patronage. During the twenties he learned that
if he went to a publisher with nothing but a manuscript in his
hands he was at the mercy not only of the shaky financial
structure of the book trade but of the publisher's interpretation

of public taste. The publisher might, and frequently did, say, "No, I cannot risk my capital on this book; take it away, and write it differently, or write something else"—or, just "Take it away." But the writer was not so vulnerable if he could reply, "I will take the risk of manufacturing costs; you will simply distribute for me. I will decide the probable market and the number of copies to be printed; I will dictate the terms of discount to retailers; I will tell you how much and what kind of promotion I will endure. In short, I will decide who and where my public is, and on what terms I will meet it." There were other ways of controlling the book trade and resisting reader pressures, but all of them, like this one, required the writer's investment of capital. Conspicuously absent from the ranks of those who had this protective margin of capital were Poe, Hawthorne, and Melville; they were also the writers who suffered most in their struggle to make some adjustment with society.

But even for writers without capital there was another strategy for maintaining a kind of independence from democratic patronage. Most of them—not, of course, fortunates like Cooper and Prescott, or unfortunates like Melville—had secondary occupations, to which they resorted either regularly or occasionally—teaching, lecturing, or public office. For the writer who either could not or would not write regularly books which the public would buy in sufficient quantity to support him, this protection was essential. But the secondary occupation was not and never has been a complete solution of the artist's problem. An artist rarely has full control of the flow of his creative energy; he can seldom keep his other energies in a separate tank, to be drained from nine to five, and then turn on the creative tap after supper. Hawthorne in the customhouse is an example, and his problem justifies a brief digression into the subject of the American writer as officeholder.

I estimate that from 1800 to 1870, from 60 to 75 per cent of all male American writers who even approached professionalism

either held public office or tried to get it. James Kirk Paulding
set the pattern, by managing, during his twenty-five years with
the Navy Department, to write seventeen books, contribute to
at least ten magazines and gift books, and grind out the equivalent of twenty or thirty volumes of political copy for newspapers. One may either suspect the quality of Paulding's public
service or question the propriety of well-paid public sinecures
which permitted an officeholder to channel so much of his
energy into another occupation; but there is no doubt that
Paulding's achievement opened new vistas to the American
writer. Officeholding seemed a perfect solution for the writer's
problem. It offered financial security, leisure to create as one
could, and freedom to say what one pleased rather than what
the public demanded. It was a kind of republican patronage,
similar to the monarchical variety, but better. Some editors
even suggested that such employment of writers be put on
an official basis, as a way of subsidizing the arts, and that
beneficiaries also be granted pensions.

By 1860 some customhouses and foreign legations resembled
salons, but no miracles occurred. Some writers, like Hawthorne
and Irving, took their jobs too seriously to have any creative
energy left over. Others found that monotonous routine killed
their literary spirit, or that enforced loyalty to the party that
held them under obligation damaged their integrity. Still others
discovered that it was easier simply to live in an official rut
than to use the job as they had originally intended. In the end
this new resource left the American author where it had found
him: in the trap that always catches the creative artist who is
also economic man.

The tensions within the artist, and between himself and
society, are revealed in the very form and substance of his work.
In the last twenty years of Cooper's career we see political novels
and tracts sandwiched in among romances of land and sea and
the past, and we call it versatility. But we do not see the stubborn
three-cornered battle between him, the reader, and the pub-

lisher in which he tried to force upon the reader sugar-coated political doctrine which he thought medicinal. In the long run the reader was right in rejecting the medicine: Cooper's best novels were those which the public liked and bought most. We see Hawthorne as a short-story writer whose tales are often blighted by bald explanations of obvious symbolism; but we do not see the magazine and gift book audience which demanded these awkward and extraneous clarifications; nor do we see the trade conditions which led to his abrupt abandonment of the short story entirely in 1850. We see in his novels wretched final chapters in which he tied the threads of story lumpily together as if he were afraid the whole plot might unravel; but we do not see that such devices were forced upon him by publishers in response to the demands of readers who wanted to know what finally happened to Miriam and Donatello, and whether Hilda and Kenyon got married. We see Emerson's recent and able biographer transforming him from an aspiring transcendental essayist into a worldly observer of English civilization and a stale repeater of his own ideas. But is it not more important to recognize that twenty years of professional lecturing on the lyceum platform taught Emerson how to communicate, and transformed him from a spokesman for a small coterie into a spokesman for a nation? We see Melville's *Pierre* as a complicated philosophical performance, not as the desperate and unsuccessful attempt it really was to write a novel in the popular vein.

We, as modern readers of these writers, have gained about as much as we have lost by the pressures which contemporary readers and the book trade exerted upon them. Men like Poe, Melville, Hawthorne, and Emerson, who had the humility to recognize reader taste and reader resistance not as a blank wall of banality and superficiality but as a challenge to their ability as craftsmen, were at their best when they accepted the challenge. Emerson's *Essays* of 1841 and 1844 are superior to his *Nature* of 1836 because in the intervening years his lyceum audiences had made him express himself more plainly and more concretely. Poe's great short stories might never have been written had not the public, by rejecting his first three books of verse, forced him into the field of fiction. The superb balance of physical and imaginative adventure in *Moby-Dick* is partly traceable to the contemporary reader's preferring *Typee* and *Omoo* to *Mardi*. Hawthorne might never have turned to the novel had not a publisher—a shrewd interpreter of reader taste—persuaded him that his professional future lay in that field.

To sum up, the artist was sometimes at his best when the two pressures—creative and social—were in equilibrium. Many of the books which we still read, and most of those which we reject, reflect an imbalance—too much artist, or too much society. But it was the artist in balance with society who produced *Tales of the Grotesque and Arabesque, English Traits,* and *Moby-Dick*.

The limitations of the approach I have presented are obvious. It has little relevance, for example, to the historical study of non-professional writers like Thoreau, Whitman, and Emily Dickinson. It is ancillary—and subordinate to—the historical study of ideas, of nationalism, of regionalism, and of cultural dynamics. But for all of these fields it is a potential corrective.

CHAPTER FIFTEEN

The People's Patronage

EVEN BEFORE the onset of the Civil War, the Middle West had become a crude power, a quantitative if not a qualitative force, in the collective life of the nation—and a mission field ripe for the eager, if at times momentarily discouraged, evangels of culture from the East. Emerson at St. Louis in 1852 doubted that there was a "thinking or even reading man" among 95,000 souls; and in 1866, in an Iowa town, he perceived that, though here was "America in the making, America in the raw . . . it doesn't want much to go to lecture, and tis pity to drive it."

This impression was confirmed by some of the newspapers. Cleveland was scornful that this "perpendicular coffin" should talk to the West about the "law of success," and Detroit reported that he was palming off the "sayings of old almanacs and spelling books; . . . putting transcendentalism on stilts for the admiration of natives." Quincy, Illinois, described him as "Another Bore," and Bloomington as "Ralph Cold-Dough Simmerson." Yet, year after year, in late autumn, he set off wearily to the land of promise, pushing as far and as fast as the new railroads would take him, for like all professional lecturers he knew that he must now seek his market west of the Hudson. And year after year listeners continued to come. Perhaps they hoped that next week John Godfrey Saxe would turn up with funny verse, or Bayard Taylor with his genius for bringing Persia to Peoria, or John B. Gough to give them a near-view of a reformed drunkard. It was significant, however, that though an Iowa town might, one week, listen to Emerson on "Power" and, next week, to

"Professor" Oscanyan (dressed in Turkish costume and accompanied by three females in harem pajamas) on "The Domestic Life of the Turks," it was Emerson who derived his basic income from lecturing for thirty-five years, not the "Professor." Emerson once explained, "In every one of these expanding towns is a knot of loving New Englanders who cherish the Lyceum out of love of the Charles and the Merrimac and the Connecticut rivers," but this was a limited and insular version of the truth. The fact was (and Emerson knew it) that the cultural isolationism and localism of the old Northeast was breaking down: the whole of the North, from Boston to the Mississippi, with Baltimore, Pittsburgh, and Cincinnati as a southern boundary, was becoming a cultural unit.

The key to this momentous development was the railroads which spread from the Alleghenies to the Mississippi Valley between 1850 and 1870—ten thousand new miles of them before the war. Any observant trainman (on the run from Albany to Cleveland, for example) could have seen the symbols. In the coaches were not only Emerson, but Horace Greeley, George William Curtis, and Anna Dickinson, all with lectures newly tried out in New York or in New England villages; Dion Boucicault's road company taking the successful *Colleen Bawn* from New York to the hinterland, probably unaware that in so doing they were revolutionizing the American stage; James R. Osgood, Ticknor and Fields's first traveling representative, carrying the firm's fall list to bookstores in Detroit and Cincinnati (another innovation); and subscription agents with handsome sample volumes from New York or Hartford. As they rode, many of these passengers passed the time by reading paper-covered volumes produced specifically for railroad travelers—Putnam's Semi-Monthly Issue for Travelers or Appleton's Popular Library. In the baggage car were bundles of the weekly edition of Greeley's *New York Tribune,* of Bonner's New York *Ledger,* of *Harper's Weekly* (cheaply carried in bulk under the postal regulations of

1852). In the freight train just behind were packing cases of Harriet Stowe's latest volume, a special shipment of Holmes's *Autocrat* bearing on its title page a Cincinnati book dealer's imprint along with that of the Boston publisher; and even bigger boxes of novels by Augusta Jane Evans, Miriam Harris, and Mary Jane Holmes; and certainly a consignment of *Hiawatha,* for by the middle of 1856 one-tenth of all copies printed had been bought by one Chicago jobber.

Such passengers and such freight had been moving out of the East for decades, but they had been subject to the uncertainties of river currents and floods, and to the slow plodding of horses on canal tracks and mired roads. The difference now was in quantity, speed—and direction. Northeastern migrants having moved west rather than south, Northeastern cultural goods flowed to western bookstores, lecture halls, art galleries, and theaters. More important, perhaps, than either speed or quantity was the fact that these goods were blocked by none of the cultural embargoes and tariff walls that were appearing along the Mason and Dixon line.

What had happened to the southern market? Up to 1840 it had been a major outlet for New York and Philadelphia book and magazine publishers, whose alliances with booksellers in large southern cities were certain evidence of the cultural homogeneity of the Atlantic seaboard. Even in the early fifties, few northern publishers dared to alienate southern buyers, or failed to apply pressure to writers who were indifferent to their prejudices. In 1845, for example, a Philadelphia publisher removed Longfellow's antislavery poems from a collected edition because they would damage his southern business. The popular "Grace Greenwood" (Sara Jane Lippincott) was warned by her Boston publisher in 1851 that the question whether her remarks on slavery would cut off the sales of her work south of the Mason and Dixon line was "one of some importance to a writer whose reputation should make her books sell extensively thro'out the country." But the lady had better business sense than her publisher. Not at all concerned about southern opinion, she begged him to see to the distribution of her books in western towns, where there was a constant and unsatisfied demand for them. Within a year another Boston publisher turned down *Uncle Tom's Cabin* because it would not sell in the South; when a competitor took a chance with it, the new North bought 100,000 copies in eight weeks. James T. Fields saw the point when he removed the *Southern Literary Messenger,* the most important of all southern magazines, from his review-copy list in 1849; so did G. P. Putnam when he ignored dire threats from southern readers of his *Monthly*: its entire sale in the South was smaller than that in Ohio alone. The fact that the enormous development of the popular lecture after 1850 took place almost exclusively in the North enforced the moral: as a literary market, the South was dispensable. As its screen against northern thought became finer and finer, its purchasing (and therefore its cultural) power became less and less.

The Midwest not only mattered—its cultural, as well as its economic and political, influence was by the fifties beginning to be crucial. Predisposed, like the Northeast, to a threefold economy—agriculture, commerce, and manufacture—it offered no serious barriers to cultural penetration from the coast. Committed, like the Northeast, to the ideal of universal, free, and eventually compulsory education, it was destined to produce an ever larger percentage of the literate adults of the nation. Once tied by railroads to New York, Boston, and Philadelphia, the centers of cultural production and the meccas of the nation's talent, the Midwest became an integral and influential part of that powerful civilization known as "the North" which was to dominate the nation thenceforward.

The accessibility of the western market to publishers depended as much upon urbanization as on railroads. Newspapers and magazines could reach isolated farms by mail, but the bookstore, which could flourish only in fair-sized towns, was still the publisher's chief outlet. If, now, Cincinnati, Buffalo, and Cleveland book jobbers served ever-growing clusters of towns capable of supporting bookstores, they were merely belated beneficiaries of an economic phenomenon which had been characteristic of the industrial Northeast for decades. In New England, countryfolk were flocking to Lawrence and Pawtucket, Fall River and Hartford; in New York, to Albany and Troy, Schenectady and Elmira; and in Pennsylvania, to Harrisburg, Reading, and Allentown. With markets geographically so concentrated, the publishers of Boston, New York, and Philadelphia had been able to achieve a leadership in book production which they have never lost.

For the literary man, Boston had importance far out of proportion to the volume of its publishing business. New York in the fifties had 107 publishers—twice as many as either Boston or Philadelphia; but its biggest houses specialized in British and in non-literary writings, as did its biggest magazines— *Harper's Monthly* and *Harper's Weekly*. When G. P. Putnam (the most "literary" of the New York publishers), and his *Putnam's Monthly* (the best literary magazine of its time), dropped out of the running in the middle fifties, Boston firms had few important rivals in the publishing of American belles-lettres. Admittedly, the best printing (especially of poetry) and the best proofreading were done in Cambridge by the University Press; and the best cloth binding was done in Boston by Benjamin Bradley. Ticknor and Fields was hospitable to poets and essayists; Little, Brown and Company, to historians; James Munroe, to philosophers; John P. Jewett, to popular novelists; and Phillips, Sampson and Company, to writers in general.

Constantly improving railroad connections with the West via Albany and the enterprise of the younger publishers (Jewett, Harriet Stowe's publisher, had a branch office in Cleveland) reduced somewhat the disadvantages of Boston's geographical position. Even so, Boston publishers could rely upon a local public long accustomed to buying and reading books, and it was a common belief among American poets that verse sold better in New England than elsewhere. Moreover, the New England public accorded to the writer a prestige which he enjoyed nowhere else in the nation; and properly introduced authors from other sections were sure of a cordial reception and good literary fellowship in dozens of homes, bookshops, and editorial offices in and near Boston. When the *Atlantic Monthly* was founded in 1857 (two months after *Putnam's Monthly* had expired), its success was assured—not only because there was enough local talent to keep its pages full (one explanation of its reputed provincialism), but because it was backed by the money and influence of publishers long accustomed to dealing with literary materials and with creative writers. Such factors as these had much to do with the renaissance of the fifties.

2

Important as were material factors in the growth of the power of the new North, education was the social foundation on which the region was building a culture radically different in quality, depth, and extent from the patrician culture which had prevailed in the old urban centers and in the South. If time devoted to formal education is an index to consumption of print, the accelerated growth of mere literacy in the North was a phenomenon of some import to the literary world. Between 1850 and 1870 the population of the country increased about 68 per cent, but attendance at public schools almost doubled—to six and one-quarter million. Educational methods, equipment, and teaching personnel may have failed to keep step with this growth, but ability to read well was an educational goal more faithfully kept in view than it is now. In spite of brave attempts in some southern states to combat difficult conditions, the great majority of these readers were being trained in the North. Illiteracy among South Atlantic whites in 1850 was five times as great as in New England; and in the relatively new South Central states it was three times as great as in the Middle West.

A presumably more sophisticated class of readers was being produced during the period (both in the North and in the South) at an even greater rate, for enrollment in academies, liberal colleges, and other private schools more than tripled to almost a million. The academies, now for the first time enduring strong competition from public high schools, were in 1850 a far greater influence in the literary market than the colleges, which enrolled a mere 27,000. It was not only that the enrollment in academies was ten times as great, but that they were hospitable to women, as most northern colleges were not, and to "modern" courses, of which the majority of colleges were still suspicious. Like the public high schools (during the period some sixty-five of these were established in large towns, only four of them in the South) they tended increasingly to offer a terminal education rather than a merely preparatory course. Inasmuch as the South in 1850, with a relatively small white population, had 40 per cent of the nation's private schools (Kentucky had twice as many academy students as Indiana), it is no wonder that northern publishers resented the alienation of southern readers.

Few colleges (total enrollment was only 56,000 on the eve of the Civil War) were doing much to improve the old classical curriculum. There was some progress in the teaching of science, modern languages, and the newer social sciences, but sectarian influence was still strong, and higher education still awaited the thorough shaking-up it was to get under new, young, German-trained presidents within a decade after the war. It was largely because the established colleges, committed to an academic program of what Veblen later called "conspicuous waste," were slow to respond to the needs of industry and agriculture that during this period technological schools sprang up as separate entities or as independent affiliates of older institutions. Most of the twenty-two technological schools and state universities founded in the sixties got federal support through the Morrill Land Grant Act (1862), the purpose of which was "to carry the advantages of education to those engaged in manual industries." Though the South before the war had sent an even larger proportion of its white population to college than had the North, the war delayed the development of technological education in the region. At any rate, higher and "useful" education for the many, like literacy for the masses, was a typically northern idea, one which was steadily undermining the old tradition of an exclusively classical and British culture for the few.

Paradoxically, increasing material prosperity was the major factor in the education of the most potent class of readers in the nation—women. Though few people as yet believed that women were worth educating beyond the elementary level, something had to be done with girls who did not have to become household drudges as soon as they were old enough to work. The solution was the female academy. Census figures for secondary education of the sexes before 1870 are lacking, but in that year more than half of all academy students were girls. As for women's colleges, the striking fact is that in 1870, though those in the Northeast were the best in the country, the number of girls enrolled in them was negligible; whereas the South, which had forty-two of the fifty-six women's colleges established during the period, was giving higher education to almost as many women as men. Except in normal schools, technical and professional curricula were intended for boys, with the result, momentous for the literary market, that education for the enrichment of life, as opposed to education for a job, was monopolized by girls. No one knows what percentage of the readers of poetry, fiction, and essays was female, but the signs are many that by mid-century most of the consumers of imaginative literature were women of the upper and middle classes. Whether, at this date, the younger female audience was made up of "vivid, responsive intelligences, which are none the less brilliant and admirable because they are innocent" (according to Howells), or whether it constituted an "Iron Madonna who strangles in her fond embrace the American novelist" (according to Boyesen), it was a force which affected literary history.

Of the informal varieties of education, the most characteristic of the period was the "popular lecture," which, though it grew out of the lyceum system, must not be confused with the typical lyceum lecture. By the fifties the superior man was no longer sharing his cultural wealth, in the local lyceum, with his less fortunate townsman; he was selling it to large groups of critical strangers who demanded their money's worth. Young Men's Associations and Library Societies, which (particularly in the West) were displacing the lyceums, now paid fees of from $50 to $100 to "names" who invariably had made their reputations in activities other than lecturing, and the reappearance of these on any platform depended on their ability to talk "interestingly" on foreign travel or on social and ethical topics. This test of popularity was not necessarily corruptive. Emerson, who made only the indispensable compromises with his audience, by much effort could earn as much as $2,000 for a season. Bayard Taylor, with his popular travel lectures, often made $5,000, and magnetic personalities like Henry Ward Beecher, Anna Dickinson, and John B. Gough earned much more. Although, inevitably, such sums tempted lecturers to cheapen their wares, the public rarely tolerated charlatanism. Dr. Holland (writer of best-sellers and, later, editor of *Scribner's*), who declared that "the public do not accept of those who are too openly in the market," believed that at its zenith the popular lecture was the champion of liberty and the foe of bigotry in politics and religion. From the forties until 1865 the platform was a medium for the expression of social opinion; and as such it served the great purpose of ameliorating prejudice; and, like the radio of today, it was a nationalizing force.

But the end of the war brought about a rapid if temporary degeneration of social and intellectual tone, one of the permanent effects of which was the destruction of the popular lecture. Commercial lecture bureaus, under the inspiration of publicity geniuses like James Redpath and Major J. B. Pond, quickly transformed it into "amusement business," and by 1870 the platform was reserved for exhibitions of the newly famous, "readings" by the latest or the oldest literary idol, and what Bayard Taylor called bitterly "non-intellectual diversion." In a little more than forty years a great cultural institution had outlived its usefuless. Thereafter the serious-minded turned to the Chautauqua for edification and enlightenment.

3

Journalism proved even more adaptable to social change. As business and industry destroyed the slow tempo of the old agrarian culture, American life speeded up. The great mass of literates produced by the schools sought reading matter attuned not to the ages but to the day, the week, and the month. Increasingly, writers were trained to write and readers to read, by periodicals. Not only literacy but inventions and improved news-gathering techniques enabled daily newspapers during the period to more than triple their circulation, though the war was responsible for a good part of the total of two and a half million.

Of these, much the most significant from the point of view of northern culture was Horace Greeley's *New York Tribune,* which sold over half of its huge weekly edition outside the city, and which, according to Bayard Taylor, ranked next to the Bible in popularity in the Midwest. It is of some significance that

Greeley thus sent into the hinterland the book and lecture reviews of George Ripley (who was kindly to social radicals like Emerson), the travel letters of Taylor, Curtis, and Clemens, and the more popular verse of the New York poets. But even Greeley could not counterbalance the weight of the scores of cheap weekly magazines and "Sunday newspapers" which flooded the nation in mid-century. The historian of our magazines has well said that the descending curve of illiteracy seems to have been matched by the ascending curve of popularity of the weeklies, for by 1870, 4,295 of them had a circulation of ten and one-half million—one copy for every two or three adults in the nation. Many of them, it is true, were insignificant religious and agricultural papers of small circulation, but some of those that emanated from New York were known in every downy hamlet in the land. Among those with circulations of over 100,000 were the *New York Weekly*, whose serials were the foundation of the Street and Smith dime-novel dynasty; the somewhat more respectable New York *Sunday Mercury*, which specialized in the J. H. Ingraham and "Ned Buntline" thrillers, and in the new popular humor of Ward, Billings, and Kerr; and the New York *Ledger*, which topped them all with a circulation of 400,000 in 1860. Robert Bonner, the owner of the *Ledger*, was, like Barnum, a master of the recently born art of publicity. His amusing use of gold—and brass—to lure such "names" as Henry Ward Beecher, Edward Everett, and Longfellow into the domain of "Fanny Fern" (Sara Payson Willis Parton), Mrs. E. D. E. N. Southworth, and Sylvanus Cobb, Jr., gives an intimate view of new cultural mutations.

Bonner's success was rivaled only by that of illustrated news weeklies such as *Frank Leslie's Illustrated* and *Harper's Weekly*. The latter, like the illustrated *Harper's Monthly*, were of less direct importance to American writers than weeklies of the *Ledger* type because they printed little American fiction. Nevertheless, the editorial policies of Bonner and the Harpers had considerable influence upon literature. Before the establishment of *Harper's Monthly* (1850), few American novels were serialized. By that date Cooper had serialized one of his last romances, the other major writers none. But by 1870 almost all recognized novelists were selling their work first to magazines and were making the necessary compromises in matters of chapter division, construction, arrangement of incident, style, and moral and social prejudice. In their new venture the Harpers had intended only to get ahead of their competitors by reprinting foreign novels as fast as they appeared in serial form abroad, but they soon discovered the potency of the phrase "to be continued." When other magazines like the *Ledger* (1850) and the *Atlantic* (1857) began to serialize American novels, the writer had a new and tempting source of income, for he could sell each novel twice—three times if he could get an English magazine to serialize simultaneously, four times if he could also sell to an English publisher.

Only slightly less important were other policies of the new magazines: they popularized the illustration of fiction, a development which was later to affect the work of novelists like Howells and James; they raised the rate of pay for magazine work and thus not only helped to stabilize further the literary profession but made New York the center of literary magazine production; they protected the copyright of their periodicals and thereby helped put a stop to the wholesale scissoring which in the forties had deprived Poe and Longfellow of the major rewards of their popularity; they helped break down the custom of literary anonymity, which had also militated against the author's interest; most important of all, by appealing to a national audience, they helped to destroy the narrow localism which damaged such respectable and even superior competitors as *Putnam's* and the *Atlantic Monthly*. The influence of these popular periodicals on literary production shows that, though Emerson may have been justified in his faith that "water and intelligence work down," it is just as true that popular influences work up.

4

The same forces were at work in the book world. The opening of railroad transportation in the Midwest, the campaign against illiteracy through the North, the habit of reading which was encouraged by lecturers, newspapers, and magazines, served to increase the sale of books on all levels. The schools contributed directly to publishers' prosperity, not only through textbooks and juveniles, which were the backbone of many a firm's list, but through district school libraries, whose holdings increased from two and one-half to three and one-half million volumes. By mid-century these libraries had become so important in the literary market that the standard Harper contract included a clause covering school editions.

The contribution of religious education was little short of spectacular: church and school libraries in 1850 owned six hundred thousand volumes; in 1870 the number was almost ten million. The ancient alliance between the church and literary culture, inevitable in colonial and early national days when the clergy wrote much of what got into print, was perpetuated up to the Civil War by close relations between the major publishers and specific denominations—Harpers with the Methodists, Appleton with the Episcopalians, Ticknor with the Baptists, Munroe and Francis with the Unitarians. But if the churches stimulated the appetite for books, they also satisfied it to some extent by doing much publishing on their own account. There were bitter complaints that such organizations as the American Sunday School Union, the Presbyterian Board, and the Methodist Book Concern, all subsidized by charity funds, were publishing and distributing general literary works of a religious cast in competition with "legitimate" houses, and that authorship suffered because copyright was paid only rarely and reluctantly. The cycle of business expansion completed the process by which literature became an important article of commerce. The enlarged book market led printers to buy improved and expensive machinery and publishers to compete with one another by paying higher royalties, sending agents out on the road, and advertising nationally. Increased overhead made larger sales necessary; so that publishers could no longer afford to be hospitable to the elite few who absorbed a thousand copies of a "good" book. G. W. Curtis in 1854 wrote the publishers to whom he was adviser that "nowadays a book seems hardly to be launched until it has a circulation of 5000."

For authors who were willing to consult the tastes of the five thousand the rewards were increasingly great. The almost universal royalty of 10 per cent and/or "author's risk" of the forties became, in the early fifties, 15 per cent, often 20, and sometimes 25 per cent if the writer paid for his own stereotype plates. Indeed, the years between 1850 and the panic of 1857 saw a boom of authors' profits unequaled in the whole nineteenth century, and royalty offers reached a high of 33⅓ per cent before the panic. During the sixties, they tended to slip back to a norm of 10 to 15 per cent, where they remained until the nineties. Authorship suffered during the Civil War, for new literary works were not in demand unless they had some special relation to the conflict, and the doubling of the cost of living about 1864 left many writers in bad straits. But retail book prices doubled too, and since deflation did not reduce them all the way to the old level, authors were left better off than they had been before.

Meanwhile, publishing methods had improved. By 1850 the old barter system by which bookseller-publishers exchanged their imprints for those of shops in other towns had been displaced by techniques of publishing for a national market. Booksellers were now encouraged to move their stocks through generous publishers' discounts which were adjusted to the salability of individual titles. Nation-wide newspaper and magazine advertising (Ticknor and Fields, publishers of the Brahmins, did not spurn the columns of the nationally circulated *Leslie's*) and new promotional methods undermined the vicious local review clique which had done great harm to professional authorship in Poe's day. Publishers learned how to exploit potential reader markets more thoroughly by adjusting format and price to differing income levels. The difficulty of reaching readers in rural areas was overcome to a certain extent by the development of subscription publishing. It was chiefly biography, history, and travel that was thus issued by such firms as the American Publishing Company in Hartford and Scribner's in New York, but Harriet Stowe in 1870 daringly contemplated sending agents into the South with an illustrated edition of *Uncle Tom's Cabin*. As she wrote her publisher, "Books to do anything here in these southern states must be sold by agents. . . . Yet *there is* money on hand even down to the colored families, and an attractive book would have a history." Mrs. Stowe's experiences illustrate another comparatively new development: the growth of intimate and trusting relations between author and publisher. Many a house like Putnam, Scribner, and Ticknor and Fields now inspired such loyalty as Emerson's, who called his publisher "the guardian of us all."

Among the new duties of the friendly publisher was arranging for simultaneous publication of his titles in England. Author and publisher alike studied British copyright, so that in spite of unfavorable decisions in the House of Lords in the early fifties, shrewd writers like Mrs. Stowe made better bargains with English publishers than Irving, Cooper, Prescott, and Melville in earlier days. Setting up a few days' residence in Canada at the time a new book was published in London was one method by which

American authors acquired a kind of standing in British courts, but careful preliminary arrangements with a reliable foreign house frequently sufficed to turn the trick. Publishing relations with Canada were excellent, though they were destined to degenerate in subsequent decades. A Canadian law of 1849 removed all tariffs on American books; another of 1850 permitted the importation of American reprints of British copyright works, with the provision that a 12½ per cent royalty for the benefit of the English author be collected at the border. In 1852 a correspondent reported that low-priced American books had almost destroyed the Canadian-English book trade, and that New York had displaced London as the purchasing center for the Dominion.

On the American side, reckless competition in the printing of English books had produced its own partial cure by mid-century: a system of courtesy by which a publisher who bought and announced a foreign title was let alone by other houses. Such arrangements raised the price of American editions of foreign works and gave native productions a better chance than they had had before. By 1860, at any rate, many American writers were deriving an adequate income from the home market, which had not been possible during the first half of the century even for such well-established authors as Irving, Cooper, and Willis. During this period writing ceased to be a part-time avocation and became a profession capable of supporting authors in middle-class respectability.

5

The forces of education and business having combined to make the popular patronage of literature an economic fact, it was inevitable that readers and publishers should exert a shaping influence upon literary work. Bald logic would suggest that such influence must have been destructive of pure creative ideals, and that the success of T. S. Arthur, Sylvanus Cobb, Susan Warner, and Josh Billings during the period of the decline of Melville, Hawthorne, and George Henry Boker was not merely coincidental. Common sense would indicate that increased literacy might have brought the new group into being without destroying the old. Between logic and common sense lay a fact: that even the best of the older writers recognized the new reading class as a force and attempted to adjust themselves to it without compromising their integrity. Unsophisticated readers throughout the North required that writers and lecturers present themselves not on the ground of their local (if impressively urban) reputations but on the ground that they had something interesting to say to "nonliterary," "nonintellectual," but intelligent people. The prerequisites for such an appeal were then what they must always be: simplicity, concreteness, lightness, eloquence, freshness, and a distinctive (if not distinguished) personal style. If the writer's ideals included also imagination, power, and relentless truth, so much the better: the public required only that he communicate and that he be interesting.

Emerson, who derived his living not from a little group of transcendentalists in Boston but from a public which extended from Bangor, Maine, to Davenport, Iowa, saw the validity of such standards. When Thoreau remarked in 1853 that any lecture which pleased an audience must be bad, Emerson demurred. "I am ambitious," he said, "to write something which all can read, like *Robinson Crusoe*. And when I have written a paper or a book, I see with regret that it is not solid, with a right materialistic treatment, which delights everybody." Melville recognized the requirements when he sought better terms from his publisher for *Pierre* because its "unquestionable novelty" would make it popular, it "being a regular romance, with a mysterious plot to it, & stirring passions at work, and withall, representing a new & elevated aspect of American life—"; and for *Redburn* because it was "a plain, straightforward, amusing narrative of personal experience . . . no metaphysics . . . nothing but cakes & ale."

It was the mark of younger and lesser writers of the period that instead of striving, like Emerson and Melville, to adapt their best gifts to the needs of their audience, they attempted a false dualism: that of subsidizing their unprofitable "art" by grinding out commercially successful work of which they were contemptuous. Bayard Taylor was humiliated that on his lecture tours women swooned, and cried, "There he is! That's *him!*" And he complained that lecturing, which built him a fifteen-thousand-dollar country house, was destroying his poetry, which he never wrote for money. Similarly, Stedman, in 1869, was conscience-striken because he had "lately written so much poor stuff for the money's sake"; and a year later he reported that the public taste was being led astray "after burlesque, the grotesque, the transitory."

There was indeed a bigger market for "poor stuff" than ever before; but those who had genuine faith in democratic man knew that the crowd was ready for better stuff if only one would learn its idiom. Whitman and Emily Dickinson did not; Mark Twain did, and reaped his reward. Melville, who never mastered it, said bitterly in 1851: "This country . . . [is] governed by sturdy backwoodsmen—noble fellows enough, but not at all literary, & who care not a fig for any authors except those who write those most saleable of all books nowadays—i e—the newspapers, & magazines." Yet he added more hopefully: "This country is at present engaged in furnishing material for future authors; not in encouraging its living ones." But it was Emerson, as usual, who saw in true perspective the dilemma of the author in this age of Barnum, Beecher, and Bonner. When a "stout Illinoian" walked out on his lectures, he reflected that "the people are always right (in a sense), and that the man of letters is to say, These are the new conditions to which I must conform . . .

he is no master who cannot vary his forms and carry his own end triumphantly through the most difficult." The time was, indeed, a difficult one for the artist, but it was not impossible. He needed only faith and humility to see that though he himself must serve Mammon as well as God, the people served God as well as Mammon.

Checklist: The Publications of
William Charvat

(This list does not include reviews.)

"Thomas Bancroft," *Publications of the Modern Language Association of America*, XLVII (September, 1932), 753–58.

The Origins of American Critical Thought, 1810–1835. Philadelphia: [University of Pennsylvania Press], 1936; London: Humphrey Milford, Oxford University Press, 1936; New York: Barnes, 1961.

"American Romanticism and the Depression of 1837," *Science and Society*, II (Winter, 1937), 67–82.

" 'Let Us Then Be Up and Doing,' " *English Journal*, College Edition, XXVIII (May, 1939), 374–83.

"A Course in the History of American Society," *Journal of Higher Education*, XI (May, 1940), 247–51.

"Francis Jeffrey in America," *New England Quarterly*, XIV (June, 1941), 309–34.

"Prescott's Political and Social Attitudes," *American Literature*, XIII (January, 1942), 320–30.

New Highways in College Composition, ed. HOMER ANDREW WATT, OSCAR CARGILL, and WILLIAM CHARVAT. New York: Prentice-Hall, 1943. Second edition, 1955.

William Hickling Prescott: Representative Selections, with Introduction, Bibliography, and Notes, ed. WILLIAM CHARVAT and MICHAEL KRAUS. ("American Writers Series.") New York: American Book Company, 1943.

"Melville's Income," *American Literature*, XV (November, 1943), 251–61.

"Longfellow's Income from His Writings, 1840–1852," *Papers of the Bibliographical Society of America*, XXXVIII (First quarter, 1944), 9–21.

"James T. Fields and the Beginnings of Book Promotion, 1840–1855," *Huntington Library Quarterly*, VIII (November, 1944), 75–94.

"A Note on Poe's *Tales of the Grotesque and Arabesque*," *Publishers' Weekly*, CL (November 23, 1946), 2957–58.

"The People's Patronage" and "Literature as Business," *Literary History of the United States*, ed. ROBERT E. SPILLER *et al.* New York: Macmillan, 1948. Pp. 513–25, 953–68.

The Cost Books of Ticknor and Fields and Their Predecessors, 1832–1858, edited, with an Introduction, by WARREN S. TRYON and WILLIAM CHARVAT. New York: Bibliographical Society of America, 1949.

"Literary Economics and Literary History," *English Institute Essays 1949*, ed. ALAN S. DOWNER. New York: Columbia University Press; London: Oxford University Press, 1950. Pp. 73–91.

Poems in English, 1530–1940, ed. DAVID DAICHES and WILLIAM CHARVAT. New York: Ronald Press, 1950.

Prentice-Hall Handbook for Writers, ed. GLENN LEGGETT, C. DAVID MEAD, and WILLIAM CHARVAT. New York: Prentice-Hall, 1951. New editions: 1954, 1960, 1965.

American Poetry and Prose, ed. NORMAN FOERSTER; *Shorter Edition*, prepared, with supplementary notes, by WILLIAM CHARVAT. Boston: Houghton Mifflin, 1952.

"Cooper as Professional Author," *James Fenimore Cooper, A Reappraisal*. Cooperstown, N.Y.: New York State Historical Association, 1954. Pp. 128–43.

James Fenimore Cooper, *The Last of the Mohicans*, edited, with an Introduction, by WILLIAM CHARVAT. Boston: Houghton Mifflin, 1958.

"Melville and the Common Reader," *Studies in Bibliography*, XII (1958), 41–57.

Literary Publishing in America, 1790–1850. Philadelphia: University of Pennsylvania Press, 1959. A. S. W. Rosenbach Fellowship in Bibliography.

"A Chronological List of Emerson's Lecture Engagements," *Bulletin of the New York Public Library*, LXIV (September, October, November, and December, 1960), 492–507, 551–59, 606–10, 657–63; LXV (January, 1961), 40–46.

Emerson's American Lecture Engagements: A Chronological List,
New York: New York Public Library, 1961. Reprinted from the
Bulletin of the New York Public Library.

"Poe: Journalism and the Theory of Poetry," *Aspects of American
Poetry,* Essays Presented to Howard Mumford Jones, ed. RICHARD
M. LUDWIG. Columbus: Ohio State University Press, 1962. Pp.
61–78.

"Henry Wadsworth Longfellow . . . James Russell Lowell . . . ,"
Major Writers of America, ed. PERRY MILLER. New York: Harcourt,
Brace & World, 1962. I, 793–803. *Shorter Edition,* 1966.

Introduction to Nathaniel Hawthorne, *The Scarlet Letter.* ("Centen-
ary Edition of the Works of Nathaniel Hawthorne," ed. WILLIAM
CHARVAT, ROY HARVEY PEARCE, CLAUDE M. SIMPSON, FREDSON
BOWERS, and MATTHEW J. BRUCCOLI, Vol. I.) Columbus: Ohio
State University Press, 1962. Pp. xv–xxviii.

" 'Everybody Writes in Ohio!' " *Ohioana,* V (Fall and Winter, 1962),
67–69, 114–17.

Nathaniel Hawthorne, *The Scarlet Letter,* edited, with an Introduction,
by WILLIAM CHARVAT. Boston: Houghton Mifflin, 1963.

Introduction to Nathaniel Hawthorne, *The House of the Seven Gables.*
("Centenary Edition of the Works of Nathaniel Hawthorne," ed.
WILLIAM CHARVAT, ROY HARVEY PEARCE, CLAUDE M. SIMPSON,
FREDSON BOWERS, MATTHEW J. BRUCCOLI, and L. NEAL SMITH,
Vol. II.) Columbus: Ohio State University Press, 1965. Pp. xv–
xxviii.

Index